CONTEST
FOR
CULTURAL
AUTHORITY

CONTEST
FOR
CULTURAL
AUTHORITY

Hazlitt, Coleridge,
and the
Distresses
of the Regency

Robert Keith Lapp

 WAYNE STATE UNIVERSITY PRESS   DETROIT

Library of Congress Cataloging-in-Publication Data

Lapp, Robert Keith
    Contest for cultural authority : Hazlitt, Coleridge, and the
distresses of the Regency / Robert Keith Lapp.
      p.   cm.
    Includes bibliographical references and index.
    ISBN 0-8143-2833-4 (alk. paper)
    1. Coleridge, Samuel Taylor, 1772–1834—Criticism and
interpretation—History—19th century.   2. Literature and history—
Great Britain—History—19th century.   3. Literature and society—
England—History—19th century.   4. Hazlitt, William, 1778–1830—
Knowledge—Literature.   5. Great Britain—History—George III,
1760–1820.   6. Criticism—England—History—19th Century.
7. England—Civilization—19th century.   8. Regency—Great Britain.
I. Title.
PR4484.L37   1999
821'.7—dc21   99-34718

To
Melody

Contents

ACKNOWLEDGMENTS

As with all projects of this kind, the generous encouragement and support of many individuals, institutions, and mentors has been indispensable in seeing *Contest for Cultural Authority* through to completion. I am particularly grateful to Ron Tetreault, whose guidance was instrumental in the conceptualization and execution of the bulk of this work, and to Michael Scrivener, whose warmly appreciative and constructive commentary at a crucial stage in its production encouraged me to proceed. With pleasure, too, I name those colleagues who have offered invaluable help, advice, and insight at various stages along the way: Ron Huebert, Judith Thompson, John Baxter, David MacNeil, Rohan Maitzen, Victor Li, Trevor Ross, Marjorie Stone, Pam Perkins, Mark Bruhn, Gretchen Mosher, Carrie MacMillan, Terry Craig, Deborah Wills, and Karen Bamford.

I received kind assistance from the staff of the British Library, the National Library of Scotland, and the Killam Library in Halifax in obtaining primary materials. Research funding was provided in part by the Social Sciences and Humanities Research Council of Canada, and I am grateful for the generous institutional support of both Dalhousie University and Mount Allison University. The editors of Wayne State University Press have been particularly helpful, and I would like to acknowledge the excellent suggestions made by two anonymous readers of the manuscript.

I thank *English Studies in Canada* for its early support of this project: a version of chapter 2 appeared in *English Studies in Canada* 20.1 (March

1994), and I appreciate the kind permission of Mary Jane Edwards to reprint it here. I also thank the Romanticists of the North American Society for the Study of Romanticism for their ongoing, stimulating influence on my work, and particularly those who responded to a version of chapter 5 when it was given as a conference paper at Duke University in November 1994.

A less calculable but no less important debt of gratitude is due to my mentors: David Shaw and Julian Patrick, who taught me the art of close reading; Robin Jackson, who shaped my thinking about Coleridge; Stanley Jones, for his warm hospitality and his vivid conversation about Hazlitt and the Regency; and Douglas Lapp, who has offered a lifetime example of intellectual endeavor, scholarly perseverance, and spiritual integrity.

Special thanks, finally, go to those whose daily lives have been intricately and inevitably bound up in the production of this book: Melody, Miriam, and Erin.

INTRODUCTION
VIGILANT AUDITOR:
Hazlitt's Regency Reviews
of Coleridge

As a body of writing, Hazlitt's eight Regency reviews of Coleridge are thought to comprise one of the most shameful episodes in British literary history. The story goes like this: Just as Coleridge was beginning to redeem his reputation as an author of genius, overcoming many personal obstacles to publish a series of important books, he was attacked in the press by one of the rising wits of anonymous review-criticism, none other than his former friend William Hazlitt. And even though Hazlitt would later go on to publish such reassuringly celebratory essays as "My First Acquaintance With Poets," he resorted in these reviews—or so the story goes—to all the crudest devices of anonymous satire and personal invective to reduce some of Coleridge's most seminal writings to utter "nonsense" in the minds of Regency readers.

Along with this scandal, however, literary history is also burdened with a contradiction. Hazlitt has since been canonized—along with Coleridge himself—as among the greatest of Romantic critics, celebrated for his incisive prose style, his enviable "clear-headedness," and his "judgements of absolute rightness and pregnant condensations of meaning" (McFarland 58).[1] Yet his judgments of Coleridge—at least those made in these reviews—are rejected as "deplorable" (Baker 355) and "malicious" (White, introduction xxxn. 3), the product of "motiveless malignancy" (Baker 356), as "strangely cruel and indiscriminate attacks" (Bate, introduction, *Biographia* lxiv), and "vicious" (Griggs 668), "poisonous" (Marrs 227n 4), "low-blows" (Carlson 133), infused "with a personal vindictiveness" (Holmes 179n).

11

It is this contradiction that first draws our attention back to Hazlitt's Regency reviews of Coleridge. Two factors are quickly identified to prompt further inquiry. First, Hazlitt himself did not regard these writings as merely momentary bagatelles of personal spleen; on the contrary, he republished five of them as *Political Essays,* under his own name, at the very climax of postwar distress in August 1819. Second, it was Coleridge who first declared these essays to be morally and generically flawed, and while his influential opinion has since become the standard view, it can scarcely be considered impartial in this case. Thus we are invited to revisit this scandal and reread the offending texts, if only because they promise to be skillfully written contemporary estimates of such seminal works as *Christabel, The Statesman's Manual,* and the *Biographia Literaria,* composed by a canonical critic whose judgments may prove in this case to be just as clearheaded as in all his other writings. Moreover, the recovery of Hazlitt's voice in a debate he explicitly classifies as "political" promises to uncover, in the vigorous rejection of his position by literary history, a certain ideological undertow—another example, perhaps, of what Jerome McGann has famously called scholarship's "uncritical absorption in Romanticism's own self-representations" (1).

Contest for Cultural Authority offers just such a rereading, but what it finds in these reviews exceeds a mere amendment to romanticized literary history. Once relocated within what Paul Magnuson calls the "public discourse" of the late Regency (13–15), and in particular the debates over what were then known as the "Distresses of the Country,"[2] the confrontation between Hazlitt and Coleridge articulated in these reviews emerges instead as an instructive epitome of much larger patterns of conflict: the political struggle between reaction and reform, marketplace competition over new reading audiences, and the friction between competing genres and modes of discursive performance in the public sphere. Hazlitt's reviews of Coleridge, in other words, offer themselves as something of a case study in Regency culture, and this book positions itself accordingly as a contribution to the more comprehensive and evolving project of a cultural history of the postrevolutionary period.[3] Ultimately the claim is this: The conflict between Hazlitt and Coleridge during the Distresses period takes the form of a contest for cultural authority between two fundamentally opposed but equally influential formations within bourgeois ideology. On the one hand, Hazlitt aligns a politicized Romanticism of dissident protest with the skillful articulation of the collective voice of "public opinion" and "common sense," a projection into nineteenth-century print culture of the universalizing and democratizing ideals of the coffeehouse culture of the eighteenth-century public sphere.[4] Coleridge, on the other hand, articulates a Romanticism of withdrawal into visionary idealism that locates cultural authority in the attractive figure of the poet-prophet. This figure is in turn a product of the more generalized ideology of individual sensibility, drawing in this instance on the emergent tradition of bardolatry and its celebration of the power of autonomous "Poetic Genius."[5]

The very attractions of poetic genius, of course, have ensured that Coleridge's version of this struggle has remained the standard one. We scarcely question his repudiation of anonymous review-criticism, for example, and in the case of Hazlitt's reviews, we look for psychological or moral explanations, confining them to biographical narratives of mentorship and betrayal.[6] The sources of this approach are readily available in Coleridge's own outpouring of "bitterness and sorrow" in his voluminous (and meticulously edited) correspondence on the subject,[7] and, more importantly, in the final chapter of his massively influential *Biographia Literaria*. Here, in the only chapter of this book written after the appearance of Hazlitt's reviews, Coleridge reflects with winning pathos on the impact such criticism has had on his person and his career. "Three years ago," he declares, referring to the point at which he began writing the *Biographia,* "I did not know or believe that I had an enemy in the world: and now . . . I reproach myself for being too often disposed to ask,—Have I one friend?" (Coburn 7.2: 238). He then justifies this query with his famous account of the reception of *Christabel,* in which he is aware of Hazlitt's role as an early reviewer of the poem in the *Examiner,* and of the influence this review exerted on Moore's later "quizzing" of the poem in the *Edinburgh.*[8] Repeating therefore his "warning to authors" in the opening chapters of the *Biographia* regarding "personal enmity behind the mask of anonymous criticism," and "the necessity of a certain portion of abuse and ridicule in a Review, in order to make it saleable," Coleridge continues with an account of Hazlitt's reviews of *The Statesman's Manual.*

> I had the additional misfortune of having been gossiped about, as devoted to metaphysics . . . [and] as therefore my character as a writer could not easily be more injured by an overt act than it was already in consequence of the report, I published a work, a large portion of which was professedly metaphysical. A long delay occurred between its first annunciation and its appearance; it was reviewed therefore by anticipation with a malignity, so avowedly and exclusively personal, as is, I believe, unprecedented even in the present contempt of all common humanity that disgraces and endangers the liberty of the press. After its appearance, the author of this lampoon was chosen to review it in the Edinburgh Review: and under the single condition, that he should have written what he himself really thought, and have criticized the work as he would have done if the author had been indifferent to him, I should have chosen that man myself both from the vigour and the originality of his mind, and from his particular acuteness in speculative reasoning. (7.2: 239–42)

This is an emotionally persuasive account, in which Coleridge's generous testimony to Hazlitt's critical powers serves to make all the more appalling his apparent breach of "all common humanity." As a result, this passage has become the implicit ethical standard by which each of Hazlitt's reviews of Coleridge's writings during the Regency have been judged by literary history.[9]

A striking example of the pervasiveness of this influence is found in the work of one of Hazlitt's most respected biographers, Herschel Baker, for whom the reviews of *The Statesman's Manual* are not simply "a deplorable performance" but an instance of "motiveless malignity" (355–56). With this phrase, of course, Baker echoes Coleridge's own use of the word "malignity" both in this passage and in the more famous description of Shakespeare's Iago, thus reinforcing Coleridge's characterization of Hazlitt as an evil intelligence bent on the inexplicable betrayal of intimate friendship. In this and similar ways, the eminently public dimensions and contexts of what Hazlitt calls "political essays" are reduced to "exclusively personal" significance, while the complex range of culturally specific practices and circumstances involved in anonymous review-criticism are collapsed into the timeless "closet drama" of Coleridge's agonistic authorship—with Hazlitt cast as the Romantically inscrutable villain.

This example of the operations of "Romantic Ideology" is by now no longer surprising. In this instance, faced with the awkwardness of a confrontation between two of its foremost critics, a romanticized literary history has turned to passages like the one quoted above to justify the relegation of Hazlitt's political reviews to obscurity. At the same time, this assessment facilitates the detachment of Coleridge's own writings from their roots in political, commercial, and, more broadly, cultural contestation. More surprising, perhaps, is the fact that Hazlitt's critique of Coleridge is still largely overlooked by recent historicist and interdisciplinary scholarship.

The groundwork for the recovery of these essays was laid as long ago as 1978 by John Kinnaird, whose treatment of Hazlitt's *Political Essays* in *Hazlitt: Critic of Power* remains definitive (105–6 and passim). Yet while Kinnaird establishes the primarily political motivations of Hazlitt's reviews of Coleridge, he does not take up the reviews themselves in any detail. Jon Cook's 1991 edition of Hazlitt's *Selected Writings* similarly stresses the centrality of the *Political Essays* to an understanding of Hazlitt's thought, though he includes none of the reviews of Coleridge in the writings selected. Such studies as Paul Magnuson's *Reading Public Romanticism* and James Chandler's *England in 1819* offer the most recent and thorough statements of the theoretical and methodological bases for a recovery of these reviews, but their focus is on other texts. Magnuson does indeed call for a fresh reading of the public discourse surrounding Coleridge's 1816 *Christabel* volume of the sort offered below in chapter 1; however, it is symptomatic that he does little to challenge the impression that Hazlitt's review (essential to such a project) was uniformly "hostile" (40). Similarly, while Chandler's landmark study helpfully recognizes Hazlitt's *Political Essays* as "his first major collection of contemporary commentaries" and therefore "a crucial forerunner to the essays later collected in *The Spirit of the Age*" (14), it nevertheless tends to reinforce a traditional emphasis by foregoing any discussion of the *Political Essays* of 1819 in favor of an extended commentary on *The Spirit of the Age,* published six years after the watershed year of Chandler's title.

Surely, however, it is significant that Hazlitt's *Political Essays* appeared just two days before Peterloo—on 14 August 1819—and that they included at their very center three sharply oppositional reviews of Coleridge's *Statesman's Manual,* a riposte to Coleridge's *Courier* essays on *Wat Tyler,* and part of Hazlitt's *Edinburgh* review-essay on the *Biographia Literaria.* These appeared, moreover, from the publishing house of the Radical dissident William Hone. Despite the political provocation implicit in this, they appeared boldly under Hazlitt's own name, (rather than anonymously, as one might have expected in the thickening atmosphere of repression that marked the summer of 1819). This, too, was at a point when Hazlitt's name carried the authority of being "one of the ablest and most eloquent critics of [the] nation" (*Morning Chronicle;* qtd. in Cook, introduction xlvi) and "one of the two most eminent speculators on literary topics"—alongside Francis Jeffrey of the *Edinburgh Review.*[10] Thus Hazlitt was putting at serious risk the cultural authority he had amassed as a literary critic through such books as *Characters of Shakespeare's Plays* (1817) and *Lectures on the English Poets* (1818) in order to take a stand with Hone and the movement for radical reform at a critical moment in its evolution. "I am no politician," his preface begins, "and still less can I be said to be a party-man: but I have a hatred of tyranny, and a contempt for its tools; and this feeling I have expressed as often and as strongly as I could. I cannot sit quietly down under the claims of barefaced power, and I have tried to expose the little arts of sophistry by which they are defended" (7: 7).[11] It is for this reason that the entire cluster of Hazlitt's reviews of Coleridge, of which the *Political Essays* contain a representative selection, must be read as more than a "motiveless" and "exclusively personal" skirmish on the margins of literary production. Once situated in the context of public debate over the Distresses of the Regency, they emerge instead as articulations of the same patterns of conflict that E. P. Thompson, in *The Making of the English Working Class,* recognized as pivotal and that Jon Klancher, in *The Making of English Reading Audiences,* has shown to have been crucial. This contest for cultural authority, moreover, was played out across a remarkable variety of genres and modes of public discourse. On Coleridge's part, these include his prefaces to *Christabel* and "Kubla Khan" (*Poetical Works* 213–15, 295–97), his premature newspaper advertisement of "A Layman's Sermon . . . on the present Distresses of the Country" (*Courier* 12 Aug. 1816: 1); his two *Lay Sermons* (Coburn vol. 6); his series of anonymous political essays in the *Courier* in defense of Robert Southey, the poet laureate, during the "*Wat Tyler* affair" (3.2: 449–78); the *Biographia Literaria,* with its final polemical chapter (7.2: 234–48); and his 1818 lectures on "The Principles of Judgement, Culture, and European Literature."

Hazlitt's responses to these texts themselves comprise a wide spectrum of textual strategies and discursive contexts. The following study is organized chronologically around each of these responses in turn, beginning (in chapter 1) with the inaugural number in the *Examiner*'s "Literary Notices" series in review of *Christabel* (19: 32–34), and then turning (in chapter 2) to the similarly sensational review "by anticipation" of "Mr Coleridge's Lay Sermon," later republished in *Political Essays* (7: 114–18). After a reexamination in chapter 3 of *The Statesman's Manual* itself, chapter 4 turns to a comparison of Hazlitt's more conventional but tellingly different reviews of this book in the *Examiner* and the *Edinburgh Review* (7: 119–28; 16: 99–114). At this point in the Distresses crisis, the paradigmatic "*Wat Tyler* affair" erupted at the forefront of public debate, to which Coleridge and Hazlitt both made significant—but now little-known—contributions. Chapter 5 therefore takes a new look at this closely followed journalistic duel in the columns of the *Courier* and the *Examiner* (7: 176–86), while chapter 6 reconsiders Hazlitt's influential extension of this debate into the *Edinburgh Review* in the form of his full-length review-essay of the *Biographia Literaria* (16: 115–38). In 1818 this contest for authority was taken into the lecture halls of London, where for several weeks Hazlitt and Coleridge held forth to packed audiences on precisely the same nights. Chapter 7 thus examines this change of venue, focusing on Hazlitt's review of Coleridge's lecture series in the *Yellow Dwarf* (19: 206–10) and his remarks on Coleridge in the last of his own *Lectures on the English Poets* (5: 165–68). Finally, in the light of these Regency writings, an epilogue offers a polemical rereading of Hazlitt's most familiar essays on Coleridge from the 1820s: "My First Acquaintance With Poets" in the *Liberal* (1823), and the article on "Mr. Coleridge" in *The Spirit of the Age* (1825) (17: 106–22; 11: 28–38).

In structuring this analysis I have used the device of anatomizing the public discourse of the Regency into three broadly overlapping and culturally specific discursive contexts: the arena of public political debate, the volatile and competitive marketplace for literature, and the shifting hierarchy of genres and modes by which authority was constructed within public discourse. The first two contexts correspond to the double classification of many of these reviews as "political essays" and "literary notices." While political and literary practices became virtually indistinguishable at the height of the Regency Distresses, we can nevertheless discern in the context of political debate an engagement with the wider issues of ideological agency, and in the context of literary production a focusing of these issues in an economic struggle for the media of that agency. These literary media were in turn marked by a tendency toward generic fusion, the defining feature of the third context. Here the discursive performance of authority ranged across such opposed genres and modes as satire and lyric, irony and "sincerity," invective and encomium, political oratory and lay sermon, journalistic "banter" and learned monologue, "[Auto-]Biographical Sketches" and "Sketches of Public Characters," each vying for ascendency between—and within—the writings of both Hazlitt and Coleridge.

To illustrate this approach—and to demonstrate at the outset the anomalous position of Hazlitt's review-criticism within traditional literary history—we may begin by turning to the briefest and perhaps most rhetorically efficient of Hazlitt's *Political Essays,* a letter entitled "To the Editor of the Examiner" (7: 128–29). This epistolary review first appeared in the *Examiner* on 12 January 1817, under the pseudonym "SEMPER EGO AUDITOR," just as the postwar distresses reached their point of greatest intensity prior to Peterloo.[12] To its first readers, this letter would have stood out for a number of reasons—particularly for its apparently bitter objection to the *Examiner*'s own recent review of *The Statesman's Manual,* and for the ironic contrast it develops between the correspondent's self-characterization as "a man of a plain, dull, dry understanding, without flights or fancies" and his obviously exuberant experiment in style, at once eclectic and rhetorically pointed. Indeed, in the sharp juxtaposition of such opposing modes as lyrical reminiscence and journalistic satire, "AUDITOR" dramatizes a moment of painful disillusionment which he suggests will be shared by many of the *Examiner*'s readers.

First, however, the attention of such readers would have been seized by the letter's long opening sequence—a rhetorical "flight" that, in a slightly altered version, has since gone on to become one of the most famous passages in the canon of British Romantic prose:

SIR,

Your last Sunday's "Literary Notice" has given me some uneasiness on two points.

It was in January, 1798, just 19 years ago, that I got up one morning before day-light to walk 10 miles in the mud, and went to hear a poet and a philosopher preach. It was the author of the "Lay-Sermon." Never, Sir, the longest day I have to live, shall I have such another walk as this cold, raw, comfortless one in the winter of the year 1798. Mr. Examiner, *Il y a des impressions que ni les tems ni les circonstances peuvent effacer. Dusse-je vivre des siècles entiers, le doux tems de ma jeunesse ni peut renaître pour moi, ni s'effacer jamais dans ma mémoire.* When I got there, Sir, the organ was playing the 100th psalm, and when it was done, Mr. C. rose and gave out his text, "And he went up into the mountain to pray, HIMSELF, ALONE["]. As he gave out this text, his voice "rose like a steam of rich distill'd perfumes," and when he came to the last two words, which he pronounced loud, deep, and distinct, it seemed to me, Sir, who was then young, as if the sounds had echoed from the bottom of the human heart, and as if that prayer might have floated in solemn silence through the universe. The idea of St. John came into my mind, "of one crying in the wilderness, who had his loins girt about, and whose food was locusts and wild honey." The preacher then launched into his subject, like an eagle dallying with the wind. *That* sermon, like *this* sermon, was upon peace and war; upon church and state—not their alliance, but their separation—on the spirit of the world and the spirit of Christianity, not as the same, but as opposed to one another. He talked of those who

17

had "inscribed the cross of Christ on banners dripping with human gore." He made a poetical and pastoral excursion,—and to shew the fatal effects of war, drew a striking contrast between the simple shepherd boy, driving his team afield, or sitting under the hawthorn, piping to his flock, as though he should never be old, and the same poor country-lad, crimped, kidnapped, brought into town, made drunk at an alehouse, turned into a wretched drummer-boy, with his hair sticking on end with powder and pomatum, a long cue at his back, and tricked out in the loathsome finery of the profession of blood.

"Such were the notes our once-lov'd poet sung,"

And for myself, Sir, I could not have been more delighted if I had heard the music of the spheres. Poetry and Philosophy had met together, Truth and Genius had embraced, under the eye and with the sanction of Religion. This was even beyond my hopes. I returned home well satisfied. The sun that was still labouring pale and wan through the sky, obscured by thick mists, seemed an emblem of the *good cause:* and the cold dank drops of dew that hung half melted on the beard of the thistle, had something genial and refreshing in them; for there was a spirit of hope and youth in all nature, that turned everything into good. The face of nature had not then the brand of JUS DIVINUM on it;

"Like to that sanguine flower inscrib'd with woe." (7: 128–29, emphasis in original)[13]

This memorable portrait of Coleridge in the annus mirabilis of British Romanticism will, of course, be recognized as part of the widely anthologized essay "My First Acquaintance With Poets," which first appeared in Byron and Hunt's *Liberal* in 1823 (17: 106–22). Modern readers, however, are unlikely ever to have focused on the political dimensions of this passage, left muted and implicit in the 1823 essay by the removal of explicit references to Coleridge's most recent lay sermon. Yet in both versions the passage itself is clearly "inscrib'd with woe," not merely from the aestheticized pain of Romantic nostalgia, but from the distinctly political imprint of "JUS DIVINUM," a phrase taken directly from Coleridge's *Statesman's Manual* and used by the *Examiner* as a sarcastic euphemism for the reactionary doctrine of "the divine right of kings"—a doctrine used in turn by government writers to sanctify the Regent's policy of repressing the movement for democratic reform.

Few readers will therefore be aware that in its original context, this moving tribute to Coleridge's discursive authority in 1798—in which "Poetry and Philosophy . . . Truth and Genius . . . Religion . . . and the *good cause*" converge with millennial transformative power—was in fact an image conjured by Hazlitt to make all the more forceful its exposure as an illusion.

Now, Sir, what I have to complain of is this, that from reading your account of the "Lay-Sermon," I begin to suspect that my notions formerly must have been little better than a deception: that my faith in Mr. Coleridge's great powers must have been a vision of my youth, that, like other such visions, must pass away from me; and that all his genius and eloquence is *vox et preterea nihil:* for otherwise how is it so lost to all common sense upon paper?

Again, Sir, I ask Mr. Coleridge, why, having preached such a sermon as I have described, he has published such a sermon as you have described? What right, Sir, has he or any man to make a fool of me or any man? I am naturally, Sir, a man of a plain, dull, dry understanding, without flights or fancies, and can just contrive to plod on, if left to myself: what right, then, has Mr. C., who is going to ascend in a balloon, to offer me a seat in the parachute, only to throw me from the height of his career upon the ground, and dash me to pieces? Or again, what right has he to invite me to a feast of poets and philosophers, fruits and flowers intermixed,—immortal fruits and amaranthine flowers,—and then to tell me it is all vapour, and, like *Timon,* to throw his empty dishes in my face? No, Sir, I must and will say it is hard. I hope, between ourselves, there is no breach of confidence in all this; nor do I well understand how men's opinions on moral, political, and religious subjects can be kept a secret, except by putting them in *The Correspondent.*

SEMPER EGO AUDITOR. (7: 129)

For this "AUDITOR," then, the "vision" of "Mr. Coleridge's great powers" was contingent upon the poet-preacher's espousal of "the *good cause"*; Coleridge's evident abandonment of that cause for a politics of pious conformism serves to nullify his authority in this area as mere "*vox et preterea nihil.*" Moreover, into the vacuum of authority suddenly created by "AUDITOR"'s recognition of this loss flows the authority of the *Examiner* itself, on which its correspondent frankly admits he depends for his entire knowledge of Coleridge's text.

Yet there are practical reasons for this transfer of authority: Coleridge's tract, after all, was addressed exclusively to "THE HIGHER CLASSES OF SOCI-ETY," and in the straightened economic circumstances of a severe, nationwide depression, such readers as "AUDITOR" were forced increasingly to rely on review-criticism for their knowledge of books that were as deliberately exclusionary in their prices as in their subtitles. "AUDITOR," of course, represents for Hazlitt the ideal consumer of his own essays within a rapidly evolving marketplace for literature. At once a vigilant and attentive "auditor" of the minute movements of public debate, he is a man of "common sense" and "a plain, dull, dry understanding," who, at the very nadir of the postwar depression, "can just contrive to plod on, if left to [him]self." Added to his vivid memory of Coleridge's Unitarian sermon, these characteristics make him typical of that sector of the reading public shaped by what Gary Kelly calls the "Nonconformist Enlightenment" and made up of a large and diverse group of "artisans and petty bourgeois reformers" (159–60). Moreover, these characteristics situate "AUDITOR" at the very intersection of three of the "reading audiences" designated by Klancher as "middle-class," "mass," and "radical," that Klancher demonstrates to have "crystallized" into mutual counter-definition at precisely this moment under pressure of the Distresses crisis (16).

This unique positioning of Hazlitt's critical persona is evident in turn in the very stylistic eclecticism that marks his correspondent's prose. The pseudonym assumes importance in this context, alluding as it does to the opening line of Juvenal's *Satires*, "Semper ego auditor tantum?"—"Must I always be a listener only?" (Duff 1; Rudd 3). This letter clearly indicates otherwise. Though "AUDITOR" declares himself to be "without flights or fancies," his letter nevertheless opens with a breathtaking "flight" of lyricized memoir, comparable in rhetorical effect to a Wordsworthian "spot of time" (or, via the allusion to *La Nouvelle Heloïse*, to Rousseau's *Confessions*), and is thus designed to appeal to the introspective tastes of the newly self-isolating "middle-class" reading audience (Klancher 47–57). Yet as we have seen, this prose experiment in the epiphanic sublime is then subordinated to the iconoclastic satire of the letter's concluding "fancies." Such images as Coleridge's newfangled "balloon" and his misanthropic "empty dishes" reach out to the growing market for the graphic and the sensational in the emergent "mass public" (Klancher 76–97). At the same time, they function as vivid allegories of the political grievances of William Cobbett's "radical" readership, at once newly enfranchised by literacy and left "empty" by the brusque rejection of political reform (Klancher 99–133).

By republishing this letter among his *Political Essays* on the brink of Peterloo, Hazlitt clearly foregrounds his appeal to this latter, Radical reader-ship, as well as the discursive context of political debate that helped define his critical practice. Yet this letter makes equally clear the interpenetration of this context with the struggle over the reading audiences in the literary marketplace and the conflicted use of genre as a vehicle for cultural authority. While "AU-DITOR" 's letter enacts a moment of poignant disillusionment in Coleridge's political authority, the immediacy of this representation is underscored by the personification of a reader willing to move beyond mere passive consumption to join the dialectical process by which "public opinion" is formed. As the pseudonym suggests, this "AUDITOR" is not content to remain "a listener only." Initially provoked by a piece of journalism ("Your last Sunday's 'Literary Notice' has given me some uneasiness on two points"), he then takes issue with his editor on the subject ("Now, Sir, what I have to complain of is this"), experiences a raising of consciousness ("I begin to suspect that my notions formerly must have been little better than a deception"), and turns finally to a direct public challenge to the literary producer: "Again, Sir, I ask Mr. Coleridge, why, having preached such a sermon as I have described, he has published such a sermon as you have described?" This awakening to activism is underscored by the subversion of lyric by satire, encomium by invective, "sincerity" by irony.

Needless to say, it is for these generic reasons that the literary history of Romanticism has taken a rather different approach to this letter. When it is recalled from the apocrypha of Romantic prose, it is customarily assigned two roles, both in negative relation to the securely canonized 1823 essay "My First Acquaintance With Poets." First, it is presented as the flawed, "primitive" draft of a subsequent masterpiece of Romantic prose, and therefore as a telling demonstration of the innate ascendency of lyric over satiric modes (Jones, "First Flight" 35, 36). Second, this "embryonic" text (Jones 40) represents for biographical criticism a hopeful turning point in the writing career of William Hazlitt—an early sign of his progressive liberation from what is held to be his brutalizing apprenticeship in political journalism and his emergence as one of the major prose stylists of British Romanticism.

These remarks may be substantiated by reference to Bill Ruddick's representative treatment in his article "Recollecting Coleridge: the Internalization of Radical Energies in Hazlitt's Political Prose." Here Ruddick notes the "harsh, impetuous, paradoxical manner of [Hazlitt's] political essays," which, in the case of the 1817 letter causes it to devolve into "a series of bitter reproaches" (251, 253). This is contrasted with Hazlitt's "most mature manner of treating revolutionary and radical themes," that in the 1823 essay manifests itself as "a joy-suffused rediscovery of the past, rapturous from beginning to end" (248, 251). Nevertheless, Ruddick regards Hazlitt's writings on Coleridge during the Distresses debate as containing "the germ" of this more "mature manner," and his 1817 letter is singled out as "the most significant" of these writings (249). It is recognized as a pivotal text, however, not in terms of the momentous events taking place in the cultural environment that gave rise to it, but rather in terms of the personal, developmental process by which Hazlitt had to "internalize" his "radical energies."

> [t]he moment of breakthrough seems to have come when Hazlitt returned to his January 1817 account of Coleridge in the pulpit, detached it from its original context as part of an attack on a particular text, and used it as the key passage which energizes the entire recreation and dramatization of the most important period in his own early life in "My First Acquaintance With Poets." Removed from a "then and now" relationship with Coleridge's later political thought . . . , Hazlitt's reminiscence proves to possess a dynamism which is far more potent than he can have realized when he published it in its original context. (250–51)

Here again we find a particularly clear instance of the way the study of Romanticism in general, and of the texts of the Distresses period in particular, have been "dominated . . . by Romanticism's own self-representations" (McGann 1). First, we note the emphasis on evaluation, both critical and moral, founded on norms that posit lyric as the highest standard for literary discourse. The "harsh" and "bitter" discourse of the political essay is contrasted unfavorably with the "joy-suffused," "rapturous," and more "mature" lyrical mode, which "proves to possess a dynamism which is far more potent" than either satire or invective. Second, as Clifford Siskin has shown in *The Historicity of Romantic*

Discourse, such discourse is preoccupied with narratives of development and "progress"—generic as well as biographical—principally articulated in paradigmatic moments of "revision" (39 and passim). In Ruddick's analysis, the "moment of breakthrough" for both text and author is also a moment of "recreation," which in turn serves a process of internalization—a development away from the public and politically engaged satiric "attack" toward the formation of a "mature" and complex interiority assisted by lyric "reminiscence." Thus the canonical value of the 1823 essay is clearly reinforced by its disengagement from the atmosphere of discursive and ideological struggle that constituted "its original context as part of an attack on a particular text," and, perhaps most tellingly, to its removal from a "relationship with Coleridge's later political thought" (Ruddick 251).

As noted at the outset, this study locates the value of Hazlitt's Regency reviews precisely in their contestatory relationship with Coleridge's later political thought. As such, they offer an indispensable vehicle for reexamining the ideological implications of this thought for the subsequent "scholarship and criticism of Romanticism" (McGann 1). More than this, however, once resituated within culturally specific contexts of political, commercial, and generic struggle, these reviews, in their very engagement with Coleridge's works, come to epitomize a distinct moment in British cultural history. In them can be read some of the most important discursive and ideological conflicts unfolding within middle-class culture at a critical moment in what Raymond Williams has called "the long revolution" (x).

1

COMMON SENSE
AND HUMANITY:

Hazlitt's Review of
the *Christabel* Volume

Hazlitt's review of the *Christabel* volume appeared in the *Examiner* on 2 June 1816, the first of five articles on Coleridge and his works to appear in the Hunt brothers' weekly political journal over the next nine months.[1] Unlike his other *Examiner* reviews of Coleridge, however, Hazlitt's "Literary Notice" of *Christabel; Kubla Khan, A Vision; [and] The Pains of Sleep* was not republished among his *Political Essays* in August 1819. Perhaps for this very reason, it has retained a higher profile within traditional literary history than any of Hazlitt's other writings on Coleridge during the Distresses period. Classified by Howe as an "Uncollected Literary Essay," and focused as it is on a volume of seemingly apolitical Romantic fragments, it has certainly never been stigmatized as an "attack" (in Ruddick's words) on Coleridge's "later political thought" (251). At the same time, however, it has attracted attention as a harshly oppositional review by a known author of a text that contains two of the most warmly canonized poems in the English language. Out of this sharp discrepancy of interpretation, Hazlitt's review of the *Christabel* volume has come to represent the scandalous rejection of Coleridge's poetic genius at the bar of anonymous review-criticism.

Yet this article, though never specifically reclassified by Hazlitt as a "political essay," was nevertheless written within the context of events in May and June 1816 that clearly prefigure the Peterloo massacre of August 1819. Indeed it bears the imprint of these events as discernibly as any of Hazlitt's more explicitly politicized reviews. A week before its appearance, for example, the *Examiner* of 26 May 1816 featured an article titled "The Riots," in which were gathered accounts of the violent uprisings that had broken out "in various parts of the country" throughout the previous month.[2] The article reports that under such banners as "BREAD OR BLOOD," houses and barns had been set aflame in a number of "disturbed districts" until in almost every case the rioters had been suppressed by detachments of the standing army. "Want of work and want of bread," the *Examiner* writes, "are indeed dreadful stimulants to outrage; and it must be confessed these are fearful signs of national suffering" (328). Though "want of bread" was familiar enough, the lack of work in May 1816 was a virtually unprecedented phenomenon. The end of the war had brought home hundreds of thousands of discharged soldiers, most of whom returned to Britain only to swell the ranks of those already thrown out of work by the collapse of the armament and textile industries—a mass unemployment that was indeed one of the "fearful signs" of the vicissitudes of a newly industrialized economy (Woodward 63; Evans 15). And as with the Manchester yeomanry three years later, the response of the Regent's Tory ministry to the resulting dissidence was to employ force, a strategy duly applauded by such ministerial journals as the *Courier* and the *Times*. Thus the *Courier* of 25 May:

> The most prompt and decisive measures have been adopted by Government to suppress the riotous proceedings which have lately taken place, and which unfortunately continue in Norfolk, Suffolk, and Cambridgeshire. . . . —It is now becoming evident that the military force, which some persons have pronounced inconsistent with the liberties of the country, is not more than sufficient for its internal security.[3]

Five days later, the *Times* adds this report:

> The decisive measures taken at Littleport had universally spread intimidation among the rioters. The coroner's jury had sate on the two persons killed at Littleport, and brought in a verdict of *Justifiable Homicide:* besides which, three troops of dragoons, with some infantry, and two pieces of light artillery, had arrived, and been distributed so as to act, if necessary, at a moment's notice.[4]

Little more than a year after Waterloo, then, and in anticipation of events three years later at Peterloo, the British army was engaged in a new form of "*Justifiable Homicide.*" And while there were "some persons" (most notably in the nongovernmental press) willing to pronounce this tactic "inconsistent with the liberties of the country," it is likely that the majority of citizens within the tiny enclave of the ruling classes felt that universal "intimidation" was in this instance an appropriate response to "national suffering."

Simultaneously with these events, and in apparent isolation from them, Coleridge's collection of romantic fragments *Christabel; Kubla Khan, A Vision; [and] The Pains of Sleep* was published on 10 May 1816,[5] and it quickly became "the standing enigma that puzzles the curiosity of literary circles" (Reiman A: 268). One measure of its success within such "circles" was the appearance of a rare review in the conservative *Times* on 20 May, hailing Coleridge's book as a "singular monument of genius" and predicting that "its publication in its present imperfect state may not improbably give an additional zest to public curiosity" (Reiman A: 890–91). This prediction proved correct, for one week later the liberal *Champion* records the ensuing stir of voices and questions "alternately heard and put" in the clubs, theaters, and drawing rooms of the bourgeois public sphere: "What is it all about? What is the idea? Is *Lady Geraldine* a sorceress? or a vampire? or a man? or what is she, or he, or it?" (Reiman A: 268). As the *Times* had suggested in its article, the "irresistible" appeal of the leading poem in Coleridge's collection lay not only in the "thought-suspending awe" inspired by Geraldine, but also in its story, that is "like a dream of lovely forms, mixed with strange and indescribable terrors. The scene, the personages, are those of old, romantic superstition; but we feel intimate with them, as if they were of our own day, and of our own neighbourhood" (Reiman A: 890).

Thus when Hazlitt came to write his review of *Christabel* for the *Examiner* in early June, it was in the context of this uncanny juxtaposition in the daily and weekly newspapers of a "zest" for "strange and indescribable terrors" and alarm over "fearful signs of national suffering." On the one hand was the phenomenon of a reading public engrossed by Coleridge's fragments of "old, romantic superstition," in which Gothic "terrors" are made to feel "intimate"—"as if they were of our own day, and of our own neighbourhood"—and on the other alarming descriptions of events actually unfolding in the "neighbourhood" of London, in which the performance of both political resistance and political authority involved recourse to actual violence and bloodshed.

Given these circumstances, Hazlitt's review is unique among the many contemporary articles on *Christabel,* both for its intuition of a link between these otherwise unrelated phenomena and for its attempt to work out this connection in a politically inflected reading of the title poem. From its opening paragraph, in which the *Examiner*'s readership is reminded that the author of *Christabel* doubles as a political writer for the reactionary *Courier* ("his mind hangs suspended between poetry and prose, truth and falsehood"), through to its final, approving quotation of lines that represent the "one genuine outburst of humanity, worthy of the author," Hazlitt's review attempts to hold *Christabel* accountable to a norm of "common sense" against which its various strategies of mystification appear ideologically pointed (19: 32, 34, 33). In the following passage, for example, Hazlitt answers the enthusiasm of the *Times* by acknowledging the aesthetic appeal of Coleridge's experiment in the Gothic sublime—in order all the more emphatically to refute it.

> In parts of *Christabel* there is a great deal of beauty, both of thought, imagery, and versification; but the effect of the general story is dim, obscure, and

visionary. It is more like a dream than a reality. The mind, in reading it, is spell-bound. The sorceress seems to act without power—Christabel to yield without resistance. The faculties are thrown into a state of metaphysical suspense and theoretical imbecility. The poet, like the witch in *Spenser,* is evidently

"Busied about some wicked gin."—

But we do not foresee what he will make of it. There is something disgusting at the bottom of his subject, which is but ill glossed over by a veil of Della Cruscan sentiment and fine writing—like moon-beams playing on a charnel house, or flowers strewed on a dead body. Mr. Coleridge's style is essentially superficial, pretty, ornamental, and he has forced it into the service of a story which is petrific. (19: 33)

It is the "effect" of such a story that Hazlitt is most concerned with here, particularly when this "dream" is measured against the "reality" of other concurrent events in June of 1816. The very "beauty" and discursive power of the poem dictate its rejection, for these work to nullify and transfix the Enlightenment norms of clarity and distinctness with a story that is "dim, obscure, and visionary." In calling the poem "more like a dream than a reality," Hazlitt clearly picks up the defining term of the *Times* review, but he deploys the word "dream" to precisely opposite rhetorical ends. In the *Times,* Coleridge's "dream of lovely forms" is praised for its capacity to make us "feel intimate with" the forms of "old, romantic superstition." Yet these are "forms" that in adjacent columns of the same newspaper— and despite a century of debate seeking to undermine or discard them— continue to function as agents of "universal intimidation" within society at large. The poem itself, we recall, speaks of Sir Leoline's "world of death," represented in Hazlitt's review by the deliberately polemical images of a "charnel house" and a "dead body." It is the poetic impulse to aestheticize such a world that Hazlitt declares to be "disgusting," a revulsion extended by implication to the eager market for such Gothic refinements among writers of the conservative press at precisely the moment that *"Justifiable Homicide,"* in defense of an effete social order, was being revived within the borders of Britain itself.

As we shall see, these political overtones in the review's central passage are reinforced by other elements of the review, but first it is important to note how differently this particular passage has been interpreted by previous commentators on it. From the response of Coleridge himself through to Karen Swann's feminist rereading of the *Christabel* controversy, the phrase "something disgusting at the bottom of his subject" has been seized upon as a sign of Hazlitt's attempt to insinuate a salacious misreading of Coleridge's title poem. The authority of this approach is once again a function of the innate priority assigned by tradition to both the poet and the poem. On the one hand there is the virtually unquestioned influence of Coleridge's own tendentious account of its reception. On the other there is the attractiveness of a companion narrative by which *Christabel* requires chivalrous rescue by scholarly posterity from the ruffian grip of anonymous critics like William Hazlitt. The combined result of these traditions is that Hazlitt's review has never been read in the context of the historical events of May 1816, nor in terms of its dialogical engagement with other, equally polemical reviews of the same text.

Coleridge's account of the reception of *Christabel,* of course, reinforces this tendency, and three elements of it in particular may be isolated for their long-term influence on literary scholarship. First, Coleridge claims in the *Biographia* that *Christabel* was "assailed with a malignity and a spirit of personal hatred" by "a man" later identified in his private correspondence as Hazlitt (2: 239; *Letters* 4: 918). By invoking the shibboleth "personal," Coleridge attempts to preclude the possibility of any other—especially political—motivation for this review. Second, "with very few exceptions," Coleridge claims to have "heard nothing but abuse" of *Christabel* from the periodical press (2: 237). In his view, Hazlitt epitomizes this "abuse" because he was the author of both the *Examiner* review and also (it seemed to him) the later, more sensationally hostile "quizz" of *Christabel* in the *Edinburgh* (*Letters* 4: 692). Third, based on this latter (and mistaken) attribution, Coleridge holds Hazlitt responsible for the "rumour" that Geraldine was actually a man in disguise.[6] The *Edinburgh*'s satire of *Christabel* famously contains a number of variously explicit sexual innuendos. For Coleridge, these provide an interpretative key to the earlier *Examiner* review, and they are further explained in his letters with a series of sensational counter-rumors about Hazlitt's alleged propensity to "vices too disgusting to be named" (4: 693).[7]

Each of these claims has been challenged from within even the most traditional forms of literary research. John Beer, for example, uses biographical evidence to question Coleridge's "conviction of a strong malevolence on Hazlitt's part," reminding us that "one searches the records of Hazlitt's life in vain for evidence which warrants [such a conviction]" (42). David Erdman's discovery in 1958 of the *Times* review—and of its reprint two weeks later in the *Courier*—demonstrated that Coleridge's book was greeted with enthusiasm as well as "abuse" (54). Indeed, as Erdman makes clear, when the total circulation of this *Times/Courier* review is taken into account and then added to other similarly appreciative articles in the *Critical Review* and the *European Magazine,* the *Christabel* volume is found to have attracted as many influentially "positive" reviews as "negative" ones. Coleridge's protestations to the contrary,[8] *Christabel* was in fact a modest market success, selling out three editions by the end of 1816 (Jackson, *Coleridge* 199n. 1). Moreover, in the late 1950s Elisabeth Schneider proved convincingly that the *Edinburgh*'s late review was written by Thomas Moore, not by Hazlitt.[9] She effectively dissociated Hazlitt from both this article's legendary hostility and its salacious innuendos regarding Geraldine's identity and intentions. Taken together, such studies open up the possibility that Hazlitt's approach to *Christabel* was shaped by quite different concerns than those Coleridge imagined.

Yet the overall impression created by Coleridge's account of this event has lingered long after its individual details have been refuted. We may take as typical Geoffrey Yarlott's brief summary of the reception of *Christabel:*

> The critics (Hazlitt particularly) pilloried these poems, especially *Christabel,* whose sexual features induced one pamphleteer to describe it as "the most obscene Poem in the English Language." *The Examiner,* of 2 June 1816, objected:
>
>> There is something disgusting at the bottom of his subject, which is but ill glossed over by a veil of Della Cruscan sentiment and fine writing— like moon-beams playing on a charnel house, or flowers strewed on a dead body.
>
> Hazlitt, the author, probably, of this review, even spread the rumour apparently that Geraldine was actually a man in disguise. In reacting against the poem's "obscenity," these reviewers proved remarkably blind to its other merits. (181)

Like other similarly traditional narratives of the event, Yarlott locates Hazlitt's review at the very center of a uniformly hostile response to Coleridge's book, with Hazlitt himself personally orchestrating a willful and salacious distortion of the title poem.

Even in more recent, "post-Romantic" criticism, Coleridge's influence ironically persists. Here we may take Swann's otherwise radical rereading of the "The Debate on the Character of *Christabel*" as typical. While she offers crucial insights into the discursive context of the literary marketplace into which both Coleridge and Hazlitt made competing and controversial interventions, her article is nevertheless premised on the surprisingly unexamined notion that the reviews of *Christabel* were "universally scathing" (404). Moreover, while Swann works to relativize the authority of Coleridge's own critical discourse on the poem—and in so doing recover a broad range of "problematically invested literary relations, including those between writers and other writers, and among authors, readers, and books"—she nevertheless reduces the intensity of these relations to masculinist "hysteria" in the face of the "fantastic [female] exchanges of Geraldine and Christabel" (398). Once again Hazlitt's review is held up as the epitome of this "hysteria"; his reference to "something disgusting at the bottom of [Coleridge's] subject" is thus routinely interpreted as an attempt to "reduc[e]" the poem's power "to its sexual content." Swann goes so far as to impute a prurient pun: "Hazlitt contains this power in the 'bottom' and invites us to declare it female" (407). Like all previous commentators on this text, Swann is concerned to locate the source of its evident polemical intensity, and in this case she falls back on a traditional (Coleridgean) impression of Hazlitt's character (with its "vices too disgusting to be named") in order to find in his review an especially virulent example of patriarchal chauvinism. Thus she too overlooks the fact that the rhetorical strategies of these "literary gentlemen" were also—and perhaps more decisively—shaped by complex political, commercial, and stylistic rivalries, patterns of contestation further intensified by the advent of "national suffering."

One crucial feature of Hazlitt's review, for example, that clearly invites us to locate it within these broader discursive contexts—but which has so far gone completely unnoticed in previous commentary—is its original title in the *Examiner* of 2 June 1816. Where Howe assigns the provisional title "Mr. Coleridge's Christabel" for the standard edition, Hazlitt's review actually appeared under the title "Literary Notices. No. 1" (19: 338). Such a title introduces far more than an isolated critique of *Christabel* motivated by personal feelings; it announces instead an article fully integrated into the larger journalistic agenda of the *Examiner,* launching in this case a new and sustained venture into literary criticism on the part of one of the most outspoken, free-thinking journals of political opinion in the British public sphere.[10] This announcement of a "Literary Notices" series takes on even greater significance when we recall that literary criticism was at this time still considered the sole province of the established monthly and quarterly reviews, rarely appearing in the columns of daily and weekly political journals (Reiman A: 890; Hayden xviii). Yet as we have seen, the *Christabel* volume was controversial enough to have already broken down this protocol, quickly attracting two reviews in the newspaper press: the first, the unexpected foray of the daily *Times* into literary criticism, and the second, a sharp retort in the liberal weekly *Champion* in its trend-setting "Literature" column. "Literary Notices. No. 1" was thus the third review of *Christabel* to appear. It was clearly designed in competitive response to these two previous reviews, and it appeared in a Sunday newspaper with a strong reputation for both dissident politics and journalistic innovation. Far from an autonomous expression of "personal hatred," this review announces, with its title, that it is primarily motivated by the *Examiner*'s engagement in the broader contexts of public debate: the arena of political struggle, the competitive marketplace for literature and literary criticism, and the shifting hierarchy of genres and modes by which discursive authority was most effectively performed within the public sphere. Hazlitt's review of the *Christabel* volume therefore deserves reconsideration within each of these contexts, in order both to clarify its role within the *Christabel* controversy as a whole and to recover its perspective on Coleridge's evolving bid for cultural authority within each of these areas.

We may begin by returning to the environment of political debate, where the polemical tone and approach of this review reflect an underlying structure of political rivalry established over years of what Jones describes as intense journalistic dueling within the London newspaper press.[11] Perhaps the clearest evidence for this lies in the immediate response of the *Courier* to the *Examiner's* review. In its very next issue (4 June 1816), the *Courier* closed ranks with its political ally the *Times* by reprinting substantial portions of the enthusiastic *Times* review (Erdman 53). With this gesture, the *Courier* answered the criticism of its foremost political adversary, the *Examiner,* while defending the work of its own long-term contributor of political essays, Samuel Taylor Coleridge. In so doing, of course, it ironically confirmed the validity of Hazlitt's attempt to suggest thematic links between Coleridge's Gothic poetry and his political prose, while at the same time it reinforced the implicit alignment of positive and negative responses to the book along the deepening ideological divisions of the British public sphere. The appearance of this reprint in the *Courier,* moreover, brought to an unprecedented total of four the number of reviews in the London newspaper press attracted by the *Christabel* volume, all within three weeks of its publication, and thus before any of the established monthly or quarterly reviews had had a chance to join the debate. In this way, Coleridge's collection of Romantic fragments became the catalyst of a marked convergence of literary and political practice, a trend in turn epitomized by the *Examiner's* review, which uses the occasion of the *Christabel* volume to announce a permanent series of such politicized "Notices." This trend was clearly accelerated by the thickening atmosphere of political crisis. Within just two months, the *Examiner* would be using its "Literary Notices" column to review "Speeches in Parliament on the Distresses of the Country." And by March 1817, at the height of the crisis, the "*Wat Tyler* affair" would bring literary and political opinion into inseparable conjunction in Parliament and in the Court of Chancery, as well as in the periodical press.

In the spring of 1816, however, the convergence of literary and political discourse was apparent only in less overt forms and contexts. The *Christabel* volume, for example, shared many of the same features that would eventually make Southey's play *Wat Tyler* the catalyst of political controversy. Both were literary works held over from the 1790s, written by former republicans now active in the reactionary press. But the underlying issue in the case of Coleridge's book was the telling absence, rather than the glaring presence, of an explicit politics in the work itself. Like Gothic fiction in general, the leading poem was thus susceptible to multiple and even contradictory political appropriations. Lord Byron's prepublication support for the poem, for example, was one reminder that Gothic fiction could be assimilated to free-thinking liberalism, as the writings of Beckford and Lewis had been in the 1790s (Sage 14). In Byron's "puff" of *Christabel* in *The Siege of Corinth,* he calls it "that wild, and singularly original and beautiful poem" (901). In an ultimately telling coincidence, this phrase was taken up as the advertising slogan for Coleridge's book[12] at the very moment that Byron became embroiled in the sensational public scandal that transformed him from Britain's most universally admired poet into a Gothic villain seeking haughty self-exile in the sultry land of Radcliffe's Montoni. In these circumstances, then, Byron's epithet "wild" became more than a merely decorous foretaste of sublimity in the poem. It represented an index of scandalous transgression—at once literary, moral, and, by association with Byron's liberalism, political.

Yet Byron's intervention also meant that the *Christabel* volume emerged from the highly respected house of John Murray, better known as the publisher of the *Quarterly Review,* bastion of Tory moral and political opinion. Hence the swift endorsement of the *Quarterly*'s political ally, the *Times,* producing a reminder that a taste for Gothic romance was just as easily assimilated to reactionary as to libertarian politics (Sage 13, 16). Such an appropriation, however, required a careful erasure of the political by emphasizing the sublime transcendence of social reality on the part of both Gothic poet and reader. Something of this kind may well have motivated Coleridge's own composition of the poem in the late 1790s, as Andrea Henderson has pointed out in her article "Revolution, Response, and 'Christabel.' " Calling attention to what Coleridge himself termed "the hubbub of revolutions" in the 1790s, and situating *Christabel* alongside such contemporaneous poems as "Fire, Famine, and Slaughter" and "France: an Ode," Henderson notes that Coleridge's "decision not to treat the political explicitly [in *Christabel*] was itself politically meaningful" (881). She then proceeds to demonstrate how the differences between the first and second parts of the poem reflect "Coleridge's mounting resistance to sensibility" between 1797 and 1800, a resistance which in turn "can best be understood in the context of his own desire to become less immediately responsive to Revolutionary enthusiasm" (887). Henderson does not, however, go on to trace the effect of finally publishing such a poem amid the "hubbub" of rioting in 1816, though certainly in Coleridge's preface to *Christabel,* written at the time of publication in 1816, can be found a corroborating elision of the political. In an effort to reconstruct "the impression of its originality," for example, and thus to "preclud[e] charges of plagiarism," Coleridge is forced to draw elaborate attention to the years in which the poem was composed (*Poetical Works* 213–14). To do so, of course, was to risk reviving the link between literary "originality" and Radical sensibility that pertained in the revolutionary decade—a link that governed Coleridge's other, more explicitly political poetry of that period, and would no doubt therefore have ensured the brisk rejection of *Christabel* by the governmental press had it been published at that time. Thus Coleridge in 1816 shrouds these dates in ornate formality, spelling out "the year one thousand seven hundred and ninety seven" and "the year one thousand eight hundred" as if to suggest the poem's provenance in an even more remote and exotic era than the simple numbers might otherwise indicate. He reinforces this impression with the striking Gothicism of his "poetic powers" being held since that time in a mysterious "state of suspended animation" (*Poetical Works* 213n. 4). Similarly, the preface to "Kubla Khan" presents the poet of sensibility as a passive visionary rather than a political activist. This fragmentary "vision"— despite its ominous "ancestral voices prophesying war" and in modest defiance

31

of Byron's recommendation—is here passed off as a harmless "psychological curiosity" (*Poetical Works* 295).

The *Times* in turn follows Coleridge's lead by celebrating the *Christabel* volume as a "singular monument of genius" that by its very nature transcends the political (Reiman A: 890). As we have seen, the very appearance of the *Times* review itself was a political gesture. Yet in the opening lines of the review this is made into an occasion for the dramatic suspension of the newspaper's "customary track"—in deference to a timeless epiphany of poetic power: "It is not often that we venture to notice the poetical compositions of the day; they have their appropriate sphere of criticism, which, indeed, is for the most part very debatable: but when a work appears of indisputable originality, forming almost a class by itself—attractive no less by its beauty than by its singularity, we may be pardoned for deviating a little from our customary track" (Reiman A: 890). By this account, the *Times* is inspired to introduce poetical criticism into the (admittedly inappropriate) sphere of political journalism not, apparently, out of partisan loyalty to a *Courier* writer and to the publishing house of the *Quarterly Review,* but out of startled respect for the "originality," "beauty," and "singularity" of Coleridge's new work. We note, however, that the article pauses just long enough to lay down a broad challenge to the "debatable" sphere of conventional criticism dominated by the monthlies and quarterlies of the Opposition press. We note, too, that the terms of praise here are all adapted directly from Byron's "puff," as quoted in Murray's advertisements for the poem—with the important exception of the key word "wild." When this politically sensitive word does in fact surface later in the review, it is with telling ambiguity: "what we have principally to remark, with respect to the tale, is, that wild, and romantic, and visionary as it is, it has a truth of its own that seizes on and masters the imagination from the beginning to the end" (Reiman A: 891). Now whether the tale bears this powerful "truth" in spite of or because of the fact that it is "wild, and romantic, and visionary," the *Times* carefully leaves up to its readers to decide. Either way—whether these terms are being appropriated or set aside for the purpose—the review makes quite clear that this "truth" is a function of the poem's fundamental detachment from political and social realities. *Christabel* is in "a class by itself," and it is the "originality" and "singularity" of both poem and poet that in this case guarantee their cultural authority over the imagination of the reading public.

Among the many responses within the Opposition press to the challenge laid down by this *Times* review, "Literary Notices. No. 1" stands out for a number of reasons. One of these is its attempt to hold "wild and romantic" genius accountable to the political and social realities of 1816. Another is its willingness to complicate a politicized response to the *Christabel* volume by alluding to Coleridge's former political authority within Enlightenment nonconformism at the time the *Christabel* poems were written. Thus by comparison, for example, with the anti-aristocratic rhetoric of the liberal *Champion* or with the one-dimensional hostility of the Whig *Edinburgh*

Review, the *Examiner* turns to such devices as wit, irony, and even allegory to register some of the manifest complexities and contradictions engendered by Coleridge's experiment in the Gothic sublime.

The *Champion*'s review presents an important and initial point of reference in this regard because it preceded "Literary Notices. No. 1" by one week, and it appeared in the only other Sunday weekly political journal of anti-ministerial opinion (Courtney 98–99). It had therefore already taken up the position of pure negation, an approach to *Christabel* governed at once by the *Champion*'s partisan antipathy to the *Times* and by a middle-class liberalism so strongly grounded in anti-aristocratic politics that it translated (somewhat ironically) into virulent anti-Byronism (Courtney 99–100). Indeed the *Champion* had recently played a decisive role in escalating the Byron scandal, and thus the word "wild" in Murray's advertisement conjured for it only a corrupt libertinism coming to the aid of a manifest product of anachronistic Toryism. It is therefore with regret that the *Champion* records in its opening sequence that "Mr. Coleridge's Poem is at present the standing enigma that puzzles the curiosity of literary circles" (Reiman A: 268). In addition to the many questions "alternately heard and put," the article goes on to record the views of its "friend[s]," one of which suggests that *Christabel* is a "mere hoax," while another declares "that the poem has just the same effect upon his temper as if a man were to salute him on the street with a box on the ear, and walk away" (Reiman A: 268). The wildness of the poem thus becomes a form of cynical, dandyesque violence; far from Romantic or visionary, it is said to produce only a "maze of impenetrable mystery" that is "nothing more nor less than the evasive and unsatisfactory resource of conceited negligence and perverseness" (Reiman A: 268).

The phrase "conceited negligence and perverseness" draws the *Champion*'s political and literary agendas together, linking Coleridge's poetry with Byron's and both, by implication, with the corrupt practices of an effete ruling class. More important even than Byron's promotion of the poem, Coleridge's use of the fragment form to produce mystery implicates it in this sort of cultural corruption, a literary genre most recently popularized by such bestselling fragments as Byron's *The Giaour.* "The principle of producing effect by means of obscurity, is very admissible . . . in the subordinate and incidental points and circumstance in the progress of a story," the *Champion* concedes,

> but here the line must be drawn, and the licence must never be applied to the main thread of the narrative. It must not be made the excuse for the utter lack of perspicuity and connexion in the main fable, or of definiteness in the characters, the passions, and the situations. The abuse of talents and the abuse of poetical principles, appear to us to have been, if not Mr. Coleridge's chief object, certainly his chief effect in this Poem. . . . In diction, in numbers, in short in everything appertaining to the Poem, Mr. Coleridge's licentiousness out-Herods Herod. (Reiman A: 269)

With this remarkable assertion, the *Champion* brings to a head the political undertones of its review, as poetic "licence" becomes a metaphor for the worst form of despotic tyranny. What the *Times* had called a "singular monument of genius" with "a truth all its own," the *Champion* exposes as a "mere hoax," a willful "enigma" designed to baffle "the curiosity" of the reading public by deliberately mystifying an "abuse of principles"—whether these be "poetical," moral, or, by strong metaphorical extension, political.

Appearing the Sunday following the *Champion*'s review, "Literary Notices. No. 1" was clearly conceived as much in competitive response to this article as it was in partisan retort to the *Times* and in critical review of *Christabel*. The *Examiner*'s politics were more a product of eighteenth-century intellectual Radicalism than of the secular moralism of the *Champion*. Thus, for example, it was predisposed to respect the opinion of the liberal Byron about *Christabel* (despite his class and way of life), yet it remained suspicious of anything that emerged alongside the *Quarterly Review* from the house of John Murray (Courtney 98–99; Sullivan viii). Hazlitt's review attempts to register as accurately as possible the uncanny ambivalence of the *Christabel* volume in political terms, while at the same time holding both Coleridge and his first two reviewers strictly accountable to such Enlightenment norms as "common sense" and "humanity." In its opening paragraph, this translates into a witty paradox that at once appropriates and supersedes the opposing views of both the *Times* and the *Champion*.

> THE fault of Mr. Coleridge is, that he comes to no conclusion. He is a man of that universality of genius, that his mind hangs suspended between poetry and prose, truth and falsehood, and an infinity of other things, and from an excess of capacity, he does little or nothing. Here are two unfinished poems, and a fragment. *Christabel,* which has been much read and admired in manuscript, is now for the first time confided to the public. The *Vision of Kubla Khan* still remains a profound secret; for only a few lines of it were ever written. (19: 32)

Taking up Coleridge's own metaphor of "suspended animation," Hazlitt produces the figure of a "genius" so capacious as to be incapacitated, tragicomically "suspended" from meaningful agency by his own urge to "universality." With this figure he both upbraids the *Champion* for its simplistic denial of "genius" in Coleridge's work and challenges the *Times*'s premature ascription of "truth" to Coleridge's "unfinished poems." In the most direct reference of any of these early reviews to the environment of political debate, Hazlitt finds Coleridge suspended in particular between the binaries of "poetry and prose, truth and falsehood." The syntactical alignment of "poetry" with "truth" and "prose" with "falsehood" produces an allusion to the provenance of these poems in the period of Coleridge's Radicalism, and to his subsequent (and apparently incapacitating) turn to writing reactionary "prose" for the *Courier.* At the same time, however, the ambivalence of the *Christabel* volume is reflected in the fact that the four categories of "poetry and prose, truth and falsehood" are in fact left strategically unfixed in their referents. The equation of "truth" and "poetry" in *Christabel,* for example, is clearly undermined by the fact that it "comes to no conclusion"; this is in sharp contrast with Coleridge's more explicitly political poetry—and prose—of the 1790s. As we have seen, moreover, this review goes on to measure the "dim" and fictive "dream" of *Christabel* against empirical "reality," using a metaphor of military impressment to suggest that Coleridge's poetry—again like his prose—has now been "forced . . . into the service of a story which is petrific"—a story, in other words, that is the precise opposite of the empowering narratives of the Enlightenment.

Meanwhile, of course, the critical "prose" of the review itself assumes its own manifest alignment with "truth," evident in the brisk enumeration of empirical fact ("Here are two unfinished poems, and a fragment"), and in an opening line that asserts with epigrammatic wit the superior capacity of review-criticism to reach conclusions—and publish them quickly. Further, as the review proceeds it becomes clear that the *Examiner'*s aim in selecting the *Christabel* volume to launch its new series of politicized reviews was more than simply to expose Coleridge's "suspen[sion] between truth and falsehood"; its intention was to reprimand his recent and apparent leaning toward the latter. When the norm of "common sense" is introduced, for example, it is in the context of examining a key revision made to *Christabel* at the time of its Regency publication. Here the *Examiner* intends to supersede the findings of the *Champion,* which based its negative verdict on the mere fact of "impenetrable mystery" in *Christabel,* symbolized by the "enigma" of Geraldine's identity: "Is *Lady Geraldine* a sorceress? or a vampire? or a man? or what is she, or he, or it?" the *Champion* asks. The *Examiner,* by contrast, is able to prove progressive intentionality in Coleridge's use of mystery by producing knowledge of a line in the original manuscript—now missing from the poem—that fixed Geraldine's identity as "a witch" (19: 33, 33n). This line, in the *Examiner'*s view, is "absolutely necessary to the understanding of the story" (19: 32), and therefore its deletion at the point of publication takes on heightened ideological significance.

> The manuscript runs thus, or nearly thus:—
>   "Behold her bosom and half her side—
>   *Hideous, deformed, and pale of hue.*"
> This line is necessary to make common sense of the first and second part [of the poem.] "It is the keystone that makes up the arch." For that reason Mr. Coleridge left it out. Now this is a greater psychological curiosity than even the fragment of *Kubla Khan.* (19: 33)

Thus the *Examiner* demonstrates what the *Champion* could only assert: that Coleridge's sole revision of the poem in 1816 is a deliberate act of mystification, a turning away from "common sense" toward the "dim" and "obscure," a suspension of "truth" even more telling than the opacity of "Kubla Khan" precisely because it is active rather than passive. In naming this phenomenon a "psychological curiosity," Hazlitt once again borrows Coleridge's own terms to arch, ironic effect, in this case to suggest that the construction of an absence at the center of the poem by removing its "keystone" is continuous with those strategies of mystification by which Coleridge constructs authority in the (new) prefaces to the volume—a form of authority in turn sustained within society at large by such voices as the *Times*.

As noted earlier, however, it is not Hazlitt's aim in this review simply to negate Coleridge's present authority but rather to hold the *Christabel* volume accountable to a former authority grounded in both "common sense" and "humanity" (19: 34). This approach becomes most evident toward the end of the review, where a severe critique of the political implications of the Gothic mode is balanced by a quoted passage held up as a vestige of Coleridge's former discursive authority and as one of those parts of *Christabel* said to contain "a great deal of beauty, both of thought, imagery and versification." What Hazlitt finds to approve, however, is certainly not what the liberal Byron promoted as "wild, and singularly original." Hazlitt's commitment to Enlightenment ideology means that whatever subversive potential may be thought to inhere in the wildness of the Gothic mode is offset, in his view, by its "spell-bound" fascination for the institutions of medieval repression. By taking up the "petrific" story of *Christabel,* therefore, Coleridge drives an unwelcome wedge between the "visionary" and the politically progressive, and once his romanticization of Sir Leoline's "world of death" is found to align itself readily with contemporary forms of repression, the story is rejected outright as "disgusting."

What Hazlitt finds to approve, by contrast, is a passage that stands out for its "humanity"—a passage on the margins of the main plot that focuses more on human "reality" than supernatural "dream," a brief moment of affection that springs up in defiance of the relentlessly tragic landscape of human relations depicted in the poem. Within the political context invoked by the review, moreover, it is clear that this passage also offers itself as an efficient allegory of the history of division and alienation among men of the British public sphere, a history conjured up by the sudden appearance of these poems of the 1790s amid the postwar distresses of the Regency.

> In the midst of moon-light, and fluttering ringlets, and flitting clouds, and enchanted echoes, and airy abstractions of all sorts, there is one genuine outburst of humanity, worthy of the author, when no dream oppresses him, no spell binds him. We give the passage entire:—
>
> > But when he heard the lady's tale,
> > And when she told her father's name,
> > Why waxed Sir Leoline so pale,

Murmuring o'er the name again,
Lord Roland de Vaux of Tryermaine?

Alas! they had been friends in youth;
But whispering tongues can poison truth;
And constancy lives in realms above;
And life is thorny; and youth is vain;
And to be wroth with one we love
Doth work like madness in the brain.
And thus it chanced, as I divine,
With Roland and Sir Leoline.
Each spake words of high disdain
And insult to his heart's best brother:
They parted—ne'er to meet again!
But never either found another
To free the hollow heart from paining—
They stood aloof, the scars remaining,
Like cliffs which had been rent asunder;
A dreary sea now flows between.
But neither heat, nor frost, nor thunder,
Shall wholly do away, I ween,
The marks of that which once hath been.

Sir Leoline, a moment's space,
Stood gazing in the damsel's face:
And the youthful Lord of Tryermaine
Came back upon his heart again.

Why does not Mr. Coleridge always write in this manner, that we might always read him? The description of the Dream of Bracy the bard is also very beautiful and full of power. (19:34)

No doubt Hazlitt's appropriation of this tale of personal estrangement and recollected love functions in part as an allegory of his own relationship with the author of these lines—"Alas! they had been friends in youth." Yet strangely enough, this reading has been almost completely overlooked in previous commentary on the review,[13] perhaps because the message conveyed is one of abiding (if nevertheless frustrated) love and respect, thus refuting the notion of Hazlitt's pure "malignity" on this occasion. Yet the poignant rhetorical question that sustains such a reading—"Why does not Mr. Coleridge always write in this manner, that we might always read him?"—is nevertheless framed in the first-person plural, a reminder that within the context of corporate journalism a biographical reading is always superseded by the conventions of anonymity, which in this case posit the reviewer first and foremost as a synedoche for the editorial staff of the *Examiner,* and, by extension, for its entire readership. Thus the primary allegorical function of the "friends in youth" passage is to articulate a desire on the part of such readers to recall, if not recover, the political authority Coleridge once held as an eloquent voice of Enlightenment nonconformism. At the same time, the passage works efficiently to conjure the collective, even national experience of painful ideological rupture—an experience particularly acute among (male) middle-class intellectuals, whose shared nostalgia for an original and underlying commonality is now permanently threatened by the emergent paradox of being at once an oppressed and an oppressing class.

The extent of this rupture would become increasingly apparent as the Distresses of the Country crisis deepened, and as the convergence of literary and political opinion became more explicit. As a final point of reference within this context of political debate, we may look ahead to the *Edinburgh*'s late review of *Christabel,* the only other article after the *Examiner* to refer directly to Coleridge's "prose." But in Moore's review (which appeared in November 1816) (Schneider, "Tom Moore" 72), the subtle structure of implication and allusion produced by Hazlitt through such devices as irony and allegory is thrown aside in favor of the blunt invective of partisan infighting. In addition to the rough "quizzing" of *Christabel* for which this article has become notorious—in which the poem is declared to be "utterly destitute of value," with "not a ray of genius"—the final lines of the review offer this telling summary of the political dynamics that underlie the entire *Christabel* controversy:

> Must we then be doomed to hear such a mixture of raving and driv'ling, extolled as the work of a *"wild and original"* genius, simply because Mr. Coleridge has now and then written fine verses, and a brother poet chooses, in his milder mood, to laud him from courtesy or interest? And are such panegyrics to be echoed by the mean tools of a political faction, because they relate to one whose daily prose is understood to be dedicated to the support of all that courtiers think should be supported? If it be true that the author has thus earned the patronage of those liberal dispensers of bounty, we can have no objection that they should give him proper proofs of their gratitude; but we cannot help wishing, for his sake, as well as our own, that they would pay in solid pudding instead of empty praise; and adhere, at least in this instance, to the good old system of rewarding their champions with places and pensions, instead of puffing their bad poetry, and endeavouring to cram their nonsense down the throats of all the loyal and well affected. (Reiman A: 473; Jackson, *Coleridge* 235–36)

Thus the *Edinburgh* lays bare the politics of its literary criticism. As the leading organ of the anti-court party, it attacks a writer for the *Courier* whose "daily prose" is "understood to be dedicated to the support of all that courtiers think should be supported" and whose poetry, because it is published by John Murray and praised by the *Times* and the *Courier,* is implicated in the system of patronage by which the Tory ministry sustains its authority within the public sphere. By contrast with Hazlitt's review, however, the fact that "Mr. Coleridge has now and then written fine verses," and that the present verses have been praised by Moore's own "brother poet" Byron, are all but lost as complicating factors in this analysis. In the discursive violence of such images as "cram[ming] . . . nonsense down the throats of all the loyal and well affected," and in the gratuitous excess of the phrase "raving and driv'ling," is conveyed instead a one-dimensional enmity that Terry Eagleton has described as a "refraction" within the bourgeois public sphere of the violence of rising class struggle in society at large (37).

The slogan "BREAD OR BLOOD" is a reminder that such class struggle was (and is) as much a matter of economics as politics, and indeed such events as the riots of May 1816 were focused more on the immediate economic causes of distress than on the long-term political effects of violent insurgency. Within the public sphere, the corresponding "refraction" of these bloody confrontations over "[w]ant of work and want of bread" took the form of increasingly aggressive marketplace competition. The very appearance of "Literary Notices. No 1" in the *Examiner* is ample evidence of this, presenting as it does a bold challenge on three fronts: to the market share of rival journals, to the established parameters of review-criticism, and to the authority—and therefore profitability—of the latest best-seller. Though this review shows that political and commercial rivalry were virtually indistinguishable, it is significant that at this early point in the Distresses crisis, the sort of discursive violence conspicuous in the *Edinburgh* is expressed in the *Examiner*'s review not so much in its finely tuned structure of political implications but rather in those passages that reflect the harsh economics of a volatile marketplace. Resituated within this second discursive context, "Literary Notices. No. 1" proves once again to be a remarkably efficient index of change.

In June of 1816, the literary marketplace was in the process of radical transformation, not only under the immediate impact of a severe postwar depression but also via such long-term trends as the commercialization of authorship and the emergence of a mass "Reading Public." Exponential population growth and the success of literacy programs were creating a rapidly expanding consumer base just as consumer spending was being sharply curtailed (Altick 82–83, 100). To survive, writers and publishers were forced to adapt and innovate in the face of considerable uncertainty, with sometimes unexpected results. As the Edinburgh publisher Archibald Constable notes in August 1816: "Trade in the South is generally speaking very dull and of course the book trade is affected by the stagnation. Books of first-rate merit however sell better now than at any former period; those of a middle walk of literature do not sell at all, and almost all periodical works of talent increase in circulation" ([1]). Constable identifies two growth markets in the midst of economic "stagnation": "Books of first-rate merit" and "periodical works of talent." The appearance of the *Christabel* volume from the house of John Murray (64 pages octavo, at four shillings, sixpence) was clearly designed for the first of these; the appearance of "Literary Notices. No. 1" in the *Examiner*—adding new value (at tenpence an issue) to one of London's most closely monitored "periodical works of talent"—was an unmistakable sign of the latter. Yet where the *Christabel* volume aimed to intercept the purchasing power of those either profiting by the depression or insulated from its effects by inherited wealth, the *Examiner* could gather readers hurt by the depression, especially those in the middle classes who wished to keep pace with literary fashion, but who could afford only the time and money for entertaining reviews of exclusively priced books.

Hazlitt's review of the *Christabel* volume shows itself acutely conscious of these changes. In the opening paragraphs of the review, for example, following the paradox of Coleridge's "suspended" genius, it moves quickly to locate the publication of *Christabel* within the dynamics of marketplace competition. Hazlitt begins with an analysis comparable to Constable's, though rather more graphic.

> The poem of *Christabel* sets out in the following manner:
>> " 'Tis the middle of the night by the castle clock,
>> And the owls have awaken'd the crowing cock;
>> Tu—whit! Tu—whoo!
>> And hark again! the crowing cock,
>> How drowsily it crew.
>> Sir Leoline, the Baron rich,
>> Hath a toothless mastiff bitch;
>> From her kennel beneath the rock
>> She makes answer to the clock,
>> Four for the quarters and twelve for the hour;
>> Ever and aye, moonshine or shower,
>> Sixteen short howls, not over loud;
>> Some say, she sees my lady's shroud."
>
> We wonder that Mr. Murray, who has an eye for things, should suffer this "mastiff bitch" to come into his shop. Is she a sort of Cerberus to fright away the critics? But—gentlemen, she is toothless. (19: 32)

With this jest, we are given a kind of Cruikshank cartoon of the literary marketplace in 1816. On the one side there is the first-rate "shop" of "Mr. Murray," defended by the howling mastiff of *Christabel;* on the other side are "the critics," a growing cluster of "gentlemen" from the various periodicals, addressed on this occasion by the newest talent among them. One striking feature of this scene is that it is the publisher, not the poet, who is the immediate target of witty attack. This foregrounding of literary commerce is in part traceable to the convergence of politics and literature: the mastiff is "a sort of Cerberus," after all, because she guards the entrance to a corresponding Hades of Tory ideology, well stocked with issues of the *Quarterly Review.*

Yet in this way Hazlitt correctly identifies Murray's profits—in manuscripts already purchased outright from the poet (Bate, introduction, *Biographia* lxi)—as the commodity that requires unusual measures of protection in a marketplace subject to the increasingly violent (and telling) attacks of "the critics." Murray is caricatured as the savvy capitalist "who has an eye for things," whose shop already contains the lucrative works of Byron and the well-funded *Quarterly,* but who in the case of *Christabel* may well have seriously misjudged. For on Byron's recommendation, he has allowed this "wild, and singularly original" infraction of the norms of poetic diction to enter his shop, and to *attract* the scorn of "the critics" with its howling rather than "to fright [them] away."

These critics, meanwhile, are interpellated as fellow "gentlemen," a telling gendering of the institution of review-criticism (as Swann has noted, passim), but an equally important designation of the intended readership of the review itself. By addressing the punch line of his jest to a chummy coterie of "gentlemen," Hazlitt implicitly aligns his readers with the practice of criticism, thus invoking the ideal interchangeability of critic and reader carried over from the coffee house culture of the eighteenth-century public sphere. This context is crucial to the construction of authority in the review, for the speaker himself is an entrepreneurial voice among "the critics," standing forth boldly in the ideally unfettered discursive space opened up by the Enlightenment to offer what seems the only plausible—if pointedly satiric—explanation for the anomaly of the "mastiff bitch" in Murray's "shop." At the same time, the term "gentlemen" associates the practice of review-criticism with the cultural authority once accorded gentility but now appropriated as a measure of bourgeois respectability—and in defiance of the low social status still accorded those known to be "mere" journalists.[14] "Mr. Murray," in marked contrast, though well-known as one of the great captains of the industry, is reduced to the merest shopkeeper.

Hazlitt pursues his analysis of the marketplace into the next paragraph, where the poet reenters the picture. Like Murray, Coleridge is found to have made a grave error in allowing the image of the "mastiff bitch" to enter and dominate the opening lines of his poem. No longer a defensive measure, however, these lines are now interpreted as deliberately offensive, a sign of the poet's "contempt" for the new protocols of literary commerce.

> There is dishonesty as well as affectation in all this. The secret of this pretended contempt for the opinion of the public, is that it is a sorry subterfuge for our self-love. The poet, uncertain of the approbation of his readers, thinks he shews his superiority to it by shocking their feelings at the outset, as a clown, who is at a loss how to behave himself, begins by affronting the company. This is what is called *throwing a crust to the critics.* If the beauties of *Christabel* should not be sufficiently admired, Mr. Coleridge may lay it all to two lines which he had too much manliness to omit in complaisance to the bad taste of his contemporaries. (19: 32)

Now it is "*the critics*" who are figured as dogs—at least in the eyes of the supercilious poet, as he throws them the opening lines of the poem like a "*crust*" over which to bark and snarl, leaving the rest of his poem unmolested. Hazlitt's use of italics here underscores the latent violence in the tone and diction as well as the imagery of this passage, a discursive intensity that in turn reflects the cultural and historic significance of the confrontation described. On the one hand we have the poet, cast out of the patronage system onto the open market and thus "at a loss how to behave himself," forced to court "the approbation of his readers" even as he rejects "the bad taste of his contemporaries." On the other hand his new patron, "the opinion of the public," is now frankly identified with "*the critics*," whose ascendent authority is based on their long experience in the art of embodying—even as they create—the opinions of their anonymous readerships. On this occasion especially, as the critic himself débuts as the voice of public opinion, the authority of review-criticism must be asserted with particular intensity. Thus in addition to the obvious flourish of penetrating the "secret" of the poet's "sorry subterfuge," the critic demonstrates his superior familiarity with the shifting protocols of public entertainment by appropriating to witty effect the very lines he criticizes as an affront. In this way he ironically earns "the approbation of his readers" precisely by "shocking their feelings at the outset."

More than a merely gratuitous flaunting of authority, however, lies behind the intensity of Hazlitt's focus on these opening lines of *Christabel.* Several other factors are at play here as well: Coleridge's attack on the critics in his preface to *Christabel;* the impact of Byron and the recent Byron scandal on public attitudes toward "poetic genius"; and the *Examiner*'s own struggle for market share with its closest commercial rivals, principally the *Champion.* If the image of Sir Leoline's toothless "mastiff bitch" is a "*crust*" thrown to Coleridge's tasteless contemporaries, then the preface to *Christabel* might be figured as a full gauntlet, thrown down in rather more explicit challenge to the opinions of Coleridge's critics-as-readers. Here, in the context of anxiously "precluding charges of plagiarism," Coleridge lashes out at his projected accusers: "For there is amongst us a set of critics, who seem to hold, that every possible thought and image is traditional; who have no notion that there are fountains in the world, small as well as great; and who would therefore charitably derive every rill they behold flowing, from a perforation made in some other man's tank" (*Poetical Works* 214–15). Coleridge's obtrusive concern with his property rights in *Christabel,* fostered in part by the unusual circumstances of its manuscript transmission, is another sign of the new uncertainties of commercialized authorship in an open market. From his perspective, "the set of critics" poses a double threat to creative genius. Misguided by a false notion of the collective and anonymous, they undermine the moral integrity of genius by reducing the poet's claims to originality to mere thefts from tradition. In so doing, they also elide the very sources of his power, a power figured here in the strikingly "traditional" image of the providential "fountain." Whether *Christabel* is intended in these terms to be a mere "rill" proceeding from one of the "small" fountains is a question better answered later in the volume, when this image reappears as the "mighty fountain" that erupts in the midst of the "Vision" of "Kubla Khan" (*Poetical Works* 297).

One effect of this prefatory challenge, of course, is to focus critical attention on the very opening "image" of *Christabel*. Given the prevailing norms of poetic decorum, the image of the "toothless mastiff bitch" becomes in these terms an arresting attempt to exceed the boundaries of the "traditional" and demonstrate the presence of a new and mysteriously fresh "fountain" of creative originality. Hence Hazlitt's use of the term "affectation." Coleridge's evident willingness to edit the poem (as proven later in the review) lends this image an additional aura of deliberation, and within the contestatory atmosphere of 1816 it is magnified into a bizarre weapon with which the poet asserts the singularity of his creative genius in defiance of the leveling criticism of "common sense."

This increasing polarization of poets and critics was the result in part of Byron's recent struggle with "the opinion of the [British] public." We have already seen how this scandal over the private life of Britain's most high-profile creative genius dictated the terms of the *Champion*'s review. Echoes of this event are also heard in such phrases as the poet's "pretended contempt for the opinion of the public," by which he "thinks he shews his superiority" to his readers by retaining "two lines which he had too much manliness to omit in complaisance to the bad taste of his contemporaries." The heavy irony of the word "manliness" depicts the false authority of patrician "contempt," imaginary "superiority," and withheld "complaisance"—all of which sketch a portrait of Coleridge in Byron's clothing, awkwardly mimicking the Gothic hauteur of his now disgraced and self-exiled benefactor. Of course, one source of discursive intensity in these lines is the very strength of such a bid for cultural authority. Byron's popularity had indeed succeeded in forging a strong link between the notions of sublime autonomy and poetic genius, a link only partially undone by his spectacular fall from public grace. Thus we see both Coleridge and Hazlitt pressing their advantage in these circumstances: Coleridge presenting himself in possession of "poetic powers" that make him one of the world's mysterious "fountains" of "originality," and Hazlitt decrying such rhetoric for its "dishonesty," insofar as it mingles the gestures of class privilege with the emergent cult of genius.

On this point, the *Examiner* fully concurs with the anti-aristocratic politics of London's other Sunday weekly, the *Champion*. Yet for this very reason, the *Examiner*'s analysis of the opening lines of *Christabel* is further animated by the dynamics of direct marketplace competition. On closer examination, we find that the *Champion* also quotes the opening lines of the poem, but it does so merely in passing, as one example of the poem's "most objectionable parts" (the words "mastiff bitch" are underscored with italics), and as the sort of passage in which the poet's "coterie of ardent admirers . . . may discover,—(though God knows, we cannot),—a great deal of undefinable sublimity" (Reiman A: 269). In following up this lead, the *Examiner* distinguishes its new contribution to review-criticism by outmatching its closest commercial rival in the wit and incisiveness of its treatment of these lines. What the *Champion* merely indicates with italics to be "objectionable," the *Examiner* seizes on and holds up as a trenchant symbol of emergent patterns of conflict and authority within an otherwise chaotic marketplace. This explanatory device clarifies, among other things, the new role to be played by the politicized criticism of Sunday weekly newspapers. One feature of such a role is to go well beyond simply charging a poem with "undefinable sublimity" as the *Champion* had done; instead, the *Examiner* makes a point of penetrating the poet's rhetorical "secret," in this case uncovering Coleridge's "sorry subterfuge" for the authority of review-criticism. As we have seen, this competitive strategy recurs on a larger scale when the *Examiner* goes on to solve what the *Champion* was content to dismiss as "a maze of impenetrable mystery," producing knowledge of the missing line "necessary to make common sense" of *Christabel* as a whole (19: 33). By substantiating the bombastic assertions of the *Champion* with empirical proofs, the *Examiner* gives point and force to its own use of invective. Discursive intensity is no longer merely the blunt instrument of factional enmity. Rather it becomes a sharp tool with which to demonstrate and denounce strategies of mystification and "subterfuge."

Such a discursive tool, of course, was considerably sharpened by wit. After all, subtlety of analysis alone would not be enough to draw a sufficient audience for this new series of reviews from a reading public as anxious to be inexpensively entertained as intellectually edified. "Literary Notices. No. 1" thus introduces a form of criticism designed to stand out for its style as well as its content, supplementing the analytical and referential modalities of the traditional review with performative gestures that seek "literary notice" in their own right. The *Examiner* had already proven itself innovative in this regard with its eclectic and loquacious series of "Round Table" essays. Building on this precedent, it now promises to distinguish itself in the field of literary criticism by forging, in effect, a new genre of review that will be characterized by an intense fusion of such elements as paradox, irony, invective, and caricature, laced with literary allusion, and gathered under the bantering, colloquial idiom of Regency "table-talk." In so doing, it impinges upon a third discursive context: the hierarchy of genres by which cultural authority was most effectively invoked—or contested—within the British public sphere of 1816. And here too, pressured by the evolving dynamics of both political debate and marketplace competition, "Literary Notices. No. 1" emerges as a paradigmatic innovation in genre. One measure of its impact within the institution of review-criticism may be found in the format adopted by the mighty *Edinburgh Review* for its late intervention in the *Christabel* controversy. In a rare abandonment of its customary full-length review-essay, the *Edinburgh* condescends on this occasion to imitate the brief, bantering style of the *Examiner*'s "Literary Notices" series for its famous "quizzing" of the poem. As we have already seen in another context, however, the differences between the *Edinburgh* and the *Examiner* reviews of *Christabel* are as important as their similarities. Here we may simply note that when Peacock came to satirize this genre of "Fashionable Literature" two years later, he took as his example the *Edinburgh*'s less felicitous experiment in it, while making an important—and rarely noted—exception in favor of "one or two *weekly* publications" (100). Unlike the general run of periodicals, such weeklies as the *Examiner,* in Peacock's view, lie outside the "*legatur* of corruption" and therefore "have the courage to push enquiry to its limits" (100).

The *Examiner* was nevertheless determined to seek a viable audience for such courageous "enquiry." To the extent that it strove to incorporate what Peacock calls "the faculty of amusing" into its new genre of review, its "Literary Notices" series clearly falls well within Peacock's pejorative category of "Fashionable Literature" (94). Yet by the same token, one of the most attractive features of the opening number in the series was the fact that the book selected for the inaugural review was equally "fashionable" in precisely these terms. In Peacock's view, "the newspaper of the day, the favourite magazine of the month, the review of the quarter, the tour, the novel, and *the poem which are most recent in date and most fashionable in name* furnish forth the morning table of the literary dilettante" (94, emphasis added). And in the spring of 1816, there can be no doubt that *Christabel* was "the poem . . . most recent in date and most fashionable in name." As even the *Champion* ruefully admitted, the *Christabel* volume was at this time "the standing enigma that puzzles the curiosity of literary circles," rising on what Peacock calls "the spring tide of metropolitan favour" and passing quickly through three editions (Reiman A: 268; Peacock 94).

Even more significant in this context was the fact that the success of this volume—and the controversy it raised—can be attributed to Coleridge's own turn to generic innovation as a vehicle for cultural authority. In this instance, he supplements the otherwise declining appeal of the Gothic ballad by capitalizing on a rising interest in the poetic "fragment." The phenomenal popularity of Byron's *The Giaour* two years earlier had created what Francis Jeffrey at that time named "The Taste for Fragments."[15] Byron's influence is clearly visible in the publication of *Christabel* as an incomplete poem, for which "the whole" is nevertheless said to be "present" to the mind of the poet (according to the preface) "with the wholeness, no less than the liveliness of a vision"—a vision that (analogous to the successive editions of *The Giaour*) he promises "to embody in verse . . . in the course of the present year" (*Poetical Works* 213n. 4). At the same time, the status of this poem as a self-contained fragment is reinforced by its inclusion in a volume with two other poems distinctly classified, in the preface to "Kubla Khan," as "fragments" (*Poetical Works* 295, 297). Anne Janowitz, in her article titled "Coleridge's 1816 Volume: Fragment as Rubric," demonstrates convincingly how Coleridge's strategy on this occasion makes him at once "a reader of the fashion, and a shaper of the genre" (28). This becomes most apparent in his odd designation of the third, and highly finished, poem, "The Pains of Sleep," as a "fragment." Where the prefaces to both *Christabel* and "Kubla Khan" thematize the incommensurability of language to the "vision" of the poet, Janowitz notes how "The Pains of Sleep" is marked both thematically and structurally by patterns of "highly reinforced closure" (37). Thus, she reasons, by including this poem " in his volume of three fragments, the generic stability of the first two poems becomes a site for the third to attach itself to the genre," with the result that the "rubric" of the fragment is made into an ever widening category by which the poet invites readers "to read every poem, however definite its construction, as only a hint of its potentiality" (37–38). This strategy in turn serves to mystify the authority of the poet, whose "mind" is held up as both source and site of the imagined "whole." And despite Coleridge's complaints to the contrary, there was a growing sector of the reading public as fully responsive to such authority as academic posterity has since proven itself to be. The *Critical Review,* for example, correctly identifies the genre of the *Christabel* poems as that of the "romantic fragment," "triumph[ing]" in this "fresh display of talent and genius" wherein "the absurd trammels of physical possibility are . . . thrown aside, like the absurd swaddling clothes of infants, which formerly obstructed the growth of the fair symmetry of nature" (Reiman A: 505). Meanwhile, as we have seen, the *Times/Courier* review celebrates the "fragmental beauty" and "thought-suspending awe" of a form of poetry "that interests . . . more by what it leaves untold, than even by what it tells," generating in this way "a truth of its own, that seizes on and masters the imagination from beginning to end" (Reiman A: 891).

In both the *Christabel* volume, then, and in "Literary Notices. No. 1," generic innovation is used as a vehicle by which to generate and sustain cultural authority. On the one hand Coleridge's collection of Romantic fragments caters to an emergent "Taste for Fragments," a trend that is indicative of a growing (and ultimately hegemonic) willingness to locate authority in the mind of "genius" as the exemplar of free subjectivity. On the other hand Hazlitt's review-satire uses wit to attract and shape "the opinion of the public," where authority is figured as a decentered function of anonymous urban numbers under the compelling—if ultimately elusive—norm of "common sense." As competing forms of "Fashionable Literature" in the spring of 1816, then, the Romantic fragment and the review-satire may be said to be evenly matched within the hierarchy of genres comprising authoritative public discourse. Yet one clear advantage held by the review-satire lay in the fact that it was designed not only to claim but to contest authority. We have already seen numerous ways in which "Literary Notices. No. 1" is used to this purpose: in the eminently quotable bon mot of the opening line ("The fault of

Mr. Coleridge is, that he comes to no conclusion"); in the comic caricature of the poet as a "witch" or as a "clown"; in the dogged "quizzing" of the "mastiff bitch"; and in the arch understatement of the line "Now this is a greater psychological curiosity than even the fragment of *Kubla Khan*" (19: 32–33). We may conclude this discussion, however, by focusing on the closing lines of the review, where Hazlitt turns from *Christabel* to address the question of genre in "Kubla Khan." Here the performatory wit of the journalistic review serves once again to reinforce the contestatory thrust of the review as a whole. At the same time, however, the impulse to generic innovation—in conjunction with Hazlitt's own characteristic willingness to "push enquiry to its limits"— produces an unexpected, and distinctly Romantic, resistance to closure.

It is important to note that the final lines of the review follow immediately on the lengthy, approving quotation of the "friends in youth" passage in *Christabel,* with its subsequent acknowledgment that "the Dream of Bracy the bard is also very beautiful and full of power" (19: 34). As if, therefore, to return to a dominant key of critical censure, the review ends with a brief coda of satiric judgment:

> The conclusion of the second part of *Christabel,* about "the little limber elf," is to us absolutely incomprehensible. *Kubla Khan,* we think, only shows that Mr. Coleridge can write better *nonsense* verses than any man in England. It is not a poem, but a musical composition.
> "A damsel with a dulcimer
> In a vision once I saw:
> It was an Abyssinian maid,
> And on her dulcimer she play'd,
> Singing of Mount Abora."
> We could repeat these lines to ourselves not the less often for not knowing the meaning of them. (19: 34)

And thus the review concludes. What has traditionally stood out in these lines, of course, is Hazlitt's apparently unimaginative retailing of the third in Peacock's incisive list of "excellent jokes," the fashionably philistine charge of "incomprehensib[ility]" (Peacock 104). And indeed the brisk, ad libitum haste of the journalistic review, with its reliance on stock phrase and current idiom, is clearly evident in this remark, as Hazlitt strives for some degree of critical closure. Yet in the quip that follows about "Kubla Khan" as *"nonsense,"* the blank counter of the common joke is tempered by paradox, recalling the high satiric polish of the opening lines of the review. It was from Coleridge's "universality of genius," after all, and from his "excess of capacity," that he is said to have done "little or nothing" in this volume (19: 32). So here, too: though "Kubla Khan" is summarily dispatched to the category of *"nonsense* verses," the fact that Coleridge is said to produce these "better . . . than any man in England" crosses the critical thrust of the remark with a vestige of monumental respect that infuses and complicates the entire review.

It is perhaps with this in mind, then, that the satirist proceeds to refine his classification of "Kubla Khan": "It is not a poem," he declares, "but a musical composition." Now two possibilities emerge: either that all "musical composition[s]" are mere "*nonsense*" or, more likely, that the purely aesthetic appeal of "Kubla Khan" can be compared only to the nonrepresentational art of music, an art form with growing resonance at this time as a metaphor for acute "sensibility" to the suprarational forces of nature. The asperity of judgment unleashed in such phrases as "absolutely incomprehensible" and "*nonsense*" hovers over the recital of several lines of this "musical composition," inviting readers to measure these lines against the rough, exoteric norm of "common sense" while also noting Coleridge's uncanny facility in creating such "*nonsense.*" The drive for critical closure, however, is suddenly undermined by the tone of bemused reflection that concludes the review. Like *Christabel,* it seems, "Kubla Khan" has rendered its critic "spell-bound," throwing his faculties "into a state of metaphysical suspense and theoretical imbecility." Yet here, significantly enough, we are asked not to recoil in (ideological) disgust but rather to embrace an unexpected resistance to closure. For in the end the search for "meaning" itself comes "to no conclusion," short-circuited by Coleridge's Abyssinian song into a pattern of potentially endless, mesmeric repetition: "We could repeat these lines to ourselves not the less often for not knowing the meaning of them."

In this way, the very brevity and ex tempore informality of the journalistic "Notice" proves itself flexible enough to assimilate features of the "fragment" itself—along with the attendant authority that accrues to a "suspended" judgment of both poet and poem lodged in the mind of the (anonymous) critic. Yet this judgment would not remain suspended for long. Within two months, Coleridge's announcement of his intention to publish "a Layman's Sermon addressed to the Higher and Middle Classes of Society on the Present Distresses of the Country" would invite the rebuke of "a politics turned—but not to account," along with the reawakened injunction, "let him not write, or pretend to write, nonsense" (7: 118). Meanwhile, the exploratory observation "It is not a poem, but a musical composition" would emerge little more than a year later in the pages of the *Edinburgh Review,* reformulated by Hazlitt into the phrase "Poetry is the music of language, expressing the music of the mind"—the centerpiece of a counter-Romantic criticism designed to contest the authority of Coleridge's most seminal work in prose, the *Biographia Literaria* (16: 136).

2

PRETENDING TO
WRITE NONSENSE:

Hazlitt's Preview of
The Statesman's Manual

If Hazlitt's first article on Coleridge has been traditionally read as a scandal, his second has been rejected out-of-hand as an outrage. Where the review of *Christabel* is depicted as a willful misreading of a now canonical text, Hazlitt's satiric preview of *The Statesman's Manual* is thought to represent no reading at all, based as it is on the mere advertisement for a work that had not even been written at the time of this "review," let alone published.[1] Critics and biographers have therefore focused their attention almost exclusively on Hazlitt's psychological motives for writing such an article rather than on the article itself. And here, as before, their explanations have fallen back with little qualification on Coleridge's own claims in the *Biographia:* that this preemptive satire of an unpublished book could only be the product of "a malignity" that is "avowedly and exclusively personal" (7.2: 241). Hazlitt's own biographer, Herschel Baker, singles out this review as an especially "deplorable performance" marked by "motiveless malignity" (355–56), while others have similarly characterized it as a "vicious attack" (Griggs 668), "malicious" (White, introduction xxxn. 3), "poisonous" (Marrs 227n. 4), and "cruel" (Campbell 225n. 1).

Yet the tone of moral outrage infusing such epithets suggests at least some degree of critical distortion. Coleridge himself can hardly be expected to have held an impartial view of the matter. Moreover, Hazlitt's first readers did not all respond with similar opprobrium. Even Henry Crabb Robinson, who was himself fond of the term "malignity," thought this article "admirable" enough to read it aloud at a dinner party—along with another of Hazlitt's "Literary Notices"—whereupon one knowledgeable commentator, the veteran essayist William Taylor of the *Monthly Review,* declared both articles to be "masterpieces of banter" (Howe, *Life* 190).[2]

Taylor's response reminds us that what is missing from the received modern reading of Hazlitt's preview of *The Statesman's Manual* is any thoroughgoing account of its public, rather than merely "personal," contexts. Here, for example, Taylor locates the authority of this article in the skill with which Hazlitt has adapted review-criticism to a specific—and ascendent—genre of public discourse, a genre with roots in the satiric persiflage of the eighteenth-century "public sphere" and now shaped to the arch repartee of Regency drawing rooms. Meanwhile, other available classifications of this review provide evidence of its engagement in similarly public discursive contexts. Hazlitt himself, for example, saw fit to republish it as one of his *Political Essays* in 1819 (7: 114–18), a clear indication that this one of his "masterpieces of banter" was also designed as a substantial intervention in a moment of public crisis, with lasting enough relevancy to be applicable to a similar moment of crisis on the eve of Peterloo. Furthermore, like the review of *Christabel,* this article originally appeared under the *Examiner*'s rubric of "Literary Notice," where, as before, it takes on the broad, corporate agenda of the newspaper as a whole as well as the specific mandate to "notice" and "examine" forms of discursive authority in a marketplace alive with momentous transformation. Taken together, then, these three classifications of the article present us once again with a text firmly situated within at least three overlapping contexts of public discourse and debate: the arena of political struggle, the volatile marketplace for literature, and the conflicted hierarchy of genres and modes by which authority was performed—and recognized—at a moment of crisis and uncertainty.

Before proceeding, however, to resituate Hazlitt's preview of *The Statesman's Manual* within each of these contexts, a rereading of it must recover the actual text that provoked its composition. In this instance—and by contrast with the *Christabel* volume—the utter obscurity of Coleridge's early advertisement for his first lay sermon has in the past served to reinforce the notion of willful and nonsensical invention on Hazlitt's part in producing a "mock review" of an unpublished text (Beer 47). It is surprising that the advertisement itself has remained in obscurity: even the most recent editor of the *Lay Sermons* did not see fit to locate or cite what Coleridge himself refers to as his "first annunciation" of *The Statesman's Manual* (7.2: 241).[3] It has been enough, apparently, to know that Coleridge mistakenly "suffered" this work to be advertised before it was written (*Letters* 4: 672), and that, as a consequence, "a long delay occurred" between its "annunciation" and its actual appearance in December 1816 (7.2: 241). Yet this tiny advertisement reached far more readers in 1816 than the controversial *Christabel* volume,[4] and, quite apart from its obvious relevance to Hazlitt's review, it contains a previously unrecorded title for Coleridge's first lay sermon as well as the unknown fact that Coleridge (and his new publisher Gale and Fenner) experimented with the idea of a charitable benefit to attract readers to the lay sermon project. Most important for our purposes, and again in contrast with the *Christabel* volume, this advertisement serves as a remarkably efficient index of the environment of sociopolitical tension in which all texts at this time were written.

Thus, in the "Books Published this Day" column of the *Courier* for 12 and 14 August 1816, and of the *Times* for 14 and 15 August, we find the following announcement:

> In a few days will be published, price 1s 6d,
> THE DAY OF ADVERSITY, a Layman's Sermon addressed to the Higher and
> Middle Classes of Society on the present Distresses of the Country
> By S. T. COLERIDGE.
> The Profits of this Pamphlet will be given to the Association
> for the Relief of the Manufacturing and Labouring Poor.

Several features of this notice immediately command our attention. First, Coleridge's title "THE DAY OF ADVERSITY" suggests a quite different sermon from the one finally written as *The Statesman's Manual*—one that more readily reflects the atmosphere of crisis that by mid-August 1816 affected all levels of society, from the "Higher and Middle Classes" through to "the Manufacturing and Labouring Poor." Yet Coleridge's very specification of these different "Classes" suggests, in the second place, that any potentially leveling effects of economic "ADVERSITY" were in fact outweighed by a politically charged sharpening of class divisions. This is especially apparent in his careful distinction here between the recipients of his charity on the one hand and of his political homily on the other. Third, Coleridge's act of charity is itself notable, both as a worthy personal gesture and, as we shall see, an astute marketing device, for it serves in this instance to align his intervention in the crisis with a scheme of charitable subscriptions recently endorsed by the Prince Regent himself. In this context, finally, Coleridge's choice of genre—"a Layman's Sermon"—is newly foregrounded, for in conjunction with his act of charity this genre was no doubt intended to convey to his proposed readers a renewed moral and spiritual authority in contrast with the hotly disputed Gothic "fragments" that were still, three months after their publication, at the center of literary controversy.[5]

Together these various features of Coleridge's advertisement present a useful index of the severity of the evolving crisis, and the prevailing responses to it on the part of the "Higher and Middle Classes of Society." The title "DAY OF ADVERSITY," for example, was clearly dictated in part by the stark images of destitution and despair among the "Manufacturing and Labouring Poor" that began to fill the daily press throughout the summer. One such image proved emblematic, and it may be cited here as the most likely catalyst for

Coleridge's impulse to charity. In early July, a group of starving colliers from Bilston-moor in Staffordshire achieved national notice by yoking themselves like beasts of burden to several huge wagons laden with coal and petitions for parliamentary reform, which they then began to haul along the main highways to London as symbolic gifts to the Regent himself. As the *Times* reports:

> About fifty men are yoked to each waggon to drag them to town. One of the waggons proceeds by the route of Worcester; another by Coventry and Birmingham: the route of the third we have not heard. The men proceed at the rate of about twelve miles a day, and receive voluntary gifts of money, &c. on the road as they pass along, declining of themselves to ask alms; their motto, as placarded on the carts, being—"Rather work than beg." Two of these extraordinary teams passed through Birmingham on Thursday last, and excited on their approach considerable alarm; but it proved without cause, as the men demeaned themselves with the utmost propriety. ("London" 2 July 1816)

Though the Bilston colliers were intercepted by police magistrates and turned back before reaching London, their act of symbolic self-abasement nevertheless "went home to the public imagination and pricked the conscience of the country," in Stanley Jones's words, because it implied "a destitution so extreme and inhuman that an animal yoke was its only appropriate symbol" (*Hazlitt* 230).

Indeed, even the Regent was moved. Though he never received—or even considered—the colliers' petitions for reform, he decided to perform his own act of symbolic condescension toward the end of July, sending his brother, the duke of York, to the City of London Tavern, where he was to preside over a meeting of the Association for the Relief of the Manufacturing and Labouring Poor—the very association named in Coleridge's advertisement.[6] With Parliament adjourned till January despite the mounting crisis, this meeting at the London Tavern was clearly designed as a substitute for governmental policy, attended as it was by the chancellor of the exchequer and other prominent members of Parliament, not to mention a glittering roll call of aristocratic and ecclesiastical dignitaries. These joined the royal family in publicly acknowledging a "stagnation of employment, and a revulsion of trade, deeply affecting the situation of many parts of the community, and producing many instances of great local distress." In response, then, "a subscription [was to be] immediately opened, and contributions generally solicited, for carrying into effect the objects of the Association, &c. &c" (*Examiner* 4 Aug. 1816: 485–86). The Regent's name was put down for £500, the queen's for £300, and the dukes of York and Cambridge contributed £300. Thereafter a detailed list of such donations became a prominent feature of the daily newspapers, beginning in each case with the Regent and proceeding down through all those who wished to associate themselves publicly with this extraordinary exercise of noblesse oblige.

Coleridge's donation to this association is therefore to be interpreted as more than a merely personal gesture. In both the *Times* and *Courier,* his announcement appears in a column directly adjacent to the growing list of noble donors,[7] and so it takes on enhanced cultural authority through deliberate alignment with the royally sanctioned response to the "Distresses." This response, moreover, appears to reach across the boundaries of class in a gesture of leveling solidarity amidst "ADVERSITY," but it also serves to reinforce these boundaries by recreating the sentimental roles of patrician donor and plebeian recipient. These roles in turn helped bolster the view that "the Present Distresses of the Country" were merely temporary and purely economic, requiring no fundamental adjustment to the British political structure. Even the Whig *Edinburgh Review,* for example, confirmed this approach in a magisterial essay on the Distresses that appeared just days before Coleridge's advertisement, in review of two prominent speeches from the last session of Parliament:

> AT no former period of the history of this country, was so great and so general a distress known to prevail, as that which has lately visited us. . . . During the last twelve or eighteen months, . . . the country has been suffering severely in every direction; in its agriculture and its manufactures; its home trade and foreign commerce. The return of peace, after unexampled victories, has brought no relief, but has rather confirmed our apparent ruin; and all classes of men more or less feel the effects of some hidden rottenness in our system, the causes of which no one seems able to discover, much less to remove.[8]

The essay goes on to probe in considerable detail the economic "effects" of this "hidden rottenness," while delicately eliding any possibility that it might have political "causes."

No doubt this *Edinburgh* article precipitated Coleridge's intervention in the crisis,[9] if only because his advertisement also reflects the pressure of other, more direct—and politically divisive—approaches to this "hidden rottenness." By addressing his sermon only to "the Higher and Middle Classes of Society," for example, his title suggests to the mainly Tory readership of the *Courier* and the *Times* that it is they who face an almost apocalyptic "DAY OF ADVERSITY," in contrast to—or perhaps at the hands of—the burgeoning numbers of those genuinely distressed by the unprecedented effects of the new industrial economy (Aspinall, *Politics* 200, 206). Indeed, violent insurgency had continued unabated since May, despite the well-publicized hanging of thirty-two of the May rioters.[10] In the industrial midlands especially, a resurgent Luddism created a new "DAY OF ADVERSITY" among middle-class factory owners.

> A gang of . . . miscreants . . . entered the premises of Mr HEATHCOTE of Loughborough, on Saturday last, for the avowed purposes of breaking to pieces the whole of his lace-machinery, on account of having learnt that this gentleman intended to reduce the price of labour. . . . The guard, being

faithful to his trust . . . was shot dead immediately . . . and in the course of one hour from that time these ruffians destroyed, in machinery and goods, property to the amount of 15,000l [£15,000]., which will prove the total ruin of the proprietor. (*Times* 2 July 1816)

What made such attacks all the more alarming for "the Higher and Middle Classes of Society" was that unlike the riots in May, they proceeded from well-defined political motives rather than merely economic or even personal ones. As the *Times* goes on to note, these particular "ruffians" had come under the influence of "democratic and disorganizing principles among their neighbours of somewhat superior rank and education."

In London, meanwhile, these same principles inspired a corresponding discursive insurgency among newly prominent Radical leaders and orators. The duke of York's meeting at the London Tavern, for example, was interrupted by the Radical Lord Cochrane, who called for the abolishment of sinecures and a reduction of taxes as a more effective, and politically appropriate, response to the distresses than mere charity (*Examiner*, 4 Aug. 1816: 481, 483). Similarly, just one week after Coleridge's advertisement appeared, the lord mayor of London held a "Common Hall" attended by such speakers as Henry ("Orator") Hunt, who drew up an aggressive petition for reform to be delivered by the Mayor himself to the Regent. In a series of resolutions, this petition describes "the Distress" as "the natural result of a corrupt system of Administration," declares a "Reform of Parliament" to be "indispensably necessary to the safety and honour of the Crown," and, in similarly threatening terms, names the "free, full, and frequent Representation of the People in the Commons House of Parliament" as "the only tranquil, sure, and effectual mode of obtaining *indemnity for the past and security for the future*" (*Examiner*, 25 Aug. 1816: 543).

This was the atmosphere, then, of both economic and political "ADVERSITY" that had accumulated within the tiny enclave of the ruling classes by the late summer of 1816. In the midst of this, Coleridge's advertisement emerges as an instructive metonymy of prevailing responses to the crisis: On the one hand it presents the nominal charity proffered by "the Higher Classes . . . of Society," and on the other it typifies the response of urgent, discursive intervention adopted by middle-class writers of every political persuasion. Here, as seen before, the vertical pressure of rising class struggle in society at large is "refracted" into the series of bitter, horizontal conflicts that characterized the discourse of the bourgeois public sphere at this time (Eagleton 37). The absence of an active parliamentary session reinforced this process, creating a vacuum of discursive authority into which poured a veritable cascade of conflicted articles, essays, editorials, pamphlets, "Remed[ies],"[11] and "WARNING[s]"[12] from the bourgeois press, all disputing the causes and outcomes of national distress. Dominating the debate was the *Edinburgh* article quoted above, as well as a similar article in its rival the *Quarterly* titled

"Reports on the Poor."[13] Within the more confined arena of London newspaper journalism, the political rivalries witnessed above in the controversy over *Christabel* were intensified, exacerbating the practice of journalistic dueling that paired off newspapers, editors, and "anonymous" writers in an almost quotidian series of journalistic conflicts. In this context, then, Coleridge's proposed intervention in the debate was inevitably read for its markers of partisan affiliation, including, in this case, his choice of genre. In conjunction with the appearance of the advertisement itself in the ministerial newspapers, and with its scrupulous participation in the Regent's subscription scheme, the genre of "Layman's Sermon" would serve to underscore its alignment with Tory ideology by claiming for this "Pamphlet" a pious adherence to the doctrinal authority of the Established Church.

In the midst of this, of course, the *Examiner* had not remained silent. On the contrary, it had taken up a leading role as a voice for reform within the Opposition press, making up in frequency of contributions what it lacked in the total circulation of its rival periodicals.[14] Several days before the *Edinburgh*'s influential essay appeared, for example, the *Examiner* set the pace of the debate with the first in a five-part, front-page editorial series titled "RELIEF OF THE NATIONAL DISTRESSES," begun in direct response to the Regent's initiative at the London Tavern. In the opening number of this series, "The Political Examiner" applauds Lord Cochrane's radical politicization of the meeting, goes on to deplore "the gross attempts of the ministerial papers to attribute all the danger of the present crisis to the mere mention of it, and not at all to the abuses of power," and concludes by offering the warning that "bear as people may, . . . a day comes now and then, when they do *not* bear" (4 Aug. 1816: 481–82). This outspoken reformism was reinforced in the "Literary Notices" column of the *Examiner,* which had since June become progressively more explicit in its political content.[15] Now, alongside the editorial series of "The Political Examiner," it began to review rival interventions in the Distresses controversy, beginning on 4 August with Robert Owen's utopian manifesto "A New View of Society" ("Literary Notices. No. 6"; 7: 97–103), and then turning on 11 August to answer the *Edinburgh Review* itself with the first of a three-part series on "Speeches in Parliament on the Distresses of the Country" ("Literary Notices. No. 7," "8," and "9"; 1: 103–13; 19: 151–57).

The result was a publishing coincidence crucial to an understanding of Hazlitt's subsequent preview of *The Statesman's Manual.* The very day after Hazlitt's first article on "Speeches in Parliament on the Distresses of the Country," Coleridge's own proposed contribution to the debate was first advertised in the *Times* and the *Courier,* thus creating the basic structure of a journalistic contest for political authority. Not only were Hazlitt's review and Coleridge's announcement competing responses to the *Edinburgh*'s influential review-essay, but the timing of Coleridge's notice made it also construable as a hastily improvised response to the *Examiner* itself. Indeed, Hazlitt had openly challenged Coleridge to such a response in his essay of the previous day. "Literary Notices. No. 6" begins with the point-blank assertion that "[a]lmost all that has been said or written upon [the Distresses] is a palpable delusion—an attempt to speak out and say nothing." Whether it be "Speeches in Parliament," the *Edinburgh*'s reviews of them, or the "resolutions" of the Regent's designated charity association, Hazlitt declares that "[t]he great problem of our great problem-finders seems to be, *to take nothing from the rich, and give it to the poor*" (7: 103–4). He then locates one obvious cause of the Distresses in the expense of £900,000,000 on a war designed to restore "the Pope, the Inquisition, the Bourbons, and the doctrine of Divine Right"—a war which he presents as an object lesson in the difference between an economy based on "unproductive labour" and one based on "what the industry of man, left to itself, produces in time of peace for the benefit of man" (7: 106, 105). "This whole question," he goes on to observe with heavy irony, "which from its complexity puzzles many people, . . . has given rise to a great deal of partly wilful and partly shallow sophistry"—one example of which is "an article on this subject in Mr. Coleridge's *Friend*" (7: 106, 106n).

With this challenge laid down, Hazlitt must have read Coleridge's advertisement the next day with considerable interest and immediately conceived the idea of reviewing this new "Layman's Sermon on the Present Distresses of the Country" as soon as it was published "in a few days." But as the weeks passed and no sermon appeared, its announcement must have seemed, with increasing irony, to confirm rather than belie the claim that such interventions were "an attempt to speak out and say nothing," and "*to take nothing from the rich, and give it to the poor.*" In each of his succeeding "Notices," Hazlitt attempts to provoke Coleridge into fulfilling his promise to speak out on the crisis. In "Literary Notices. No. 8," for example, he personifies "the other side" of the debate as "Mr. Burke, Mr. Coleridge, Mr. Vansittart, [and] the *Courier*" (7: 111). The following week, in his final article on "Speeches in Parliament" ("Literary Notices. No. 9"), he throws down an even more emphatic journalistic gauntlet, opening with a double epigraph from *King Lear* which he offers to Coleridge as an appropriate "text" for his competing intervention in the crisis:

> ——"Take physic, pomp;
> Expose thyself to feel what wretches feel,
> That thou may'st shake the superflux to them,
> And shew the Heavens more just."—*Lear.*
> "Ha! here's three of us are sophisticated. Off, off, you lendings."—*The same.*

We see Mr. Coleridge has advertised a Lay-Sermon on the present situation in this country, *addressed to the higher and middle classes.* If he is at a loss for a text to his Lay-Sermon, with the proper mixture of divinity and humanity in it, he cannot do better than take the above two mottos from Shakespear. They are much at his service. (19: 151)[16]

Finally, at the conclusion of "Literary Notices. No. 10" (an extension of his earlier notice of Owen's "New View of Society"), Hazlitt announces his intention to review "*Mr. Coleridge's Lay-Sermon in our next*" (*Examiner,* 1 Sept. 1816: 556). With this, Hazlitt may be said to challenge Coleridge one last time to publish his "Pamphlet" within the week. In so doing, however, he alerts his readers to the nonexistence of the proposed review-text and prepares them for a new venture in the already sensational art of the journalistic review.

The resulting effort, first published as "Literary Notices. No. 11" on 8 September 1816, was first and foremost a "political essay," according to Hazlitt's own later reclassification of it. As such, and in tandem with the ongoing editorial analysis of the "National Distresses" in "The Political Examiner,"[17] it was designed at once to expose the general inadequacy of ruling-class responses to the crisis and criticize in particular Coleridge's proposed intervention. By overtly associating Coleridge with the ministerial politics of the *Courier,* Hazlitt presents his rival as part of an overall threat to the agenda of progressive reform. And drawing on his unusually detailed familiarity with Coleridge's previous political writings (catalogued here as "*the Friend,* the Preliminary Articles in *the Courier, the Watchman, the Conciones ad Populam,* [and] any of the other courtly or popular publications of the same author"), Hazlitt defines Coleridge's unique position within the debate as "a politics turned—but not to account" (7: 115, 118).

Though the tactic of reviewing an unpublished work was clearly unprecedented, the rhetorical tone and strategy of the essay's political agenda were largely products of convention. From both sides of the debate, a typically heightened pitch of declamatory intensity was combined with a focus on details of personal character and opinion designed to undermine the political, moral, and intellectual authority of the opponent (Gilmartin 92–93). Equally typical was the way the intensity of this focus often worked to transform individual particulars into ideological abstractions. In the following passage, for example, Hazlitt draws on Coleridge's most recent political writings (principally "*the Friend,* [and] the Preliminary Articles in *the Courier*") to paint a vivid picture of his Toryism:

> [Mr. Coleridge] takes his notions of religion from the "sublime piety" of Jordano Bruno, and considers a belief in a God as a very subordinate question to the worship of the Three Persons of the Trinity. The thirty-nine articles and St. Athanasius's creed are, upon the same principle, much more fundamental parts of the Christian religion than the miracles or gospel of Christ. . . . He highly approves of *ex-officio* informations and special juries, as the great bulwarks of the liberty of the press; taxes he holds to be a providential relief to the distresses of the people, and war to be a state of greater security than peace. He defines Jacobinism to be an abstract attachment to liberty, truth, and justice; and finding that this principle has been abused or carried to excess, he argues that Anti-jacobinism, or the abstract principles of despotism, superstition, and oppression, are the safe, sure, and undeniable remedy for

the former, and the only means of restoring liberty, truth and justice in the world. (7: 115–16)

From foregrounding a suitably startling example of Coleridge's obscurantism with the reference to Bruno, Hazlitt moves in this passage with the certainty of any Radical orator to the rhythmic and emphatic rehearsal of the bywords "liberty, truth, and justice." Similarly, the sheer repetition of the finger-pointing "he" (which recurs twenty-three times in the full paragraph) turns this pronoun too into one of those "abstract principles," its referent sliding imperceptibly from individualized political agent to one of the faceless enemies of reform who propagate "despotism, superstition, and oppression."

Yet against this typical polarizing movement lies the implication that in the sophistical juggling of such "abstract principles" as "Jacobinism" and "Anti-jacobinism," Coleridge has sacrificed meaningful political agency for the feeble evasions of the self-conscious apostate. Like Southey, Coleridge has turned away from the republicanism of the 1790s to embrace the reactionary politics of the Regency court. Yet unlike Southey, whose laureate odes and *Quarterly* essays guarantee him a measure of cultural authority, Coleridge's "powers," on his own admission, remain paradoxically "suspended": "He would have done better if he had known less. His imagination thus becomes metaphysical, his metaphysics fantastical, his wit heavy, his arguments light, his poetry prose, his prose poetry, his politics turned—but not to account" (7: 117–18). Inevitably, then, a certain tension develops in Hazlitt's essay. There is both an apparent need to preempt the political influence of Coleridge's pamphlet and a claim that Coleridge has effectively taken care of this himself. The seeming absurdity of his political ideas, based as they are on a "transposition of reason and common sense," has resulted in the "everlasting inconsequentiality [of] all that he attempts" (7: 116, 117). The nonappearance of the announced sermon thus becomes an apt metaphor for the spectacle of co-opted genius, of "a politics turned—but not to account."

At the rhetorical climax of this essay, then, we find once again that it is not so much an epiphany of Coleridge's present authority that is to be resisted as it is the loss of a former authority that is to be regretted, especially in face of a far more insidious threat to "liberty, truth, and justice": "We lose our patience when we think of the powers that [Mr. Coleridge] has wasted, and compare them and their success with those, for instance, of such a fellow as the ———, all whose ideas, notions, apprehensions, comprehensions, feelings, virtues, genius, skill, are comprised in the two words which *Peachum* describes as necessary qualifications in his gang, "To stand himself and bid others stand!" (7: 118). Consistent with the *Examiner*'s reputation for outspokenness, the article's most resounding verbal barrage is here discharged not against Coleridge but against an unnameable source of coercive tyranny, presumably the unperturbed Regent himself. For in the midst of the country's economic destitution, and despite his nominal donation to the "Labouring Poor," it was the spendthrift Regent who, with all the unanswerable efficiency of Peachum's drunken highwayman (Gay 1.3), seemed to hold "taxes . . . to be a providential relief to the distresses of the people."[18] Thus in a brilliant because unexpected maneuver, this passage comes as close as possible to seditious libel by using Coleridge's suspended intellectual "powers" as a foil for the complete and utter negation of intellect to be found at the center of applied political power. More than just angry regret, this loss of "patience" becomes a kind of strategic chafing under political restraints symbolized by the lacuna at the climax of the text. While this lacuna ironically parallels Coleridge's own apparent reluctance to commit himself to print—and is in fact a sign that the exercise of discursive resistance produces only the certainty of its containment—it nevertheless functions rhetorically to foreground this containment by licensing an outburst that in its very excess flaunts the "powers" of the reformist press.

One of these powers, it seems, is that of allusiveness. The comic irruption of Peachum and his gang as the capstone to this philippic is a sign of the convergence of "political" and "literary" discourse under pressure of the Distresses; it is also a reminder that this "political essay" appeared in the *Examiner* under the rubric of "Literary Notice." Though these two contexts were by now virtually inseparable, we may nevertheless discern in the second of these a focusing of the wider issues of ideological agency in a contest for the media of that agency. As a piece of review-criticism rich in literary allusions, Hazlitt's article simultaneously challenges Coleridge's bid for discursive authority in a highly competitive marketplace and promotes the ascendancy of review-criticism itself as a medium of choice within the emergent "Reading Public." This is particularly evident in the article's pivotal opening sequence, where the literary tastes of the *Examiner*'s projected readership are reconstructed in a rapid series of metaphorical allusions, beginning once again with a double epigraph:

> ——"Function
> Is smother'd in surmise, and nothing is
> But what is not."

> "Or in Franciscan think to pass disguis'd."

THIS LAY SERMON puts us in mind of Mahomet's coffin, which was suspended between heaven and earth, or of the flying island at Laputa, which hovered over the head of Gulliver. Or it is like the descent of the Cloven Tongues. (7: 114, 380)

From tragic drama to oriental romance, from Christian epic to prose satire, these allusions project a commonality of reference and association among the literate middle classes apparently limitless in its resources (suggested by the repeated "or") and yet safely centered in the key pronoun "us." With the epigraphs taken from *Macbeth* and *Paradise Lost* left unattributed, the literary accomplishments of those readers able to recognize them are subtly flattered at the same time that the sheer popularity of these works, and the corresponding cultural ascendency of Shakespeare and Milton as national poets, lend an aura of indisputable authority to the article that follows. The entire passage addresses a reader sufficiently au courant with current opinion about Coleridge to decode the wit with which his new project is to be scrutinized; certainly readers of "Literary Notices. No. 1" would have no difficulty seeing in the epigraphs how the dawning of Macbeth's deranged ambition and the futile schemes of those lost to the Limbo of Vanity are here conjured up to reflect with withering irony on Coleridge's desire to exchange the mantle of the Gothic poet for the robes of the lay divine. Meanwhile, the comic insubstantiality of the lay sermon itself is suggested with a cluster of allusions to the iconography of popular prose in which the attractiveness of the products of the imagination is balanced by the stout refusal to be mystified by the forms of superstition or by parodies of self-evident truth. The governing norms of "reason and common sense" are skillfully evoked in the allusion to Swift, whose authority here helps align the witty judgments of review-criticism with the iconoclastic tradition of English satire.[19]

The continuity of this satiric tradition within the practice of anonymous review-criticism was strong enough to sustain and incorporate the startling moment of self-parody that occurs when this "Literary Notice" acknowledges it is about to review "a work, not a line of which is written, or ever likely to be written" (7: 114). Suddenly the "Function" of the review itself is briefly "smother'd in surmise," and the otherwise tacit displacements of what Peacock was to call "Fashionable Literature" thrown into bold relief. Yet like the lacuna at the crux of its political argument, this absence of a review-text paradoxically affords the review an opportunity to exhibit the force of its hold over the public by co-opting its own subversion in a stunning excess of wit. The unavailability of Coleridge's new lay sermon is thus transformed into a symbol of the general obscurantism of the conservative hegemony, while presenting itself for facetious analysis as part of Coleridge's individual strategy to create authority through the mystification of his genius: "he considers it the safest way to keep up the importance of his oracular communications, by letting them remain a profound secret both to himself and the world" (7: 114). The Enlightenment norms of clarity and intelligibility can then be invoked to underwrite a review that becomes in effect a series of nimble variations on a single satiric conceit: "We see no sort of difference between [Mr. Coleridge's] published and his unpublished compositions. It is just as impossible to get at the meaning of the one as the other" (7: 114). The difficulty of having no text to review is thus fully elided by making the material unavailability of Coleridge's "unpublished compositions" a metaphor for the cognitive inaccessibility of his "published" ones. These writings are then pressed into service as legitimate referents for critical review.

Meanwhile, of course, the manifest availability of the "Literary Notice" in hand is the best proof of its normative superiority. It shows itself charged with a new and progressive form of authority that is a function of its relatively wide and rapid circulation,[20] its demotic appeal to the intellectual tastes and pretensions of a newly enfranchised readership, and (in this case) its uncanny adroitness in eclipsing the ideas—and even the writing—of the text under review. It is suggested, for example, that Coleridge has shrouded himself and his text in inaccessibility to ensure that "he may escape in a whole skin without being handled by the mob or uncased by the critics" (7: 114). The role of criticism in the literary marketplace is thus clearly identified with the sheer power—and violence—of anonymous urban numbers, a political force organized by the vigilance of its commercially elected spokespersons in "uncas[ing]" the nervous evasions of its politicians and the obfuscating "paradoxes of the learned" (7: 116). Moreover, any question of the ethics of review-criticism is set aside in the following forthright proposition, which combines the trope of the honest wager with the impeccable procedures of scientific method: "Let the experiment be tried, and if, on committing the manuscript to the press, the author is caught in the fact of a single intelligible passage, we will be answerable for Mr. Coleridge's loss of character" (7: 115). In one bold stroke, the judicial powers of review-criticism are vaunted at the same time that their proper "answerab[ility]" is assured. For concealed in the hyperbolic flourish of this challenge is the ameliorative appeal of satire: Coleridge's "loss of character" on these terms could only involve the potential recovery of his authority with the public by rendering his "powers" accessible once more to its urgent needs.

In the meantime, of course, this statement functions as a disclaimer, authorizing an unfettered depiction of the public "character" Coleridge is thus challenged to lay aside. As might be expected, it is in this facet of the review that it moves well beyond the analytical and referential modalities of "political essay" and "Literary Notice" toward the performative gestures of a masterly piece of "banter" seeking literary notice in its own right. Here then we enter on a third discursive context, reflected in a textual practice that Hazlitt himself later described as combining the "two styles [of] the *literary* and the *conversational*" (8: 333). Hazlitt's contestation of Coleridge's authority in this area, however, is much subtler than a mere "quizz" of eccentricity. As we shall see, in a remarkable coda he draws explicit attention to Coleridge's own extraordinary powers of "conversation," paying fulsome tribute to them as a kind of latter-day epiphany of the discursive sublime (7: 118). In so doing, however, he also draws an implicit contrast between the ultimate "inconsequentiality" of this individual's "talk" and the potent cultural agency of "*conversational*" journalism: a newly textualized medium constructed from—and in turn constitutive of—the quotidian discourse of the bourgeois public sphere.[21]

As a discursive genre, Regency "banter" may be located on a diachronic scale between the early "wanton" and the later "good-humoured" forms of ridicule (*OED*), and synchronically between the aggressive raillery of the dandies and the semiprivate, intellectual license of "table-talk." At its most self-consciously "literary" it takes on the cosmological scope and energy of mock-epic:

> Doubt succeeds to doubt, cloud rolls over cloud, one paradox is driven out by another still greater, in endless succession. . . . All [Mr. Coleridge's] notions are floating and unfixed, like what is feigned of the first forms of things flying about in search of bodies to attach themselves to; but *his* ideas seek to avoid all contact with solid substances. Innumerable evanescent thoughts dance before him, and dazzle his sight, like insects in the evening sun. (7: 116, 117)

In an ironic reversal of satirist and "dunce," the newly empowered descendent of the Grub Street hack here draws on the influential precedent of *The Dunciad*, reinforcing his allusion stylistically by studding his prose with patterns of repetition and alliteration.

Elsewhere, mock-epic simile gives way to metaphors of identity as Coleridge is associated with various stock characters from Restoration comedy: "He is the 'Secret Tattle' of the Press, . . . an intellectual Mar-Plot" (7: 115). Such references suggest a bridge between the "*literary*" and the "*conversational*" elements of textualized "banter"; both these characters had appeared recently on stage as part of the continuing popularity of the comedy of manners among Regency theatergoers (5: 270, 278). Clearly the performance of Restoration dialogue had a direct influence on the mordant exchanges of the Regency "refined," reflected here in the clustering of jests in seemingly inexhaustible appositional chains: "Through the whole of [his *Friend*], Mr. Coleridge appears in the character of the Unborn Doctor; the very Barmecide of knowledge; the Prince of preparatory authors! . . . His mind is in a constant state of flux and reflux: he is like the Sea-horse in the Ocean; he is the Man in the Moon, the Wandering Jew" (7: 115, 117).[22]

The most sensational gestures of the review, however, are traceable to two nonliterary precedents, both of which are particularly clear "refractions" of the physical violence in society at large. On the one hand, such a line as "He is only saved from the extremities of absurdity by combining them all in his own person" is typical of the aggressive verbal posturing of the dandies, who were currently making fashionable the exchange of affronts as the quintessence of civility (7: 116; George 164).[23] On the other hand, the popularity of graphic caricature is reflected in such depictions as "His genius has angel's wings, but neither hands nor feet" (7: 117). Analogous to a Gillray or Cruikshank cartoon, the license for distortion is here limited only by the need to convey a recognizable likeness. And finally, in perhaps the most fashionably transgressive stroke of this kind, Hazlitt reaches into the settled iconography of so-called vulgar literature to remark: "Mr. Shandy would have settled the question at once:— "You have little or no nose, Sir" (7: 117, 381).[24]

The calculated excesses of this "quizzing" of Coleridge's public image are in turn justified within the moral and rhetorical norms of the satire by reference to his political apostasy, figured at the climax of the essay as an irredeemable fall from grace. Graphic distortions of "character" are thus warranted as reflections of an even more shocking spiritual ruination.

> If [Mr. Coleridge] had had but common moral principle, that is, sincerity, he would have been a great man; nor hardly, as it is, appears to us—
> "Less than arch-angel ruin'd, and the excess
> Of glory obscur'd." (7: 118)

By a seemingly inexorable process of exaggeration, the satiric subject becomes identified in these lines with nothing less than the character of Satan himself. Yet this resonant allusion to *Paradise Lost* leads directly into the fulminating loss of patience over the "wast[ing]" of Coleridge's "powers" and their subsequent comparison with those of the execrable "fellow." The combined effect is to leave Coleridge's "character"—despite its "glory obscur'd"— charged with something of the gothic grandeur of the first and greatest apostate, in sharp contrast to the bathetic importunity of Peachum's drunken functionary (Gay 1.3).

Though these images help to bring the political agenda of the essay to an emphatic conclusion, they nevertheless threaten the satiric aims of its *"literary"* and *"conversational"* elements with the remystification of autonomous genius. The final paragraph of the review therefore pursues an entirely different rhetorical and tonal strategy by turning to the figures of "Unitarian Romance" and the ingenuous garrulity of "table-talk" (4: 52). This new tonal register answers to the task of conjuring Coleridge's own redoubtable capacity for "conversation," and this phenomenon in turn serves at once as generous evidence of his remaining "powers"—distant echoes of his unobscured "glory"—and as a final surrogate "text" for review at the tribunal of public opinion.

> When his six friends, the six Irish gentlemen . . . after an absence of several years, discovered their old acquaintance John Buncle, sitting in a mixed company at Harrowgate Wells, they exclaimed with one accord—"There he is—making love to the finest woman in the universe!" So we may say at a venture of Mr. Coleridge—"There he is, at this instant (no matter where) talking away among his gossips, as if he were at the Court of Semiramis, with the Sophi or Prestor John." The place can never reach the height of his argument. He should live in a world of enchantment, that things might answer to his descriptions. His talk would suit the miracle of the Conversion of Constantine, or Raphael's Assembly of the Just. It is not short of that. His face would cut no figure there, but his tongue would wag to some purpose. He is fit to take up the deep pauses of conversation between Cardinals and

Angels—his cue would not be wanting in presence of the beatific vision. Let him talk on for ever in this world and the next; and both worlds will be better for it. But let him not write, or pretend to write, nonsense. Nobody is the better for it. (7: 118)

As another of his "unpublished compositions," Coleridge's "conversation" is here afforded favorable review precisely because it safely resists materialization as text. Moreover, the hyperbolic praise accorded these remaining "powers," along with the generous edict to exercise them freely, make all the more forceful the sudden, censorious injunction: "But let him not write, or pretend to write, nonsense."

The authority of these gestures, however, is grounded in several important assumptions. One of these is that mere "talk" has no effective cultural agency; another is that the attempt to press the wagging "tongue" of conversation into print risks the production of nothing but "nonsense." At this point there arises another sharp moment of irony in this review, for this piece of "banter" has itself just supplemented the gratuitous jests of a dandyesque "quizz" with the loquacious excess of "table-talk." As before, however, this glimpse of its own potential meaninglessness becomes an occasion for a redoubled display of its discursive power. As when the unbridled invective of the "political essay" was made possible only by eliding the name of its intended object, or when the quintessence of wit in a "literary notice" was reached only by exposing its own function to be essentially "floating and unfixed," so here the full imperative force of "public opinion" is felt only by effectively obscuring the possibility that its dictates are grounded not in universal standards of "taste" but in the mutable and often arbitrary ordinances of the "gossips." In the end, then, the persuasiveness of this passage depends on two further assumptions: first, that great cultural authority is available to the writer who can in fact reproduce the beguiling fluency of conversation in the relatively fixed medium of print; but second, that this translation is possible only by striving to produce "common sense" rather than "nonsense"—by striving, that is, to adjust the accents of discourse to match the current consensus of "the town" rather than by calling down from the sublime "height[s]" of exploratory insight in the glossolalia of autonomous genius.

The *Examiner*, of course, had a writer on staff who could produce just such a translation. What is more, he did so swiftly enough to outpace Coleridge's ponderous homily by several crucial months, with the result that the dissenting reformer, the anonymous critic, and the journalistic "banterer" emerged at this point the unequivocal victor in this particular contest for cultural authority. For in each of the discursive contexts we have examined—political, literary, conversational—alacrity of response had become essential to the success of any intervention. In the political environment, for example, as rising class struggle pressured the formation of bourgeois ideology, the continued unavailability of Coleridge's pamphlet served only to confirm the apparent abstraction and even incapacity of the Tory intelligentsia. Hazlitt's article, meanwhile, could take its place among a growing number of "political essays" from the pen of intellectual dissent declaiming the less and less subtle arts of "despotism, superstition, and oppression." Similarly, in the literary marketplace, as accelerated competition for readerships transformed the media of ideology, the absence of Coleridge's lay sermon from the booksellers' shops could only have confirmed the effectiveness of the new legislative power of anonymous criticism, however much its use of the plural and the imperative was in ironic parody of the repressive dictates of Georgian "legitimacy." And as Coleridge continued to expend his energies in ineffable drawing room monologues, the newest mode of "*conversational*" journalism would survive its immediate consumption in the periodical press and become the focus of repeat performances—in this instance, to be read aloud at a dinner party one full month after its publication and there recognized as a masterpiece of banter. As we shall see, even after the publication of *The Statesman's Manual*— an event which should have nullified the authority of this satiric preview— Hazlitt had no difficulty recuperating its value as a fitting preamble to his analytical sequel: "We have already given some account of this Sermon," begins "Literary Notices. No. 21" with brisk dispatch. "We have only to proceed to specimens in illustration of what we have said" (7: 119).

A more instructive epilogue to this particular episode, however, is to be found in the final version of this article as one of Hazlitt's *Political Essays* in 1819. As seen at the outset, the positive reception of "Literary Notices. No. 11" by the "Reading Public" was very much a function of a precise moment in British cultural history. Thus while its republication in book form represented an important renewal of its cultural agency, its participation in the various contexts of public discourse was significantly altered. The most important change on this occasion was the abandonment of the trope of anonymity. By 1819 Hazlitt had become "one of the ablest and most eloquent critics of [the] nation."[25] This new cultural authority encouraged him to refocus the politics of dissent, the prestige of criticism, and the appeal of communally constructed discourse in an alternative version of individualized—as opposed to collective—authorial agency. As a "political essay," then, freshly situated among his other ideologically engaged writings and published by the outspoken radical William Hone just two days before the climactic massacre at Peterloo, its intervention in the protracted crisis is now characterized by an ethos of personal courage rather than by a self-effacing enactment of the "intellect of the people" (7: 269). Hazlitt's new visibility in the literary marketplace, meanwhile, put him in the unaccustomed position of promoting the metaphysics of his own talent while sustaining the attacks of anonymous satire. Thus we find the following added footnote: "It may be proper to notice, that this article was written before the Discourse which it professes to criticize had appeared in print, or probably existed anywhere, but in repeated newspaper advertisements" (7: 114n. 1). In the phrase "professes to criticize," Hazlitt uncloaks the dissembling strategies of review-criticism while at the same time laying claim to the ingenuity with which he had once deployed them. Finally, in becoming similarly "answerable" for the more abrasive gestures of "banter," the ventriloquism of public opinion is now recast as the idiosyncrasy of a "personal" style. In his only revisions to the article, Hazlitt trims the most jagged edges of its wit, silently omitting the references to the "Cloven Tongues" and the Shandean "nose." The result is a subtle adjustment to the essay's overall tonality, one that suggests such titles as *Table Talk* (1821) and *The Plain Speaker* (1826) in its counterpoise of the known and the anonymous, the genial and the forthright.

3

Preaching to the Learned:

Coleridge and
The Statesman's Manual

By the time Coleridge's *Statesman's Manual* finally appeared in mid-December 1816, two events had dramatically transformed the sociopolitical landscape of Great Britain and launched the Distresses crisis into an acute phase. First, William Cobbett's introduction in November of a cheap, two-penny version of his *Political Register* had succeeded in galvanizing virtually overnight a vast new reading audience among the laboring classes. As the Radical Samuel Bamford records, "the writings of William Cobbett suddenly became of great authority; they were read on nearly every cottage hearth in the manufacturing districts [of England and Scotland]. Their influence was speedily visible; he directed his readers to the true cause of their sufferings—misgovernment; and to its proper corrective—parliamentary reform. Riots soon became scarce" (quoted in Evans 111). Riots may have soon become scarce, but not before a second event, the "Spafields riot" of 2 December, served to consolidate reactionary opinion and justify government repression of the movement for parliamentary reform. On this occasion, some 10,000 people had gathered at London's Spafields to hear the Radical "Orator" Hunt report on a petition he had delivered to the Regent. Despite his pleas for nonviolence, governmental agents provocateurs incited a portion of the crowd to attack the city, loot gun shops, and make a ramshackle attempt to storm "the Bank and the Tower."[1] This faint echo of 1789 was enough to reopen the question of political authority among middle-class intellectuals, and, among the ruling elite, to prepare the way for one unequivocal answer to such a question—a bill to suspend Habeas Corpus as soon as Parliament resumed in January (Thompson 636).

The impact of these events is registered in the revisions made by Coleridge and his publisher to the lay sermon project as it was re-announced on 10 December 1816:

> This day is published, price 4s, sewed,
> THE STATESMAN'S MANUAL, or the Bible the best Guide to Political Skill and Foresight; a lay sermon addressed to the higher classes of society,
> By. S. T. COLERIDGE, Esq.
> In the press, by the same author, a second and third Lay Sermon addressed to the middle and labouring classes, on the present distresses of the country. The three Tracts together will be so published as to make an uniform volume.
> Printed for Gale and Fenner, Paternoster-row [etc.].
> ("Books Published This Day," *Morning Chronicle* 10 Dec. 1816)[2]

In response to an escalating crisis, then, the mere "Pamphlet" advertised in August has now grown to become the first in a series of three full lay sermons, each one addressed to a different, class-defined, reading audience. In place of "THE DAY OF ADVERSITY" is a new title that clarifies Coleridge's approach to the question of political authority: his first sermon is now addressed only to the de facto rulers of society—"the higher classes"—and locates the ground of their authority in the "Political Skill and Foresight" preeminently available in the Bible or in "THE STATESMAN'S MANUAL." Meanwhile, the impact of Cobbett's two-penny *Register* on the literary marketplace is observable here in the new distinction between a "middle class" and a "labouring class" reading audience, and in the replacement of charity with discourse—the original concept of donating "the Profits of this Pamphlet" to the "Manufacturing and Labouring Poor" has here given way to a third lay sermon. Moreover, where the price and quality of the text in hand has risen from 1s, 6d to "4s, sewed," a further advertisement on the back wrapper of *The Statesman's Manual* announces that the third sermon in the series will be "Printed in a cheap Form for Distribution" with the motto "The Poor have the Gospel preached unto them" (White, introduction xxxi). Thus both commercially and generically, this final lay sermon offers a challenge to both Cobbett and Hunt, projecting at once a religious tract to compete with the vast "Distribution" of Cobbett's two-penny *Register* and something of an open-air Methodist sermon to match the rising authority of "Orator" Hunt among the laboring classes.

Coleridge was not alone in this new pattern of response to the multiple uncertainties of the discursive environment. Hazlitt too, in contesting *The Statesman's Manual* after its publication, addresses a single message to divergent readerships in diverse discursive modes. We saw at the outset, for example, the epistolary review signed "SEMPER EGO AUDITOR," in which Hazlitt challenges this first lay sermon in the persona of a "man of a plain, dull, dry understanding," who, like Cobbett's Radical readers, experiences an awakening to activism as he contemplates the apparent apostasy of a former Bristol republican and Unitarian preacher (7: 128–29). Meanwhile, just two weeks after the appearance of the advertisement cited above, Hazlitt published a detailed analysis of *The Statesman's Manual* in the "Literary Notices" column of the *Examiner,* quoting generously from both Coleridge's sermon and the Bible itself to produce a kind of dissenting counter-sermon in the pages of a Sunday weekly political journal (7: 119–28). In so doing, Hazlitt ironically redirects portions of a text addressed exclusively to "the higher classes of society" to the middle- and lower-middle-class readers of the *Examiner.* Finally, for the *Edinburgh Review* he composed a full-length review-essay in which he actually confronts *The Statesman's Manual* among its intended readership, making use of his position within Francis Jeffrey's stable of anonymous critics to address a reading audience that lay in significant part among "the higher classes of society" (16: 99–114). As we shall see, in searching out an appropriate discursive mode for this essay, he strives on the one hand to match Jeffrey's own series of magisterial strictures against "the Lake School," while on the other hand creating a worthy successor to Moore's ribald "quizz" of the *Christabel* volume that had appeared in the immediately previous edition of the *Edinburgh.* Ironically, of course, the decision to review *The Statesman's Manual* in the pages of the *Edinburgh* contains an implicit acknowledgment of the book's significance as a contribution to public debate. However harshly its authority is refused by both Hazlitt and Jeffrey, Coleridge's first lay sermon is thus brought to the attention of the largest single readership among the ruling classes—including many among the "higher classes" who might otherwise have passed it by.

Indeed *The Statesman's Manual* represents one of Coleridge's most determined bids for cultural authority, a forceful restatement of many of the ideas introduced in his little-read *Friend* (1808–10), and one that at the same time looks forward to another major work inspired by the issue of parliamentary reform, *On the Constitution of Church and State* (1830). Yet this text has always remained on the outer margins of the Coleridgean canon and is rarely read in its entirety. Quietly understood to be "polemical, extreme, and frequently absurd,"[3] it has been decorously abstracted by literary historians from the highly politicized circumstances in which it was composed and delivered to posterity via the distorting metonymy of selective quotation—a text valued primarily for the passage in which Coleridge makes his famous distinction between "symbol" and "allegory."[4] More recently, however, cultural historians have begun to reconsider this lay sermon in its original form and context, and hold it up as crucial to an understanding of the changes taking place at this time in political ideology, in the formation of British reading audiences, and in the role played by genre and style in these processes. Jerome McGann, for one, begins his "critical investigation" of the "Romantic Ideology" with several lengthy (and previously unfamiliar) quotations from *The Statesman's Manual,* noting that Coleridge's ideas on "the concept of ideology, [and] its relevance to the works of Romanticism" are "trenchant and, in certain respects normative to this day in certain lines of critical thought" (3–4). This first lay sermon, he notes, is founded on an understanding of "the necessary interdependence of knowledge and belief" (4). Knowledge must be grounded in "ultimate principles," Coleridge insists, "while every principle is actualized by an idea, and every idea is living, productive . . . and . . . containeth an endless power of semination" (6: 23–24; McGann 4). Thus for McGann,

> Coleridge's position is a defense of what we would now call "ideology," that is, a coherent or loosely organized set of ideas which is the expression of the special interests of some class or social group. . . . From a Marxist perspective, Coleridge's views are praiseworthy in so far as they argue that knowledge is a social rather than an abstract pursuit. But because his position is a conceptualist-idealist defense of Church, State, and the class interests which those institutions support and defend, Coleridge's ideas are, in a Marxist view, clearly deplorable. (5)

Nevertheless, McGann goes on to note, their relevance to cultural history is indisputable: "From Mill and Arnold to Mannheim, Trilling, and their successors, theories of ideology were reproduced which can be traced back to the models developed by Coleridge (and his German counterpart Hegel)" (7).

Meanwhile, certain key passages of *The Statesman's Manual* run like a leitmotif throughout Jon Klancher's seminal study *The Making of English Reading Audiences, 1790–1832*. Klancher identifies "the twelve months between November 1816 and October 1817" as a pivotal moment in the process of British audience-formation, because during this brief period such texts as Cobbett's two-penny *Register*, Coleridge's *Statesman's Manual*, and William Blackwood's *Edinburgh Magazine* helped fundamentally "to crystallize the tension between modes of reading prefigured in the 1790s" (48). This resulted in the formation of what Klancher identifies as "middle-class," "mass," and "radical" reading audiences, and eventually—beginning with Coleridge's critique of the "Reading Public" in *The Statesman's Manual*—in the projection of an "institutional audience" Coleridge would later name "the clerisy" in *Church and State* (Klancher 17). *The Statesman's Manual* anticipates this idea by addressing itself not only to "the higher classes" on the title page, but also to "THE LEARNED" or "*ad clerum*" in the body of the sermon (6: 49, 36). Klancher is particularly interested in the way Coleridge must distinguish this readership from others forming at the same time outside the criteria of "*sound book learnedness*" (6: 39), especially the amorphous "READING PUBLIC" which "diet[s]" (in Coleridge's terms of disgust) at "the two public *ordinaries* of Literature, the circulating libraries and the periodical press" (6: 38). Klancher comments,

> In *The Statesman's Manual*, Coleridge decrie[s] the "luxuriant misgrowth" of a middle-class audience, but his diagnosis was by no means clear to even his most attentive readers. When Hazlitt, writing for the *Edinburgh Review*, read

Coleridge's complaint—"I would that the greater part of our publications could be thus *directed,* each to its appropriate class of readers"—he queried in a footnote: "Do not publications generally find their way there, without a *direction?*" The *Edinburgh's* reviewer can scarcely imagine the phantasm of a mass, chaotic, alien public Coleridge called the "promiscuous audience." Coleridge directed his own sermons *ad populum* or *ad clerum,* but between the populace and the learned, an amorphous middle class had become readers of the great public journals. (47)

In 1816, then, still many years before he had fully formulated the idea of the "clerisy" in *Church and State,* Coleridge can only "gaz[e] unhappily at this emerging discursive event" and reassume "the stance of a preacher, sermonizing against the world of reading and writing coming into visible form" (Klancher 48).

Yet as Marilyn Butler recognizes, it was precisely Coleridge's sermonizing in this case that succeeded in carving out the audience he desired. The lay sermons, she notes, "first provoked the hostility of young liberal intellectuals, and then more slowly helped to lay the foundation for Coleridge's influence on the next generation" (90). For, "[b]y the 1820s, the religious revival for which Coleridge was calling had come, led as he wished by the upper orders," and it was the genre and style of such works as *The Statesman's Manual,* as much as their specific content, that guaranteed Coleridge's position as one of the central ideologues of the movement (90). In Butler's view,

> Coleridge meant to use his writings to find out an élite, and to help remould it in better accordance with his ideal. The style of his writing helped him to his audience, since the strangely specialized tone made a kind of compact with the reader, flatteringly promoting him to membership among the elect. . . . Coleridge is surely the first example, in England at least, of the sage who turns himself into a cult-figure for the next student-generation. (91)

As we shall see, one feature of this style, ultimately crucial to his exposition of the leading ideas in *The Statesman's Manual,* is what Butler names "the barely controlled, inspirational flight," the lyric turn that links the political homilist and cultural commentator with the poet of Romantic fragments (92).

Taken together, then, these studies of McGann, Klancher, and Butler show *The Statesman's Manual* to be crucially engaged within each of the discursive environments identified in the present study. What remains for our purposes is to examine this text further in these terms while resituating it as a specific intervention in the Distresses controversy. Coleridge himself facilitates this task by developing in his sermon a series of personae corresponding to the three contexts respectively of political debate, readership formation, and generic struggle. For the first of these he takes on the role of the latter-day poet-prophet, who, like the "Hebrew legislator, and the other inspired poets, prophets, historians and moralists of the Jewish church," issues a "threatening call to repentance" and a new paradigm for the true *"spirit and credentials of a*

Law-giver" (6: 17, 10, 42). For the second he warrants his specific appeal to a readership of "THE LEARNED" by positioning himself as the "recluse genius" whose role is quietly to shape "the rise and fall of metaphysical systems" (6: 14–15). And for the third he invokes the presence of "the gladdened preacher," who, in passages of resonant lyrical prose, "speak[s] under the influence of Love," inspired by a "genuine enthusiasm" that his reader/hearers are meant to distinguish, by stylistic and generic signs, from texts inspired only by the opposing "enthusiasm of wickedness" (6: 92, 23).

The extravagance of these gestures may once again be understood as a function of the general intensification of discourse under pressure of the Distresses crisis. From the first, Coleridge's lay sermon project as a whole was intended primarily as a political intervention in this moment of crisis. In this initial context, however, by addressing his opening lay sermon exclusively to "the higher classes of society," Coleridge's rhetorical position may be seen as ironically analogous to the petitions of the laboring poor generated by such events as the Spafields meetings. Like them, *The Statesman's Manual* is directed upward toward the ruling elite and, like them too, it mingles the requisite deference of the humble petitioner with the bold assurance that comes from consciousness of possessing a superior, if clearly unofficial, authority. This is most evident in the "motto" of the work, which Coleridge does not take from *Lear* (as Hazlitt suggested) but rather from the untranslated Latin of Giordano Bruno (as Hazlitt predicted): "[Tr:] "I beg you, pay attention to these things, however they appear at first sight, in order that, though you perhaps may think me mad, you may at least discover the rational principles behind my madness" (6: 3, 4n. 2). Unlike the Spafields petitioners, however, the apparent "madness" which the higher classes must condescend on this occasion to overlook is not that of male suffrage or the immediate abolition of sinecures. By contrast, part of Coleridge's deferential strategy in the sermon that follows is to avoid direct reference to the specific, practical issues of the crisis. "In this time of distress and embarrassment," he notes with a bow, to "touch on the present state of public affairs in this kingdom" would be to "tread on glowing embers" (6: 46, 33). Instead the apparent "madness" of his appeal is aligned with that of the archetypal prophet, whose role is to issue a harsh if timely warning from the margins of society, and whose "rational principles" in this case consist in locating the ground and source of all political authority in "the acts and constitutions of God, whose law executeth itself, and whose Word is the foundation, the power, and the life of the universe" (6: 7).

This, of course, was no more welcome a message among the higher classes than demands for immediate political reform from the working class, despite the gentry's nominal adherence to the tenets of the Established Church. The ascendency of Enlightenment rationalism, and with it the swift inroads of the "higher criticism" of the Bible, had done much to erode the cultural authority of "Holy Writ" in general, let alone its specific value as a "Guide to Political Skill and Foresight" among the nation's policy-makers (6: 5, 3).[5] Thus what Coleridge refers to as "the orthodox philosophy of the last hundred years" he also decries as "that atheistic philosophy, which in France transvenomed the natural thirst of truth into the hydrophobia of a wild and homeless scepticism" (6: 108, 22). Indeed Coleridge does not hesitate to identify the rationalist orthodoxy as "the Spirit of Anti-christ" (6: 22), arising first in the "disguised and decorous *epicureanism*" of the empiricist Locke (6: 108) and then epitomized in the "heartless sophist" Hume (6: 22). This orthodoxy in turn animates the false prophets of the age, "the critical benches of infidelity" that Coleridge names as his direct opponents in the press (6: 17). Doubtless he has in mind such political journals as the *Examiner,* and even such articles as Hazlitt's own on the "Distresses of the Country," when he characterizes these competing authorities as "the dark hints and open revilings of our self-inspired state fortune-tellers, '*the wizards, that peep and mutter,*' " who are "alarmists by trade, and malcontents for their bread" (6: 7).

Invoking this archetypal struggle between true and false prophecy, Coleridge has the advantage of aligning himself with the "permanent prophecies" and "eternal truths" of the Bible in opposition to the "*wizards*" and "champions . . . of Baal" (6: 7, 111). Yet to do so with sufficient vigor in the emergency of the Distresses, he must supplement the provisional interpretative authority allowed by Protestantism to the lay preacher with the more controversial agency of the self-appointed (if not "self-inspired") poet-prophet. Moreover, Coleridge was struggling at this time with a public persona that gave him rather more notoriety than authority as the poet of *Christabel* and "Kubla Khan." Continuity of purpose, however, allows him to situate his present work in a line of cultural authority that extends from the biblical writers through Milton to the present day:

> Recent occurrences have given additional strength and fresh force to our sage poet's eulogy on the Jewish prophets:
>> As men divinely taught and better teaching
>> The solid rules of civil government . . .
>> In them is plainest taught and easiest learnt
>> What makes a nation happy and keeps it so,
>> What ruins a kingdom and lays cities flat.
> PARADISE REGAINED, iv. 354. (6: 8)

For both Milton and Coleridge, the "Jewish prophets" present an indisputable paradigm for the cultural authority of writers who, regardless of their social class, believe themselves "divinely taught" and who are therefore in a position to instruct their temporal rulers in "[t]he solid rules of civil government." Such a role also suggests an authority that is in no way diminished by the possibility that the prophet in question may end up being thought "mad"—particularly if his emphasis falls too threateningly on "[w]hat ruins a kingdom and lays cities flat."

In the immediate context of the Distresses, and of the Spafields riot in particular, Coleridge's prophetic task is twofold. First, he must remind the rulers of Britain that "what makes a nation happy and keeps it so" is contained preeminently in the Scriptures, for "in the Scriptures alone is the *Jus divinum,* or direct Relation of the State and its Magistracy to the Supreme Being, taught as an indispensable part of all moral and all political wisdom" (6: 10, 33). Second, he issues the warning that what "ruins a kingdom and lays cities flat" is precisely the neglect of scriptural wisdom in favor of "that atheistic philosophy" which, in political terms, issues inevitably in Jacobinism. It is here, perhaps, that Coleridge's political homily would have its most cogent appeal among "the higher classes." Jacobinism is described as a

> *monstrum hybridum,* made up in part of despotism, and in part abstract reason misapplied to objects that belong entirely to experience and understanding. . . . In all places, Jacobinism betrays its mixt parentage and nature, by applying to the brute passions and physical force of the multitude (that is, to man as a mere animal,) in order to build up government and the frame of society on natural rights instead of social privileges, on the universals of abstract reason instead of positive institutions, the lights of specific experience, and the modifications of existing circumstances. (6: 63–64)

By implication, then, any current threat to the "positive institutions" of government mounted by the (false) agents of reform must be resisted as forcefully as in the war against Napoleonic France. In particular, "the majestic Temple of the British Constitution" is beyond any need for immediate transformation, least of all by "the brute passions and physical force" of such multitudes as those gathering regularly at Spafields, because it has been clearly "perfect[ed] and secure[d]" by the "especial controul of Providence" (6: 109)—a divine favoritism most recently proven by Britain's victory over the "madhouse of jacobinism," and by the correspondingly "fearful chastisement of France" (6: 109, 33).

This evidence of a "providential counterpoise" to the "Spirit of Antichrist" in Britain underlies Coleridge's principle assertion that the Bible is "the Best Guide to Political Skill and Foresight," and that it should be regarded by the higher classes as *The Statesman's Manual* of first resource. After all, Coleridge points out,

> [t]he humblest and least educated of our countrymen must have wilfully neglected the inestimable privileges secured to all alike, if he has not found, if he has not from his own personal experience discovered, the sufficiency of the Scriptures in all knowledge requisite for a right performance of his duty as a man and as a christian. Of the labouring classes, who in all countries form the great majority of inhabitants, more than this is not demanded, more than this is not perhaps generally desireable—"They are not sought for in public counsel, nor need they be found where politic sentences are spoken.—It is

enough if every one is wise in the working of his own craft: so best will they maintain the state of the world." (6: 7)

The reading of the Bible, then, is among the "privileges secured to all alike" by British Protestantism, and therefore it is especially incumbent upon the higher classes. Yet we note that for "the labouring classes . . . more than this is not perhaps generally desireable." Political authority is here said to reside in the ability to speak "politic sentences," which, by virtue of another, unnamed set of differential privileges, is not among the "craft[s]" assigned by Providence to the "least educated of our countrymen."[6] By contrast, among those whose work is statecraft— among "men moving in the higher classes of society" (6: 7)—the Scriptures operate in an entirely different way to "maintain the state of the world." Coleridge calls upon the gentry to "contemplate the ANCIENT OF DAYS" because "this, most of all things, will raise you above the mass of mankind, and therefore will best entitle and qualify you to guide and controul them!" (6: 25).

The Bible thus teaches different things to different classes of society, differences that are at least in part explained as a matter of textual emphasis. In this sermon, for example, Coleridge lays his greatest emphasis on the Old Testament in proving the Bible to be *The Statesman's Manual,* as opposed to "the gospel" that he proposes to "preach unto [the poor]" in his third lay sermon. While of course the New Testament also remains applicable to the higher classes—offering them the ironically reassuring prospect of "a kingdom that is not of this world, thrones that cannot be shaken, and scepters that cannot be broken or transferred" (6: 8)—it is the Old Testament that at this juncture offers them much more practical "instruction" in "the paths by which Providence has led the kingdoms of *this* world through the valley of mortal life—Paths, engraved with the foot-marks of captains sent forth from the God of Armies! Nations in whose guidance or chastisement the arm of Omnipotence itself was made bare" (6: 8). Clearly Britain and France are meant to be numbered among the modern equivalents of such "Nations"—the one with a Constitution secured by "Providence" and the other still smarting from the "fearful chastisement" that inevitably followed its "revolution" (6: 33). By far the most important lesson to be learned from the Old Testament by the statesmen of such nations is that this "Providence" is the sign of the inexorable authority of the law of God, "the *Jus divinum,* or direct Relation of the State and its Magistracy to the Supreme Being" (6: 33).

Yet in order to establish the preeminence of the Bible as a practical manual for statesmen, Coleridge must carefully balance the doctrinal assertion of its utter uniqueness as revelation—its "especial claims to divine authority"—with the reassurance that this source of authority remains permanently available to those who would aspire to reenact the "*Jus divinum*" in early nineteenth-century Britain. And it is this crucial link between revelation and political authority that lies at the heart of what Coleridge defines as the "*credentials of a Law-giver.*" On the one hand we are reminded that "the Hebrew legis-lator and the other inspired poets, prophets, historians and moralists of the Jewish church" have a prodigious advantage over modern writers on political philosophy. This advantage consists in the fact that

> their particular rules and prescripts flow directly and visibly from universal principles, as from a fountain: they flow from principles and ideas that are not so properly said to be confirmed by reason as to be reason itself! Principles, in act and procession, disjoined from which, and from the emotions that inevitably accompany the actual intuition of their truth, the widest maxims of prudence are like arms without hearts, and muscles without nerves. (6: 17)

The unique authority of the Bible is thus grounded in the fact that unlike the "maxims" of rational skepticism, its "rules and prescripts flow directly and visibly from universal principles." Yet such principles, on account of their very universality, must on the other hand remain available at all times to an "actual intuition of their truth." Thus in Coleridge's most far-reaching definition of political authority, the "intuition" of "universal principles" is equated with the possession of a priori ideas—in defiance of Lockean empiricism—and presented as one of the foremost qualifications of statesmanship:

> *The first man, on whom the Light of an* IDEA *dawned, did in that same moment receive the spirit and credentials of a Law-giver:* and as long as man shall exist, so long will the possession of that antecedent knowledge (the maker and master of all profitable Experience) which exists in the power of an Idea, be the one lawful qualification of all Dominion in the world of the senses. (6: 42–43)

In terms of the overt rhetorical aims of *The Statesman's Manual,* this definition of "*the spirit and credentials of a Law-giver*" represents the culmination of Coleridge's ideal of biblically informed statesmanship among "the higher classes of Society," linking political with ideological authority, legislative power with a certain quality or capacity of mind, and "Dominion in the world of the senses" with "the possession of that antecedent knowledge" that comes from contemplation and recognition of those "ideas and principles" revealed in the Scriptures generally and in Old Testament history in particular.

At the same time, however, in this very convergence of political with ideological authority, and in the noticeable elision here of the categories of social class set up elsewhere in his text, Coleridge produces a definition of the ideal "*Law-giver*" that radically exceeds the overt rhetorical premises of *The Statesman's Manual.* If legislative power is indeed contingent not upon rank, inheritance, or even election but rather upon powers of cognition and the consequent possession of "IDEA[s]," Coleridge proposes a model of cultural authority based not on class but on an alternative hierarchy of intellect and erudition. Moreover, in his use of a philosophical vocabulary at once recondite and avant-garde to frame such a definition of authority, the tone of deference appropriate to the lay petitioner of inferior rank modulates here into the more "imperative and oracular" mode of an author conscious of possessing precisely the sort of authority that is being defined (6: 18). If "the one lawful qualification of all Dominion in the world of the senses" is the possession of "that antecedent knowledge . . . which exists in the power of an Idea," any author able to discern and declare the truth of such a "qualification"—indeed to legislate it—must already possess this "power" and must therefore share in some sense *the spirit and credentials of a Law-giver.*"

In such a passage, then, Coleridge's concern to clarify the sources of political authority vested in the de facto *"Law-giver[s]"* of Britain among the higher classes of society shifts toward the equally important task of defining the sort of authority by which he himself intervenes in public debate to address such an audience. To supplement the biblical role of the prophet, Coleridge adopts a second persona of the "recluse genius" whose "visions" are accessible only to the intellectual—as opposed to sociopolitical—elite of "THE LEARNED" (6: 49). Like his definition of *"the spirit and credentials of the Law-giver,"* Coleridge's definition of this role is polemical, in that it implies a fundamental relocation of the grounds of cultural authority away from the traditional categories of social class toward a new and rapidly evolving social hierarchy based on literacy, education, and intellectual capacity. One of the important advantages of biblical history, Coleridge notes, is the way it "balances the important influence of individual Minds with the previous state of national morals and manners" (6: 28). In similar fashion Coleridge boldly traces "the true proximate cause" of "national events," not "to particular persons" among "the great"—as his readers among the higher classes might naturally have supposed—nor "to the errors of one man, [and] to the intrigues of the other [among] the cabinets of statesmen," but rather to those minds more fundamentally able to influence "the predominant state of public opinion" and "the scheme or mode of thinking in vogue" (6: 13–14). Such minds are not, of course, to be found among the anonymous *"wizards that peep and mutter"* on behalf of the various organs of public opinion. Rather they are to be found in "the closets and lonely walks of uninterested theorists . . . in the visions of recluse genius" (6: 14–15). Precisely because of their lack of recognition, such minds have in the end a prodigious influence on cultural history:

> all the *epoch-forming* Revolutions of the Christian world, the revolutions of religion and with them the civil, social, and domestic habits of the nations concerned, have coincided with the rise and fall of metaphysical systems. So few are the minds that really govern the machine of society, and so incomparably more numerous and more important are the indirect consequences of things than their foreseen and direct effects. (6: 14–15)

This, then, is the model of cultural authority that lies at the basis of Coleridge's intervention in public debate. It is the men *"on whom the Light of an* IDEA *[has] dawned"* that are in a position to determine "the rise and fall of

77

metaphysical systems." These are the "uninterested theorists" who, through a combination of intellect and *"sound book learnedness,"* are in a position to exercise ideological authority by legislating those meanings within a culture that ultimately determine or transform "the speculative principles . . . or mode of thinking" (6: 14) operative at a given moment in cultural history. And in the fierce opposition Coleridge sets up between what he calls "the mechanical philosophy" of empirical rationalism and his own unique synthesis of biblical, neo-Platonic, and German Romantic transcendentalism, it gradually emerges that one of the fundamental aims of *The Statesman's Manual* is to initiate nothing less than a counterrevolution in British philosophy.

With this goal in mind, and midway through his sermon, Coleridge unexpectedly readdresses his text to a reading audience more likely to be in a position to decode and appreciate the authority of his philosophical "visions." This occurs in the midst of the crucial passage cited frequently by Klancher for its distinction between a text addressed "exclusively *ad clerum*" (or "to men of *clerkly* acquirements") and one addressed indiscriminately to that "promiscuous audience," the "READING PUBLIC" (6: 36). The historically relevant self-consciousness of this distinction is further heightened by a moment of confusion in the passage itself (quoted in full below), where Coleridge notes that his specific appeal to an audience of *"clerkly"* readers appears in the very title page of the sermon. As Hazlitt was later to remark, "All that we know is, that there is no such title-page to our copy" (7: 124). In a private letter at this time, Coleridge claims he "directed" the title page to read "to the Learned and Reflecting of all Ranks and Professions, especially among the Higher Class" (*Letters* 695). Yet he subsequently emended only one of the extant copies of the book to this effect, which suggests that this crucial alteration of his intended readership came too late to be communicated clearly to his publisher.[7] The effect of the confusion created by all this, however, is simply to draw more attention to the change itself. This passage is worth quoting at length, for it represents Coleridge's most overt as well as his most controversial reflections on the literary marketplace and the projected place of his text within it:

> When I named this Essay a Sermon, I sought to prepare the inquirers after it for the absence of all the usual softenings suggested by worldly prudence, of all compromise between truth and courtesy. But not even as a Sermon would I have addressed the present Discourse to a promiscuous audience; and for this reason I likewise announced it in the title-page, as exclusively *ad clerum;* i.e. (in the old and wide sense of the word) to men of *clerkly* acquirements, of whatever profession. I would that the greater part of our publications could be thus *directed,* each to its appropriate class of Readers. But this cannot be! For among other odd burs and kecksies, the misgrowth of our luxuriant activity, we have now a READING PUBLIC—as strange a phrase, methinks, as ever forced a splenetic smile on the staid countenance of Meditation; and yet no fiction! For our Readers have, in good truth, multiplied exceedingly, and

have waxed proud. It would require the intrepid accuracy of a Colquhoun[8] to venture at the precise number of that vast company only, whose heads and hearts are dieted at the two public *ordinaries* of Literature, the circulating libraries and the periodical press. But what is the result? Does the inward man thrive on this regime? Alas! if the average health of the consumers may be judged of by the articles of largest consumption; if the secretions may be conjectured from the ingredients of the dishes that are found best suited to their palates; from all that I have seen, either of the banquet or the guests, I shall utter my *Profaccia* with a desponding sigh. From a popular philosophy and a philosophic populace, Good Sense deliver us! (6: 36)

Coleridge's recourse to wit in this passage comes in striking contrast to the "staid," portentous tone struck in the earlier parts of the sermon. Yet this forcing of "a splenetic smile" serves to define even more narrowly the audience of *"clerkly"* readers Coleridge hopes will join with him in his desponding *"Profaccia."* This, clearly, will be an audience that will not only revel in the rolling, parenthetical periods and orotund, Latinate diction but will share his vigorous rejection of the very possibility of "a popular philosophy" with a distaste that mingles Malthusian horror at the prospect of readers "multipli[ying] exceedingly" with patrician contempt for the various kinds of "misgrowth" that have "waxed proud."

Yet as Klancher makes clear, it is not just William Cobbett's upstart readers among the laboring classes that Coleridge satirizes here. Klancher distinguishes between Cobbett's "radical" readership and two others he names "mass" and "middle-class" respectively, and it is these latter two that Coleridge conflates in the derisive phrase, "READING PUBLIC."[9] The nascent "mass" audience was characterized, in Klancher's view, by a fascination with commodities (in which "social relations take on 'the fantastic form of relations between things' " [49]), while the newly self-aware "middle-class" audience is characterized by a new and widening gap between the literate consumer of periodicals on the one hand and "a corporate, collective 'author' institutionally set apart from its readers" on the other (48). Coleridge correctly identifies in this larger "READING PUBLIC" a common denominator of "consumption," deploying this now familiar metaphor to witty effect by following it through, with Swiftian zest, to its conjectured "secretions."

We note, however, that it is ultimately not the "guests" but the "banquet" that most concerns Coleridge here—not the "vast company" newly delivered by literacy to the "two public *ordinaries* of Literature" but the *"ordinaries"* themselves: "the dishes that are found best suited to their palates" and, among these, "the articles of largest consumption." These latter are Coleridge's direct opponents, both ideologically and commercially, in an urgent struggle over the "heads and hearts"—and metaphorical bellies—of British readers. Such "articles of largest consumption" as the *Edinburgh Review,* for example, now wielded unprecedented cultural authority in their capacity to shape "public opinion" directly and immediately, thus threatening with total eclipse the subtler, long-term "influence of individual minds" (6: 28). Meanwhile, to revisit Constable's terms, the "stagnation" of the commercial marketplace meant paradoxically that "books of first-rate merit" such as *The Statesman's Manual* ("4s, sewed") were "sell[ing] better now than any former period"— a commercial advantage, however, that served only to place them in direct competition with such "periodical works of talent" as the *Examiner,* which, at less than a shilling per copy, were the only other commodities "increas[ing] in circulation" (Constable fol. 615).

Eventually Coleridge's response to the challenge of the periodical press would be to propose a counter-institution to that of anonymous review-criticism—a *"clerisy"* made up of an elite caste of reader-writers whose task would be (in Klancher's words) "to instruct all other audiences, each according to its social space, how to read and how to distinguish between proper readings and those readings that must be ruled out" (151). At the time of the Distresses, however, this idea is confined to the immediate task of distinguishing an appropriate readership for *The Statesman's Manual* from the "promiscuous" mass of the "READING PUBLIC": "At present, however, I am to imagine for myself a very different audience. I appeal exclusively to men, from whose station and opportunities I may dare anticipate a respectable portion of that *"sound book learnedness,"* into which our old public schools still continue to initiate their pupils. I appeal to men in whom I may hope to find, if not philosophy, yet occasional impulses at least to philosophic thought" (6: 39). To create such an audience, Coleridge calls for "a recurrence to a more manly discipline of the intellect on the part of the learned themselves" (6: 42); more significantly, he commands such discipline immediately by writing in a prose style of consummate difficulty. As Klancher notes, this style is "more convoluted than any periodical could reasonably withstand," yet for this very reason it may be regarded as "an audience-forming strategy to counter all other strategies being deployed in the early nineteenth century" (152–53). This is particularly evident in the "Appendix" of "Comments and Essays," which fully double the size of the sermon and in which Coleridge undertakes (among other things) to redefine, in the terms of the German Transcendentalist philosophy—and in defiance of British empiricism—such key concepts as "Reason," "Understanding," "Religion," "Will," and "Idea."[10] Such redefinitions create the telling need for a concluding "Glossary . . . of the principle terms that occur in the *elements* of speculative philosophy, in . . . the sense in which I myself have employed them" (6: 113–14). Hence the "strangely specialized tone" that Butler describes, a "tone" and style that aroused consternation among the sermon's first readers but which eventually succeeded in "finding out an élite," not only among the gentrified students of Cambridge and Oxford in the 1820s (for whom this recluse genius became something of a "cult-figure"), but within the modern academy as well, where Coleridge's very notebooks now provide an endless source of puzzlement and enquiry (91).

Beyond its intellectual challenge, however, one element of the "specialized tone" of this sermon is what Butler calls its "emotional appeal," a crucial feature of Coleridge's prose that has, in her view, "outlasted the immediate situation, and also outweighed flaws in the argument" (92). This is a feature of the sermon that exceeds both politics and philosophy, a rhetorical strategy that serves at once to loosen the text from its immediate circumstances of the Distresses and supplement the complexities—and the aporias—of its audience-forming metaphysics. Thus to the "madness" of the inspired prophet, and to the abstruse elaboration of his "rational principles" by the "recluse genius," is added the "barely controlled inspirational flights" of the lyric poet, linking the genre of "lay sermon" with the Romantic "fragments" of *Christabel* and "Kubla Khan." To this end, Coleridge develops a third rhetorical persona, defined toward the end of the volume as that of the "gladdened preacher" who "speaks under the influence of Love, and is heard under the same influence!" (6: 92). In this role he is able to thematize the ironic incommensurability of language to the task of communicating biblical "principles" and "Ideas," yet he can also enact rhetorically the moment of epiphany in which such "Ideas" dawn upon the mind—and dramatize "the emotions that inevitably accompany the actual intuition of their truth" (6: 17).

The passage in which this role is defined occurs as the peroration of a lengthy essay on the "ideas" of reason and religion. "In RELIGION," Coleridge finally declares, "there is no abstraction. To the unity and infinity of the Divine Nature, of which it is the partaker, it adds the fulness, and to the fulness the grace and the creative overflowing" (6: 90). This "creative overflowing" is in turn recognized, in both form and content, by a "budding and blossoming forth in all earnestness of persuasion, and in all words of sound doctrine" (6: 91). This rhetorical burgeoning is immediately dramatized in a climactic series of rhetorical questions that probe the central paradox of the sermon: that belief must in fact precede a proper apprehension of biblical truth. Here Coleridge once again boldly reimagines his audience, this time exploiting the residual orality of the lay sermon to project a passive auditory of listeners, in which the previously invoked categories of social class and intellect are now leveled in the timeless attitude of the "grateful and affectionate fellow-christian" seated "at the feet" of the heaven-sent preacher.

> From God's Love through his Son, crucified for us from the beginning of the world, Religion begins: and in Love towards God and the creatures of God it hath its end and completion. O how heaven-like it is to sit among brethren at the feet of a minister who speaks under the influence of Love and is heard under the same influence! For all abiding and spiritual knowledge, infused into a grateful and affectionate fellow-christian, is as the child of the mind that infuses it. The delight which he gives he receives; and in that bright and liberal hour the gladdened preacher can scarce gather the ripe produce of today without discovering and looking forward to the green fruits and embryons, the heritage and reversionary wealth of the days to come; till

he bursts forth in prayer and thanksgiving—The harvest truly is plenteous, but the labourers few. O gracious Lord of the harvest, send forth labourers into thy harvest! There is no difference between the Jew and Greek. Thou, Lord over all, art rich to all that call upon thee. But how shall they call on him in whom they have not believed? and how shall they believe in him of whom they have not heard? and how shall they hear without a preacher? and how shall they preach except they be sent? And O! how beautiful upon the mountains are the feet of him that bringeth good tidings, that publisheth peace, that bringeth forth glad tidings of good things, that publisheth salvation; that saith unto the captive soul, Thy God reigneth! God manifested in the flesh hath redeemed thee! O Lord of the harvest, send forth labourers into thy harvest!!

Join with me, Reader! in the fervent prayer, that we may seek within us, what we can never find elsewhere, that we may find within us what no words can put there, that one only true religion, which elevateth Knowledge into Being, which is at once the Science of Being, the Being and the Life of all genuine Science. (6: 92–93)

This is the emotional appeal of the ecstatic evangelist, in which the crucial aura of spiritual presence is skillfully textualized in the apparent immediacy of the author's inspiration. A mounting series of rhetorical questions gradually identifies the task of the archetypal "preacher" with that of the present writer, an identity which in turn authorizes—"in all words of sound doctrine"— the climactic paean to the preacher himself as "him that bringeth good tidings," him "that publisheth peace . . . [and] salvation." From this position of consummate spiritual authority, in which the preacher seems to reexperience the very moment of divine commission, he then reaches out in a gesture of sudden and spontaneous intimacy—"Join with me, Reader! in the fervent prayer"—a prayer, ironically, that requires the reader to seek "within . . . what no words can put there."

Indeed, the intercessory prayer is the primary rhetorical function served by the lyric flights of the "gladdened preacher." It is required to bridge the acknowledged gap between the discursive mediation of the sermon and the "actual intuition" of biblical truth on the part of Coleridge's readers (6: 17).[11] Thus toward the end of the sermon proper we find a similar prayer to the one quoted above, in which Coleridge suddenly bows his knees "unto the Father of our Lord Jesus Christ, that he would grant [readers of the sermon] . . . to be strengthened by his Spirit . . . to comprehend with all saints what is the breadth, and length, and depth and heighth" (6: 48). Shortly afterward the sermon itself concludes with a passage of similarly fervent invocation, in this case to the "Light" necessary to rediscover "the hidden treasures of the Law and the Prophets" (6: 50–51). Here, however, the pious appropriation of biblical diction gives way to the rococo profusion of Coleridge's own metaphysics in a breathtaking series of variations on his principal longing for "some gracious moment" in which "one solitary text" of the Bible "should but dawn upon us in the pure untroubled brightness of an IDEA, that most glorious birth of the God-like within us" (6: 50).[12]

By far the most engaging use of lyric intercession, however, occurs once again in one of the supplementary essays, where Coleridge suddenly pauses to remark: "If you have accompanied me thus far, thoughtful reader! Let it not weary you if I digress for a few moments to another book, likewise a revelation of God—the great book of his servant Nature" (6: 70). With this, of course, the task of the "gladdened preacher" coincides with Coleridge's more familiar public persona as a Romantic poet, an association which he encourages by declaring that "it has been the music of gentle and pious minds in all ages, it is the *poetry* of all human nature, to read [the book of Nature] . . . in a figurative sense, and to find therein correspondencies and symbols of the spiritual world" (6: 70). On this premiss, he then embarks on a passage of appropriately lyrical prose, in which the same intimacy and immediacy of the "fervent prayer" quoted above is combined with an effort to describe and evoke the emotions necessary to an "actual intuition" of this "spiritual world":

> I have at this moment before me, in the flowery meadow, on which my eye is now reposing, one of its most soothing chapters, in which there is no lamenting word, no one character of guilt or anguish. For never can I look and meditate upon the vegetable creation without a feeling similar to that with which we gaze at a beautiful infant that has fed itself asleep at its mother's bosom, and smiles in its strange dream of obscure yet happy sensations. The same tender and genial pleasure takes possession of me, and this pleasure is checked and drawn inward by the like aching melancholy, by the same whispered remonstrance, and made restless by a similar impulse of aspiration. It seems as if the soul said to herself: from this state hast *thou* fallen! Such shouldst thou still become, thy Self all permeable to a holier power! thy Self at once hidden and glorified by its own transparency, as the accidental and dividuous in this quiet and harmonious object is subjected to the life and light of nature which shines on it, even as the transmitted power, love and wisdom, of God over all fills, and shines through, nature! But what the plant *is,* by an act not its own and unconsciously—*that* must thou *make* thyself to *become!* must by prayer and by a watchful and unresisting spirit, *join* at least with the preventive and assisting grace to *make* thyself, in that light of conscience which inflameth not, and with that knowledge which puffeth not up. (6: 71)

The tone and imagery of this passage are in striking contrast to the rest of the sermon. Absent here is the denunciatory zeal of the poet-prophet, the sardonic wit of the elitist genius, even the bold enactment of spiritual authority in earlier passages in a similar persona. The emotional appeal of this passage resides instead in the tone of earnest but humble introspection on the part of a man of sensibility, whose dialogue between self and soul in the presence of a breast-fed infant and a "flowery meadow" is only with the most decorous subtlety contrived to identify reader and author in the pronoun "thou." Once this identification is made, however—once the reader understands that it is he or she who is asked to *"make* thyself to *become"* like the plant—the rhetorical task of this passage is found to be the same as previous ones: to model a necessary receptiveness to the "Ideas" of the Bible and, by extension, an openness to their ideological proxy, *The Statesman's Manual.* Like the preacher-poet vis-à-vis the "vegetable creation," so we as readers are enjoined to become "permeable to a holier power," allow the "genial pleasure" of these images to possess us, and cultivate a "watchful" but ultimately "unresisting spirit."

This is the "hermeneutics of belief" that has guaranteed the continued authority of Coleridge's prose and poetry well into the present day. Indeed, quoted in isolation from the rest of the sermon, the "flowery meadow" passage could well survive "the immediate situation" of its composition (in Butler's terms) and even transcend "flaws in the argument" of *The Statesman's Manual* as a whole. Yet this is a passage just as firmly rooted in the context of intense and historically specific struggle as the others quoted above. As it continues, for example, into the subsequent pages of the essay, the feeling of "awe" inspired by the contemplation of nature is reinforced by a renewed intensity of rhetorical gesture ("Lo!—with the rising sun it commences its outward life. . . . Lo!—at the touch of light how it returns an air akin to light. . . . Lo!—how upholding the ceaseless plastic motion of its parts. . . ." [6: 72]), until Coleridge suddenly exchanges the lyric sublime of the "gladdened preacher" for the bitter jeremiad of the prophet against "Antichrist."

> O!—if as the plant to the orient beam, we would but open out our minds to that holier light, which "being compared with light is found before it, more beautiful than the sun, and above all the order of stars," (Wisdom of Solomon, vii. 29.) ungenial, alien, and adverse to our very nature would appear the boastful wisdom which, beginning in France, gradually tampered with the taste and literature of the most civilized nations of christendom, seducing the understanding from its natural allegiances, and therewith from all its own lawful claims, titles and privileges. It was placed as a ward of honour in the courts of faith and reason; but it chose to dwell alone, and became an harlot by the way-side. . . . [U]surping the name of reason [the Human Understanding] openly joined the banners of Antichrist, at once the pander and the prostitute of sensuality, and whether in the cabinet, laboratory, the dissecting room, or the brothel, alike busy in the schemes of vice and irreligion. Well and truly might it, thus personified in our fancy, have been addressed in the words of the evangelical prophet. . . . "Thou hast said, none is my overseer!—thy wisdom and thy knowledge, it hath perverted thee!—and thou hast said in thy heart, I am, and there is none beside me!" (Isaiah, xlvii, 10) (6: 73–75)

Thus the "emotional appeal" of the "gladdened preacher" is once again aligned with the political and ideological agenda of the poet-prophet and "recluse genius." An openness to that "holier light" evidenced in nature is here found to be contingent upon a rejection of that "boastful wisdom" that represents the entire philosophical and scientific achievement of the eighteenth century.

The very extravagance of these claims—the "madness" referred to in Coleridge's motto—is the clearest sign of their historical specificity, and it represents one index of the scope and urgency of this particular contest for cultural authority. For this "French wisdom," Coleridge continues in warning to the higher classes, is "[p]rurient, bustling, and revolutionary," and must therefore be an object of immediate resistance in face of such events as the Spafields riot (6: 76). It is, moreover, characterized by

> a heartless frivolity alternating with a sentimentality as heartless—an ignorant contempt of antiquity—a neglect of moral self-discipline—a deadening of the religious sense, even in the less reflecting forms of natural piety—a scornful reprobation of all consolations and secret refreshings from above—and as the caput mortuum of human nature evaporated, a French nature of rapacity, levity, ferocity, and presumption. (6: 76–77)

These we may take to be the signs by which the "Learned and Reflecting" will recognize and revile Coleridge's direct opponents in the periodical press. In a final effort to define his audience against theirs, Coleridge assumes in his readers an anti-Gallic patriotism that he enlists to turn back the "heartless frivolity" of fashionable prose. And against the inevitable assaults of satiric banter, he poses his own unique and eclectic style, blending Romantic veneration of "antiquity" with the "moral self-discipline" of ascetic intellect—a stern piety seasoned with sensibility and with lyric "consolations and secret refreshings from above."

4

Two Classes of Public Opinion:

Hazlitt's *Examiner* and
Edinburgh Reviews
of *The Statesman's Manual*

Having waited almost four months for Coleridge's new book to appear, Hazlitt wasted no time in responding to it. Within days of its publication, he had prepared three different reviews: a sequel to his September preview for the *Examiner,* a full-length review-essay for the *Edinburgh Review,* and the stylistic tour-de-force signed "SEMPER EGO AUDITOR" that we examined at the outset (7: 119–29; 16: 115–38). It is the first two of these that concern us here, and in particular the instructive differences between them. By comparing the reviews for the *Examiner* and the *Edinburgh* we can trace Hazlitt's own attempt to address the divergent reading audiences identified by Coleridge in *The Statesman's Manual.* In the *Examiner* Hazlitt redirects portions of a sermon addressed to "the higher classes" to middle-class readers who will take offense at the lay preacher's scorn of their politics and their "boastful wisdom." By contrast, in the *Edinburgh* he caters to a gentrified, Whiggish readership formed in part from the same "higher classes" Coleridge himself seeks to address—and whose attitudes toward Coleridge have just been shaped by Moore's "quizz" of *Christabel* in the immediately previous number of the *Edinburgh.* Thus where Hazlitt's *Examiner* review takes on Coleridge's politics, situating him among those "modern apostates" whose former radicalism makes them particularly virulent spokespersons for the reactionary backlash, his essay for the *Edinburgh* denies Coleridge any political agency. Instead it positions him as a "Lake School" poet whose censorious attack on the "READING PUBLIC" and its "articles of largest consumption" provides an occasion for a stirring defense of "the freedom of the press" and the "exercise of public opinion" (16: 106). And while both articles set out to satirize Coleridge's "rhapsodic" style, they conclude with quite different "specimens" of this style, illustrating Coleridge's ideological "nonsense" and "Lake School" bathos respectively. Finally, however, in quoting Coleridge generously in each case, Hazlitt allows two similar moments of undecidability to arise from the tension between exposing the absurdity of Coleridge's prose and co-opting its attractions for all readers with a taste for the sublime.

In writing first for the *Examiner,* Hazlitt has the advantage of providing a sequel to his own previous remarks on Coleridge, whereas in the *Edinburgh* he will be forced to align his style with Moore's far less nuanced approach. Thus he begins his response to *The Statesman's Manual* by improvising a kind of Sunday counter-sermon from the lay pulpit of political dissent, anchored in an allegorical lesson from *The First Book of Kings* and in long illustrative "specimens" of Coleridge's own sermon. Moreover, at the time Hazlitt was writing this—in late-December 1816—the *Examiner* as a whole was addressing a series of urgent and immediate issues into which a review of *The Statesman's Manual* could readily be inserted. The violence of the Spafields riot had produced a reactionary backlash against the movement for reform, and the *Examiner* found itself increasingly isolated as one of the few middle-class journals still willing to espouse this now discredited cause.[1] Yet its response was to redouble rather than reduce its assault on the aristocratic corruption and "Ministerial" oppression that it saw as the root cause of national distress. It became Hazlitt's task in particular to express "as often and as strongly as [he] could" what he would later define as his "hatred of tyranny and [his] contempt for its tools" (7: 7).[2] Indeed, for the two weeks immediately preceding his review of *The Statesman's Manual,* Hazlitt's "Literary Notices" column actually displaced the "Political Examiner" as the paper's front-page leading article.

These front-page essays of 15 and 22 December provide an indispensable context for the review of Coleridge's lay sermon a week later on 29 December. In them Hazlitt focuses his attack on the *Examiner*'s arch-rival, the daily *Times,* and in particular on its ultra-royalist editor John Stoddart. Stoddart had once been a fervent democrat but was now among the most virulent advocates of uncompromising repression in the name of Hanoverian "Legitimacy."[3] Thus Hazlitt presents a series of "reviews" titled "Illustrations of the Times Newspaper," in which he holds up Stoddart's writings as paradigmatic of a more pervasive phenomenon he calls "literary prostitution or political apostasy"—the tendency, that is, for middle-class writers to abandon the liberal ideals of reform under the pressure of reaction and to become instead the "tools" of "tyranny" (7: 131, 7). "[P]atriots in 1793, and royalists in 1816," these are the writers who once were "loud" in their support of "the right of the people to chuse their own government," and who have now "turned around to flatter and to screen, with the closeness of their fulsome embraces, the abuses of a power which they set out with treating as monstrous, the right of a discarded family to reign over a nation in perpetuity by the grace of God" (7: 132).[4] Stoddart was only the most obvious example of this phenomenon; another was the Poet Laureate Robert Southey, whose increasingly clamant essays in the *Quarterly Review* were in sharp contrast to his republican "pantisocracy" of the 1790s.[5] And with the sudden appearance of *The Statesman's Manual*— with its jeremiad against Jacobinism in the name of "*Jus divinum*"—Coleridge too was to be clearly numbered among "The Modern Apostates."

Yet by contrast with the forthright, daily "raving" of Stoddart in the *Times* on behalf of "Legitimacy," or with the sycophantic zeal of Southey's laureate "Lays" and *Quarterly* reviews (7: 138), Coleridge's apostasy is distinguished by a unique pattern of evasions and omissions. As long as the promised lay sermon remains unpublished, for example, the *Examiner* is forced to declare Coleridge's politics to be strategically indeterminate and unreadable—"in total eclipse."[6] Its strategy is therefore to clarify for its readers what *was* determinate: namely, Coleridge's *former* politics as evidenced in his publicly available—and vividly anti-ministerial—writings of the revolutionary period. Thus on 24 November, the *Examiner* reprints Coleridge's 1798 "War Eclogue," "Fire, Famine, and Slaughter," in a gesture that anticipates on a small scale the publication of Southey's Jacobin play *Wat Tyler* by Sherwood, Neely and Jones three months later. On 15 December, in his front-page article about the *Times,* Hazlitt quotes the adage "*Once a Jacobin and always a Jacobin*" in pointed allusion to the title of one of Coleridge's anti-ministerial essays in the *Morning Post* of 1802, where Coleridge had actually challenged the pejorative use of the term "Jacobin" by those he names "the blind and furious bigots, of the late Ministry" (3.1: 368). And on 29 December, with *The Statesman's Manual* finally published and the evidence of a "politics turned" in hand at last, Hazlitt nevertheless finds its politics to be more of a twist than a turn. On the one hand he argues, Coleridge relies on "cant" to shroud the crucial doctrine of divine right in the Latinate euphemism "*Jus divinum,*" while on the other he "purposely" omits to provide any direct illustration or proof of this doctrine from the Bible itself (7: 121, 120).

The turn to "cant" was a trope already foreseen in Hazlitt's essay of two weeks earlier, where he defines it as a rhetorical "violence" that is the sign of overcompensation for political self-contradiction—for the "want of sincerity" that is the hallmark of apostasy in the reactionary press (7: 135). In *The Statesman's Manual,* it is found to comprise a smoke screen of fine distinctions and learned jargon designed to reprobate (in Coleridge's terms) the "mechanic philosophy" of "the unenlivened generalizing understanding," while mystifying the "Reason" and "Imagination" necessary to discern in the Scriptures "the Best Guide to Political Skill and Foresight" (7: 120). Hazlitt quotes a lengthy passage containing these terms in which Coleridge aims to establish the efficacy of biblical history, a passage that contains one of

Coleridge's most evidently Kantian definitions of the "Imagination"[7] and which ends with a strikingly convoluted claim: " *'Hence by a derivative, indeed, but not a divided influence, and though in a secondary, yet in more than a metaphorical sense, the Sacred Book* is worthily entitled the Word of God,' p. 36" (7: 120). To this, Hazlitt retorts:

> So that, after all, the Bible is not the immediate Word of God, except according to the German philosophy, and *in something between a literal and metaphorical sense.* Of all the cants that ever were canted in the canting world, this is the worst! The author goes on to add, that "it is among the miseries of the present age that it recognizes no medium between *literal* and *metaphorical,*" and laments that "the mechanical understanding, in the blindness of its self-complacency, confounds SYMBOLS with ALLEGORIES."— This is certainly a sad mistake, which he labours very learnedly to set right, "in a diagonal sidelong movement between truth and falsehood." (7: 121)

Thus Coleridge's entire apparatus of "learned[ness]," and in particular his recourse to the terms of "German philosophy," is reduced in Hazlitt's analysis to rhetorical sleight-of-hand, all the more dangerous for its bathetic complexity. For this is a form of cant that takes the curiously distracting shape of a "diagonal sidelong movement between truth and falsehood." The caricature at once recalls the imagery of Hazlitt's first two reviews of Coleridge and dismisses at a blow the one passage that has since been valued most about *The Statesman's Manual.*

If Hazlitt's rejection of the famous distinction between "SYMBOLS" and "ALLEGORIES" may seem at first merely tendentious, it is worth noting that his view has been corroborated as recently as 1986 in Hodgson's skillful deconstruction of this distinction in a chapter titled "Coleridge's Rhetoric of Allegory and Symbol" (4–10). The difference, however, is that in Hazlitt's analysis, the distinction between these two terms is identified as an integral part of Coleridge's political agenda rather than as part of his attempt to create an ahistorical lexicon of literary-critical terms. For the passage just quoted leads directly into Hazlitt's treatment of the notion of *"Jus divinum,"* implying that in such distinctions as that between symbol and allegory Coleridge has used his learning as a tool to reconstruct a conservative—and, in the circumstances, distinctly repressive—ideology:

> [A]nd so [Mr. Coleridge] goes on for several pages, concluding his career where the Allies have concluded theirs, with the doctrine of Divine Right; which he does not however establish quite so successfully with the pen, as they have done with the sword. "Herein" (says this profound writer) "the Bible differs from all the books of Greek philosophy, and in a two-fold manner. It doth not affirm a Divine Nature only, but a God; and not a God only, but the living God. *Hence in the Scriptures alone is the JUS DIVINUM or direct Relation of the State and its Magistracy to the Supreme Being, taught as a*

vital and indispensable part of ALL MORAL AND ALL POLITICAL WISDOM, *even as the Jewish alone was a true theocracy!"* (7: 121)

This, for Hazlitt, is the crux of Coleridge's political argument in *The States-man's Manual,* a statement that confirms Coleridge's place among "The Modern Apostates" and reveals some of the most fundamental contradictions in his present position. Thus he responds:

> Now it does appear to us, that as the reason why the *Jus divinum* was taught in the Jewish state was, that that alone was a true theocracy, this is so far from proving this doctrine to be a *part of all moral and all political wisdom,* that it proves just the contrary. This may perhaps be owing to our mechanical understanding. Wherever Mr. C. will shew us the theocracy, we will grant him the *Jus Divinum.* Where God really pulls down and sets up kings, the people need not do it. Under the true Jewish theocracy, the priests and prophets cashiered kings; but our lay preacher will hardly take this office upon himself as a part of the *Jus Divinum,* without having anything better to show for it than his profound moral and political wisdom. Mr. Southey hints at something of this kind in verse, and we are not sure Mr. Coleridge does not hint at it in prose. (7: 121)

Hazlitt's refutation of Coleridge's central thesis thus rests quite openly on what Coleridge would indeed label a "mechanical understanding" of biblical revelation. In this view, the Bible's authority in "times like these" is strictly limited by its claim that God took an active role only in the "theocracy" of ancient Israel. As for nineteenth-century Britain, "[w]herever Mr. C. will shew us the theocracy, we will grant him the *Jus Divinum.*" For Hazlitt and his readers, of course, the dissolute Regent, his reactionary ministry, and an unreformed Parliament hardly constituted evidence that God was still playing a providential role in British history—unless, of course, this were manifest in "the people" themselves, now inspired indeed for these very reasons to "pull down" a "discarded family." Moreover, in a further irony, Hazlitt points out that this "office" of "cashier[ing] kings" was traditionally assigned God's "priests and prophets," a role Southey and Coleridge seemed to have taken on in the 1790s in their Radical "verse" and "prose," and which Coleridge self-consciously reassumes in *The Statesman's Manual.* Thus Hazlitt aims to expose the ironic, underlying identity of Coleridge's present project with the agenda of Radical reform, a self-canceling identity that leaves only the rhetorical husk of "cant" to distinguish his present text from his former writings.

Coleridge's anxiety on this very point is proven, in Hazlitt's analysis, by his recurrence in *The Statesman's Manual* to the peculiar device of the "missing" text. This corresponds to the "missing line" that was "necessary to make common sense" of *Christabel* or to the missing sermon that would have made sense of the August advertisement. Hazlitt seizes upon the preacher's strange reluctance to refer directly to the Bible itself in support of his central thesis, and in particular his reticence to quote a passage from *The First Book of Kings* that he alludes to as proof of the decisive concept of *"Jus Divinum."* As before, moreover, it becomes Hazlitt's satiric role in these circumstances to supply this missing text, here by printing at length the passage in question from *First Kings* as the centerpiece of his review, thus turning his "Literary Notice" (in a Sunday journal) into a generic echo of Coleridge's text from the opposing "pulpit" of Radical dissent. To set up this maneuver, Hazlitt structures the first half of his review around a mock search for the biblical passage in Coleridge's text, using extensive quotation and interpolated asides to demonstrate his own contrasting willingness to lay bare the contents of his review-text.

> It is a pity that with all the fund of "rules and assistances" which the Bible contains for our instruction and reproof, and which the author in this work proposes to recommend as the Statesman's Manual, or the best Guide to Political Skill and Foresight, in times like these, he has not brought forward a single illustration of his doctrine, nor referred to a single example in the Jewish history that bears at all, in the circumstances, or the inference, on our own, but one, and that one he has purposely omitted. Is this to be credited? Not without quoting the passage.
>
> "But do you require some one or more particular passage from the Bible that may at once illustrate and exemplify its application to the changes and fortunes of empires? Of the numerous chapters that relate to the Jewish tribes, their enemies and allies, before and after their division into two kingdoms, it would be more difficult to state a single one, from which some guiding light might *not* be struck." (Oh, very well, we shall have a few of them. The passage goes on.) "And in nothing is Scriptural history more strongly contrasted with the histories of highest note in the present age, than in its freedom from the hollowness of abstractions." (7: 119–20)

Still searching for the promised passages from Jewish history, Hazlitt continues to quote another full page from Coleridge's book and samples from several pages following, culminating in the key statement about the *"Jus Divinum."* Here the lack of proof becomes most conspicuous:

> [Regarding the cashiering of kings,] Mr. Southey hints at something of the kind in his verse, and we are not sure that Mr. Coleridge does not hint at it in prose. For after his extraordinary career and interminable circumnavigation through the heaven of heavens, after being wrapt in the wheels of Ezekiel, and sitting with the captives by the river of Chebar, he lights once more on English ground, and you think you have him.
>
> "But I refer to the demand. Were it my object to touch on the present state of affairs in this kingdom, or on the prospective measures in agitation respecting our sister island, I would direct your most serious meditations to the latter part of the reign of Solomon, and the revolutions in the reign of Rehoboam his son. *But I tread on glowing embers.* I will turn to a subject

on which all men of reflection are at length in agreement—the causes of the Revolution and fearful chastisement of France." (7: 122)[8]

Hazlitt's aim here is to isolate the moment of telling indirection in Coleridge's turn from the businesslike "But I refer to the demand" to the enigmatic recoil *"But I [should] tread on glowing embers."* And though Coleridge does in fact go on to provide biblical illustration for "the causes of the [French] Revolution," he does so using a text taken from the highly symbolic prophecy of *Isaiah,* not from the concrete history of the Jewish "theocracy" in *First Kings.* This substitution of prophecy for history—of symbol for allegory, in effect—clearly met Coleridge's own criteria for appropriate evidence, but certainly not Hazlitt's, whose strategy is precisely to cater to the preference for "allegory" over "symbol" that marks the so-called mechanical understandings of his readers. Thus, he continues:

> As we are not so squeamish as Mr. Coleridge, and do not agree with him and all other men of reflection on the subject of the French Revolution, we shall turn back to the latter end of the reign of Solomon, and that of his successor Rehoboam, to find out the parallel to the present reign and regency which so particularly strikes and startles Mr. Coleridge. Here it is for the edification of the curious, from the First Book of Kings:— (7: 122)

And thus Hazlitt inserts a lengthy Bible lesson into his "Literary Notice," a procedure as strange in context as it is perfectly justified, not only by Coleridge's allusion and by the Protestant tenets of his sermon as a whole but also by the norms of Enlightenment enquiry, by its appearance in a Sunday newspaper aimed at dissenting readers, and even by a sly inversion of the aims of Christian evangelism with its use of Scripture to "edif[y]" the newly literate.

Hazlitt marks his Bible reading with italics, using this technique to underline for his readers all the saliently allegorical features of the story. Thus, for example, he emphasizes the fact that *"all Israel were come to Shechem to make [Rehoboam] king,"* but, led by Jeroboam, they agree to do so only on the condition that Rehoboam *"wilt be a servant unto this people"* by lightening the "heavy yoke" of his father. Instead the new king (not unlike the Regent) *"consult[s] with the young men that were grown up with him"* and, taking their advice, *"answer[s] the people roughly . . .* saying, *My father made your yoke heavy, and I will add to your yoke; my father also chastised you with whips, but I will chastise you with scorpions"* (7: 122–23).

At this point, the story's striking "parallel to the present reign and regency"—and its differences—become particularly instructive, underscored at a key point by one of Hazlitt's interpolated asides.

> Wherefore the king hearkened not unto the people; *for the cause was from the Lord,* that he might perform his saying which the Lord spake by Ahijah, the Shilonite, unto Jeroboam, the son of Nebat," (We see pretty plainly how the

principle of "a true theocracy" qualified the doctrine of *Jus Divinum* among the Jews; but let us mark the sequel.) *"So when all Israel saw that the King hearkened not unto them, the people answered the King, saying, What portion have we in David: neither have we inheritance in the son of Jesse: to your tents, O Israel: now see to thine own house, David.* Then king Rehoboam sent Adoram, who was over the tribute; and all Israel stoned him with stones that he died; therefore king Rehoboam made speed to get him up to his chariot to flee to Jerusalem. So Israel rebelled against the house of David unto this day." [1 *Kings* 11.42–43 and 12. 1–20] (7: 122–23)

With this, of course, Hazlitt is able to drive home all the crucial allegorical lessons of such a text, both for the immediate end of refuting Coleridge's tendentious reading of the Bible and for the larger goal of reinforcing the *Examiner*'s own political intervention in the Distresses crisis. Coleridge's recommendation of the story of Rehoboam to the "serious meditations" of the ruling classes must, Hazlitt suggests, either be the product of a covert Radicalism or of a particularly subtle form of apostasy, the "voluntary self-delusion" of the lapsed intellectual.

> Here [in this story] is the doctrine and practice of divine right, with a vengeance. We do not wonder Mr. Coleridge was shy of instances from his Statesman's Manual, as the rest are like this. He does not say (neither shall we, for we are not salamanders any more than he, *to tread on glowing embers*) whether he approves of the conduct of all Israel in this case, or of the *grand, magnificent, and gracious* answer of the son of Solomon; but this we will say, that his bringing or alluding to a passage like this immediately after his *innuendo* (addressed to the higher classes) that the doctrine of divine right is contained *par excellence* in the Scriptures alone, is we should suppose, an instance of a power of voluntary self-delusion, and of a delight in exercising it on the most ticklish topics, greater than ever was or will be possessed by any other individual that ever did or ever will live upon the face of the earth. "Imposture, organised into a comprehensive and self-consistent whole, forms a world of its own, in which inversion becomes the order of nature." Compared with such powers of inconceivable mental refinement, hypocrisy is a great baby, a shallow dolt, a gross dunce, a clumsy devil! (7: 123)

As in the climactic passage of the September preview, Coleridge's "powers of inconceivable mental refinement" are once again contrasted with the stark despotism of the Regent, who, like "the son of Solomon," demands only the relatively simple "hypocrisy" of such "dunce[s]" and "devil[s]" as Stoddart or Southey, tools of tyranny paid to describe his "conduct" as "*grand, magnificent and gracious.*" As before too, the hyperbole that marks the description of Coleridge's "powers"—the image of the "arch-angel ruin'd" now amplified into a form of apostasy "greater than ever was or will be possessed by any other individual that ever did or ever will live upon the face of the earth"—conveys once again the ironic respect for these "powers" that underscores the urgency with which they are brought to public notice and contested. Yet whereas in the previous absence of the lay sermon Hazlitt was able to present Coleridge's "powers" as "wasted" and therefore inconsequential, in *The Statesman's Manual* they are "exercis[ed]" in such a way as to make them even more insidious than "hypocrisy" itself. Once again Hazlitt appropriates Coleridge's own words (this time from his lay sermon) to describe the ideological tyranny of "Imposture." At the same time he reconfirms the crucial cultural role filled by the vigilant critic able to unmask such "imposture," both in its intellectual "refinement" by such writers as Coleridge, and in its more grotesque and "clumsy" manifestations within the political landscape of the Distresses crisis as a whole.

It is particularly instructive, therefore, to observe Hazlitt blunt the cutting edge of this analysis when he comes to rewrite this review for the *Edinburgh* and its readers several weeks later. In this second full-length review he virtually drops the charge of apostasy, allowing the pivotal treatment of *Jus divinum* to be reduced—perhaps by Francis Jeffrey[9]—to a mere passing remark. Coleridge is still presented as a writer with "a regular leaning to the side of power," but his new lay sermon is said, surprisingly, to have "no leaning any way" (16: 103). Its espousal of *Jus divinum* is called "curious" but "beyond our comprehension" (16: 112), and the *Edinburgh*'s readers, like Coleridge's own, are left to look up the salient passage in *First Kings* by themselves. In these changes can be read the more or less subtle cost of Hazlitt's access to the highest levels of public debate. For here, and by contrast with Robert Southey for example, Coleridge was a political nonentity: to the *Edinburgh* he was at best a minor literary phenomenon, a "Lake School" satellite of Wordsworth whose pretensions to "genius" were in irritating conflict with the Enlightenment tastes of the nation's leading periodical. This, certainly, had been the import of Moore's satire of *Christabel* in the September edition of the *Edinburgh,* in which Coleridge's collection of fragments is dismissed as "one of the boldest experiments yet made on the patience or understanding of the public"—beneath even "the other productions of the Lake School" in its recourse to "the unmeaning or infantine," to "extravagance and incongruity," and to "raving" under "the effects of [an] anodyne" (Reiman A: 473, 469, 472).

Of course, by following up Moore's article with a full-length essay on *The Statesman's Manual,* the *Edinburgh* tacitly acknowledges that Coleridge commands a kind of cultural authority that must in fact be taken seriously. And in a further irony, some of the credit for this must be given to Hazlitt himself, for by skillfully revising his review around the cultural politics of the literary marketplace, shifting his focus from issues of apostasy to Coleridge's frontal attack on the reading public and the moral authority of the *Edinburgh,* he convinces Jeffrey of the relevance of this sermon to current debate and gets his own notice of it disseminated to the same "higher classes" sought out by Coleridge. It is also in part a measure of Hazlitt's ascendency within the Opposition press—and of Jeffrey's respect for his previous contributions to the *Edinburgh*[10]—that when he submitted this essay in early January, it was quickly inserted into the belated December edition of the *Edinburgh* and appeared (with relative speed) on 24 February 1817.[11]

There can be no doubt that this review proved the decisive factor in this particular contest for cultural authority. Not only did it appear in the pages of the mighty *Edinburgh*—and close on the heels of Moore's heavy "quizzing" of *Christabel*—but it went unchallenged by any correspondingly positive notice in the *Quarterly,* as if the Tory press silently acquiesced in the *Edinburgh*'s negative verdict.[12] Moreover, a coincidence of timing and content ensured that this final review of *The Statesman's Manual* received maximum public exposure and influence. Written amidst the seething political tensions leading up to the reopening of Parliament on 28 January (tensions that issued in such landmark events as the "Convention of Delegates for Reform" and an attack on the Regent's carriage),[13] this review was published just as the new Parliament began debate over a slate of reactionary legislation that included the suspension of Habeas Corpus.[14] Though the Opposition Whigs were vastly outnumbered in the House of Commons (and the Suspension Bill passed quickly into law on 4 March), the *Edinburgh Review* led an Opposition press that dominated the formation of opinion within the public sphere at large. Even the rival *Quarterly* acknowledged this to be true. In an edition that appeared shortly before the *Edinburgh,*[15] Robert Southey unleashed a thunderous, fifty-page jeremiad against "Parliamentary Reform," declaring it the product of the "increased power which has been given to public opinion by the . . . prodigious activity of the press" (*Quarterly* Oct. 1816; 16.31: 272). Though Southey's immediate object was the Radical press epitomized by Cobbett's two-penny *Register,* he includes "Mr. Examiner Hunt" and even "the Caledonian Oracle" of Edinburgh in the swath of his tireless reprobation (248, 261). "We have laws . . . against poisoning the minds of the people," Southey declares. "Why are not these laws rendered effectual and enforced?" (275).

In the context of a debate over the suspension of Habeas Corpus, such threats in the mouthpiece of government opinion loomed large indeed. Hazlitt had thus harnessed the prodigious cultural authority of the *Edinburgh Review* at the very moment when this authority was sharply foregrounded as both an object of political debate and a crucial counterweight to the reactionary majority in the House of Commons. What is more, of the three articles addressing issues of the crisis in this pivotal edition of the *Edinburgh,* Hazlitt's came closest to refuting Southey's clamant demands for censorship and repression. Where the other two articles tackled such issues as "The Commercial Distresses of the Country" and "The Catholic Question,"[16] Hazlitt correctly anticipated the *Edinburgh*'s needs by reorganizing his response to *The Statesman's Manual* around a vigorous defense of the "freedom of the press" (16: 106). By turning back Coleridge's own conservative strictures on the "READING PUBLIC" and its "articles of largest consumption," Hazlitt's essay served as a propitious retort to Southey and the *Quarterly* as well, as it boldly argues for the continued expansion of the public sphere to include "the labouring classes" and for the unfettered "exercise of public opinion" as an indispensable "control and counter-check" on the forces of "corruption, servility, superstition, and tyranny" (16: 106, 113).

In effect, then, Hazlitt's reformist politics are now subsumed into a new contrast he develops in this review between two incompatible models of cultural authority: between "the principle of Catholic dictation" on the one hand, implied by Coleridge's system of exclusions based on class and intellect, and the liberal "diffusion of free inquiry" on the other, dating (in Hazlitt's account) to the Protestant Reformation but now championed by such Enlightenment organs of "public opinion" as the *Edinburgh Review* (16: 105). We note further that Hazlitt's contestation of *The Statesman's Manual* in these terms depends on a freshly tightened interpenetration of political, literary, and commercial concerns, a reflection in turn of a larger trend in public debate by which these different contexts of struggle had become virtually indistinguishable under pressure of the Distresses crisis. Within days, for example, this trend would be epitomized in the scandal that erupted around Southey's Radical play *Wat Tyler,* with its embarrassingly brisk sales among the labouring classes.[17] In the present instance, Hazlitt takes advantage of the opportunity to update his *Examiner* material by specifically foregrounding the plight of the laboring classes, and locating in their economic and political distress a metaphor for a less obvious but equally reactionary program of cultural disenfranchisement adumbrated in such texts as *The Statesman's Manual.*

He begins by probing the contradiction inherent in Coleridge's claim that the Bible, though ideally accessible "to all conditions of men, under all circumstances," should nevertheless be read in different ways by different classes of readers. To unpack this contradiction, Hazlitt seizes on a distinction Coleridge himself makes in the very opening paragraph of the sermon between Protestant and Catholic forms of interpretative authority. The ascendency of Protestantism in Britain is, for Coleridge, the logical result of a recognition "that the interment of such a treasure [as the Bible] in a dead language must needs be contrary to the intentions of the gracious Donor" (Coburn 6: 5; Howe 16: 103). In Catholicism, by contrast, the "sophistry" of "a jealous priesthood" has made "the very excellence of the Giver . . . a reason for withholding the gift," resulting in "a complete system of delusion" (6: 5). Hazlitt's strategy is to suggest that the struggle between these two forms of authority is far from over—that in fact the confidence with which Coleridge identifies his own practice with the Protestant model is itself delusory: "The truth is, as it appears to us, that the whole of this Sermon is written to sanction the principle of Catholic dictation, and to reprobate that diffusion of free inquiry—that difference of private, and ascendency of public opinion, which has been the necessary consequence, and the great benefit of the Reformation"

(16: 105). The opposition between Catholicism and Protestantism presents for Hazlitt the archetype of an ongoing struggle for cultural authority between reactionary and libertarian forces within the British public sphere—between individual authors who anxiously aim to control and curtail the "diffusion of free inquiry," and the "ascendency" of an anonymous, and ideally democratic, "public opinion."

To make good his inversion of Coleridge's terms, Hazlitt juxtaposes the opening paragraph of the sermon with Coleridge's key statement several paragraphs later on regarding the "sufficiency" of the Bible among the lower classes:

> The humblest and least educated of our countrymen [Coleridge writes] must have wilfully neglected the inestimable privileges secured to all alike, if he has not himself found, if he has not from his own experience discovered, the sufficiency of the Scriptures in all knowledge requisite for a right performance of his duty as a man and as a Christian. Of the labouring classes . . . more than this is not demanded, more than this is not generally desirable. "They are not sought for in public counsel, nor need they be found where politic sentences are spoken. It is enough if everyone is wise in the working of his own craft: so best will they maintain the state of the world." (16: 103–4)

To this, Hazlitt retorts:

> Now, if this is all that is necessary or desirable for the people to know, we can see little difference between the doctrine of the Lay Sermon, and "that complete system of papal imposture, which inters the Scriptures in a dead language, and commands its vassals to take for granted what it forbids them to ascertain." If a candidate is to start for infallibility, we, for our parts, shall give our casting vote for the successor of St. Peter, rather than for Mr. Coleridge. The Bible, we believe, when rightly understood, contains no set of rules for making the labouring classes mere "workers in brass or stone,"—"hewers of wood or drawers of water," each wise in his own craft. Yet it is by confining their inquiries and their knowledge to such vocations, and excluding them from any share in politics, philosophy, and theology, "that the state of the world is best upheld." Such is the exposition of our Lay-Divine. Such is his application of it. (16: 104)

What Hazlitt uncovers in this commentary is what Coleridge elides: The access to Scripture authorized by Protestantism inevitably entails access to literacy, a literacy that cannot in fact be confined to Scripture alone. Thus Coleridge's attempt to contain literacy—to insist on the "sufficiency of Scripture," to countenance only those readings that reinforce vocational as well as moral "duty," to claim that the self-evident aim of such reading is to maintain "the state of the world"—all these gestures betray his unexpected affinity with "papal" authoritarianism. Hazlitt, for his part, lays claim to an alternative authority, one that is heard in the plural and anonymous "we" of institutionalized "public opinion" with its own set of imperatives: "The Bible, *we* believe, *when rightly understood,* contains no set of rules for making the labouring classes mere 'workers in brass or stone' " (emphasis added). This is the rhetoric of Enlightenment libertarianism, driven by a unique historical moment to refurbish the slogans of the Puritan Revolution for the purposes of nineteenth-century class struggle. In this view, both the Bible ("when rightly understood") and the literacy required to read it are more likely to be transformative than conservative, fitting the laboring classes for "free inquiry" beyond Scripture and beyond "mere" labor itself. This is the true British Protestantism, Hazlitt implies, willing to risk offering "the people" their "share in politics, philosophy, and theology," thus enfranchising them to become fellow producers—and consumers—of "public opinion."

The review proceeds to reinforce this point with mounting vehemence, a multiple iteration that stands out both for its intensity and for its apparent freedom from editorial intervention. This, it would seem, was the task Jeffrey was pleased to have Hazlitt perform: to deliver a resounding defense of the "Reading Public" and of "the ascendency of public opinion" in a rhetorical crescendo appropriate to the climactic urgency of the Distresses debate within society as a whole. Immediately following the commentary given above, Hazlitt offers two vivid illustrations of the scene of instruction in Coleridge's text. The first of these depicts the drama of "Catholic dictation," in which can be discerned an allegory of the dashed political hopes of "the poor and illiterate" at the hands of the reactionary backlash:

> Great as is our contempt for the delusions of the Romish Church, it would have been still greater, if they had opened the sacred volume to the poor and illiterate; had told them that it contained the most useful knowledge for all conditions and all circumstances of life, public and private; and had then instantly shut the book in their faces, saying, it was enough for them to be wise in their own calling and to leave the study and interpretation of the Scriptures to their betters—to Mr. Coleridge and his imaginary audience. (16: 104)

Hazlitt then refigures Coleridge's "imaginary audience" in terms that reecho the bitter indignation of "SEMPER EGO AUDITOR."

> The Catholic Church might have an excuse for what it did in the supposed difficulty of understanding the Scriptures. . . . But Mr. Coleridge has no excuse; for he says, [the Scriptures] are plain to all capacities, high and low together. "The road of salvation," he says, "is for us a high road, and the way-farer, though simple, may not err therein." And he accordingly proceeds to draw up a provisional bill of indictment, and to utter his doubtful denunciations against us as a nation, for the supposed neglect of the inestimable privileges, *secured to all alike,* . . . when, all of a sudden, his eye encountering that brilliant auditory which his pen had conjured up, the Preacher finds out, that the only use of the study of Scriptures for the rest of the people, is to learn that they have no occasion to study them at all—"so best shall they maintain the state of the world." If Mr. Coleridge has no meaning in what he

writes, he had better not write at all: if he has any meaning, he contradicts himself. (16: 104)

In this "brilliant auditory" Hazlitt draws together Coleridge's Unitarian congregation of the 1790s with the vast crowds of 1816 desperate for words of encouragement regarding "privileges, *secured to all alike.*" Yet the scene of instruction has shifted once again from oral to written discourse—from "auditory" to readership. For Hazlitt this shift bears the loss of Coleridge's authority, transforming a potential for "brilliant" oratorical power into the unwitting self-contradictions of a "genius" who "[lays] himself out in absurdity" (16: 100).

To justify these harsh images, Hazlitt needs only to produce the passage in which Coleridge himself dismisses this "brilliant auditory" by naming it, with fastidious hauteur, that "promiscuous audience," "THE READING PUBLIC." This passage, we recall, contains some of Coleridge's most explicit statements regarding patterns of consumption in the literary marketplace, including his satiric depiction of the circulating libraries and the periodical press as the two "public ordinaries of Literature." The "READING PUBLIC," according to Coleridge, is a "misgrowth of our luxuriant activity," a "vast company" that has "multiplied exceedingly" and has "waxed proud." Moreover, "if the average health of the consumers may be judged of by the articles of largest consumption; if the secretions may be conjectured from the ingredients of the dishes that are found best suited to their palates," then he must "utter [his] *Profaccia* with a desponding sigh"—a sigh articulated in the elitist apothegm "From a popular philosophy and a philosophic populace, good sense deliver us!" (Coburn 6: 35–38; Howe 16: 105).

Hazlitt's response to this passage in the *Edinburgh* draws on the operative distinction between "Catholic dictation" and (radical) Protestantism to help structure one of the clearest definitions, as well as one of the most forceful demonstrations, of the cultural authority claimed by anonymous review-criticism during the Distresses crisis. "If it were possible to be serious after a passage like this," Hazlitt begins,

> we might ask, what is to hinder a convert of "the church of superstition" from exclaiming in like manner, "From a popular theology, and a theological populace, Good Lord deliver us!" Mr. Coleridge does not say—will he say— that as many sects and differences of opinion in religion have not risen up, in consequence of the Reformation, as in philosophy or politics, from "the misgrowth of our luxuriant activity"? Can any one express a greater disgust, (approaching to *nausea*), at every sect and separation from the Church of England, which he sometimes, by an hyperbole of affectation, affects to call the Catholic Church? There is something, then, worse than "luxuriant activity,"—the palsy of death; something worse than occasional error,—systematic imposture; something worse than the collision of differing opinions,—the suppression of all freedom of thought and independent love

of truth, under the torpid sway of an insolent and selfish domination, which makes use of truth and falsehood equally as tools of its own aggrandizement and the debasement of its vassals, and always must do so, without the exercise of public opinion, and freedom of conscience, as its control and counter-check. For what have we been labouring for the last three hundred years? Would Mr. Coleridge, with impious hand, turn the world "twice ten degrees askance," and carry us back to the dark ages? Would he punish the *reading public* for their bad taste in reading periodical publications which he does not like, by suppressing the freedom of the press altogether, or destroying the art of printing? He does not know what he means himself. Perhaps we can tell him. He, or at least those whom he writes to please, and who look "with jealous leer malign" at modern advantages and modern pretensions, would give us back all the abuses of former times, without any of their advantages; and impose on us, by force or fraud, a complete system of superstition without faith, of despotism without loyalty, of error without enthusiasm, and all of the evils, without any of the blessings, of ignorance. (16: 105–6)

Here, then, is "the exercise of public opinion," at once defined and displayed at the height of its elocutionary and admonitory power. Such a performance suggests, among other things, that although Coleridge's text may remain otherwise "unintelligible" to the *Edinburgh Review* (16: 100), it has nevertheless warranted this utmost assertion of the *Edinburgh*'s cultural authority at a crucial moment in public debate.

Yet as this passage unfolds, *The Statesman's Manual* becomes the occasion to strike out at much larger targets: "those whom [Mr. Coleridge] writes to please"—in other words, those who are in a position to underwrite the authority of such reactionary texts and who might, given the mood of the present ministry, go so far as to "punish the *reading public* for their bad taste in reading periodical publications which [they] do not like, by suppressing the freedom of the press altogether, or destroying the art of printing." The hyperbole here becomes a register of the rhetorical extremes to which public debate had been driven by the exigencies of the Distresses crisis. Against the looming threat of the suspension of Habeas Corpus, this impassioned plea for "freedom of thought and the independent love of truth" in the nation's leading periodical may be regarded in fact as a courageous "exercise of public opinion" in the form of a "control and counter-check" to the alarming trend toward reaction and repression symbolized by Coleridge's contempt for the "READING PUBLIC" and its "objects of largest consumption"—and indeed fully realized in Southey's simultaneous threats and expostulations in the *Quarterly*.

In these circumstances, *The Statesman's Manual* presents an important case precisely because of its potentially attractive evasions and obfuscations addressed to the "higher classes." Against these, the *Edinburgh* asserts the blunt certainties of "common sense": "[Mr. Coleridge] does not know what he means himself. Perhaps we can tell him." Then, on behalf of the "READING PUBLIC," the *Edinburgh* proceeds to clarify the high stakes of ideological struggle: the contest between what is here stigmatized as "the torpid sway of an insolent and selfish domination" on the one hand, and the (anonymous) "exercise of public opinion, and freedom of conscience, as its control and counter-check" on the other. What saves this opposition from the charge of mere partisanship is the frank admission of the risks involved in its positive terms. "[F]reedom of thought" is indeed a "luxuriant activity" of Enlightenment that may well entail the possibility of "misgrowth," whether it be in the form of "occasional error" or the uncertainties of an unregulated "collision of differing opinions." The alternative, however, is a mistaken attempt to recover the imaginary certainties and ideal unanimity of the "dark ages." This kind of reversionary quest is made romantically attractive in such poems as *Christabel,* but when it is lived out by the lower classes in the form of economic distress, political repression, and cultural disenfranchisement, it offers only "the palsy of death" and "all of the evils, without any of the blessings, of ignorance."

At the very nadir of postwar economic distress, then, and just as the accompanying political crisis was reaching a watershed in the suspension of Habeas Corpus, Hazlitt succeeds in mounting this expression of reformist cultural politics at the very highest level of public debate. While offering the *Edinburgh* a follow-up to Moore's satire of *Christabel,* he nevertheless far exceeds Moore's review in both ideological scope and cogency by clarifying the context of cultural struggle in which both *Christabel* and *The Statesman's Manual* wielded potential—even palpable—agency. In this way, too, he helps justify the *Edinburgh*'s otherwise arbitrary rejection of Coleridge's authority, while mounting a stirring redefinition of the journal's own mandate within British culture.

At the same time, of course, to provide effective continuity with Moore's review, Hazlitt frames this central passage with satiric commentary designed to entertain as well as edify the *Edinburgh*'s influential readership. This in turn produces another telling difference between the *Examiner* and *Edinburgh* reviews. In both cases Hazlitt adopts the old reviewing strategy of appropriating the "beauties" of the review-text to enhance—if only for satiric purposes—the entertainment value of his own review. In the *Examiner,* however, Hazlitt's first task is to prove his earlier assertion that Coleridge's conversational powers turn to "nonsense" in print; with his disenfranchised readership in mind, he selects "specimens" of the sermon especially vulnerable to the charge of elitism or pedantry. In the *Edinburgh,* by contrast, Hazlitt is already catering to the elite—and to the impression created among them by Moore that Coleridge is to be looked down upon as a mere "Lake School" poet of the "unmeaning or infantine" (Reiman A: 473). One result of these choices in the *Examiner* is to allow Coleridge's most impassioned paean to the "*Idea*" of "an IDEA" to inhabit the conclusion of Hazlitt's review, thus bringing this passage to the attention—and possible admiration—of an entire sector of middle-class intellectuals. In the *Edinburgh,* a different effect is achieved, as the identity of review and review-text is blurred by a satiric performance that includes inadvertent parody and a final "specimen" of bathos that contains unmistakable traces of the sublime.

Such moments of undecidability, however, emerge only as overtones of the dominant note of vigorous critical satire. Writing for the *Examiner,* Hazlitt has only to select and point out those passages that illustrate his earlier assertions about Coleridge's conversational style, especially those least likely to survive the translation from drawing-room monologues to well-thumbed copies of the *Examiner* in the window seats of inns and alehouses across the nation.[18] Thus, for example, toward the end of the review, Hazlitt reprints a portion of Coleridge's lengthy footnote to his remarks on the "READING PUBLIC" in which he digresses into a moment of gentlemanly satiric banter. As Hazlitt indicates, however, the "wit and humour" of Coleridge's remarks depend on the shared assumptions and privileges of a narrowly circumscribed readership—in this case, one defined by classical education and a profound distaste for the infelicities of the unlearned.

> To the words READING PUBLIC, in the above passage, is the following note, which in wit and humour does not fall short of Mr. Southey's "Tract on the Madras System":—
>
> " . . . I would point out to the reader's attention the marvellous predominance at present of the words, Idea and Demonstration. Every talker now-a-days has an *Idea;* aye, and he will demonstrate it too! A few days ago, I heard one of the READING PUBLIC, a thinking and independent smuggler, euphonise the latter word with much significance, in a tirade against the planners of the late African expedition: '*As to Algiers, any man that has half an* IDEA *in his skull must know, that it has been long ago dey-monstered, I should say, dey-monstrified,*' &c. But the phrase, which occasioned this note, brings to my mind the mistake of a lethargic Dutch traveller, who, returning highly gratified from a showman's caravan, which he had been tempted to enter by the words LEARNED PIG, gilt on the pannels, met another caravan of a similar shape, with the READING FLY on it, in letters of the same size and splendour. 'Why, dis is voonders above voonders,' exclaims the Dutchman, takes his seat as first comer, and soon fatigued by waiting, and by the very hush and intensity of his expectation, gives way to his constitutional somnolence, from which he is roused by the supposed showman at Hounslow, with a 'In what name, Sir, was your place taken? are you booked all the way for Reading?'— Now a Reading Public is (to my mind) more marvellous still, and in the third tier of 'Voonders above voonders.' " (7: 126)

Hazlitt abjures detailed commentary: "A public that could read such stuff as this with any patience would indeed be so," he remarks, confident that the "public" will find Coleridge's attempt at wit more self-evidently offensive than humorous. Unlike the "fashionable literature" with which it competes, Coleridge's discourse is shown to be unable to survive the transition from smoking-room banter to full public circulation. Though the story of "a lethargic Dutch traveller" might have residual appeal for the insular prejudices of Britons in all classes, the joke fails in a public text because it harnesses such prejudices on behalf of a series of overt and unguarded class slurs directed against the new majority of British readers. From the association of the new literacy with criminality (in the example of the "thinking and independent smuggler") to the equation of the contra-natural abilities of the "PIG" and the "FLY" with those of the "READING PUBLIC" Coleridge's class-based "wit and humour" are exposed as products of either sycophancy or bigotry; in either case, his credibility as a lay preacher is seriously undermined, not only in the present sermon but in those he proposes to address to more "promiscuous audiences."

Even the "READING PUBLIC," however, would not expect a lay sermon to compete with journalism in the quality of its banter, and the *Examiner* itself had asserted in its September preview that Coleridge's true forte lay in "the world of enchantment" conjured up by the lyric flights of his conversation. Thus as his final "specimen" in the *Examiner* of Coleridge's text, Hazlitt selects the peroration to the lay sermon proper in which Coleridge summarizes his argument with a impassioned paean to the power of "an IDEA," followed by a brief and "melancholy comment" on "what . . . is achievable by the human understanding without this light." By thus quoting the final two paragraphs of the sermon as the conclusion to his own review, Hazlitt sustains an impression of critical fairness and decorum, if not at the same time catering to an emergent taste among those *Examiner* readers "of *clerkly* acquirements" for precisely such resonant flights of lyrical prose.

Yet Hazlitt's ostensive aim remains that of satiric deflation, and this he accomplishes in large part by strategic juxtaposition. The subversive pressure exerted by Coleridge's sardonic remark just quoted—that "[e]very talker nowadays has an *Idea;* aye, and he will demonstrate it too!"—works in this case to unravel the authority of his own "*Idea*" of "an IDEA," turning his lyric afflatus on the subject into pure performance without meaning. Worse still, the possibility thus opened that there exists no transcendental referent for the "IDEA" conjured up by this performance reduces Coleridge's final "melancholy comment" on "the labour of the foolish" into a jarringly ironic comment on his own text. The double effect of this final passage—its lyric appeal and its inversion to bathos—requires quotation in full. This will serve to make clear how Hazlitt refrains from interpolation—adding only two italicized emphases—and allows this flight of the "gladdened preacher" to take uninterrupted rhetorical wing in the very midst of Hazlitt's own text. Moreover, we note how the terse yet efficient framing remarks recall the terms of his September preview to reinforce an overriding context of criticism and satire.

> To conclude this most inconclusive piece of work, we find the distant hopes and doubtful expectations of the writer's mind summed up in the following

rare rhapsody. "Oh what a mine of undiscovered treasures, what a new world of power and truth would the Bible promise to our future meditation, if *in some gracious moment one solitary text of all its inspired contents* should but dawn upon us in the pure untroubled brightness of an IDEA, that most glorious birth of the godlike within us, which even as the light, its material symbol, reflects itself from a thousand surfaces, and flies homeward to its parent mind, enriched with a thousand forms, itself above form, and still remaining in its own simplicity and identity! O for a flash of that same light, in which the first position of geometric science that ever loosed itself from the generalizations of a groping and insecure experience, did for the first time reveal itself to a human intellect in all its evidence and in all its fruitfulness, Transparence without Vacuum, and Plenitude without Opacity! O! that a single gleam of our own inward experience would make comprehensible to us the rapturous EUREKA, and the grateful hecatomb of the philosopher of Samos: or that vision which, from the contemplation of an arithmetical harmony, rose to the eye of Kepler, presenting the planetary world, and all their orbits in the divine order of their ranks and distances; or which, in the falling of an apple, revealed to the ethereal intuition of our own Newton the constructive principle of the material universe. The promises which I have ventured to hold forth concerning the hidden treasures of the Law and the Prophets will neither be condemned as paradox, or as exaggeration, by the mind that has learnt to understand the possibility that the reduction of the sands of the sea to number should be found a less stupendous problem by Archimedes than the simple conception of the Parmenidean ONE. What, however, is achievable by the human understanding without this light may by comprised in the epithet κενόσπουδοι; and *a melancholy comment on that phrase would the history of the human Cabinets and Legislatures for the last thirty years furnish!* The excellent Barrow, the last of the disciples of Plato and Archimedes among our modern mathematicians, shall give the description and state the value; and, in his words, I shall conclude:—

> *Aliud agere, to be impertinently busy, doing that which conduceth to no good purpose, is, in some respect, worse than to do nothing. Of such industry we may understand that of the Preacher, 'The labour of the foolish wearieth every one of them.'*"

A better conclusion could not be found for this Lay-Sermon: for greater nonsense the author could not write, even though he were expressly inspired for the purpose. (7. 126–27)

Thus Hazlitt appropriates Coleridge's own final words to convenient effect, abstaining from further comment as if the *"labour of the foolish"* has wearied even its own most indefatigable critic. In so doing, of course, Hazlitt once again trusts that the context of political and cultural criticism established by the rest of the review will render this final "specimen" of Coleridge's prose more self-evidently nonsensical than rhetorically compelling. Certainly Coleridge's decision to turn suddenly from a dazzling exercise in the lyric sublime to a "melancholy comment" on the *"labour of the foolish"* serves Hazlitt's purpose well, providing a ready-made structural echo of his own parting comments in the September preview, where the "beatific vision" of Coleridge's "talk" was turned suddenly into the bleak prospect of printed "nonsense." Within the terms of the present review, moreover, the charge of "nonsense" is justified by implication in a number of ways: by Coleridge's appeal to a priori ideas in defiance of Lockean empiricism; by his condescending rejection of what "is achievable by the [mere] human understanding without this light" in contrast to his own implicit possession of it; by the political self-contradiction inherent in using *"the history of the human Cabinets and Legislatures for the last thirty years"* to illustrate the *"labour of the foolish,"* thus suggesting, in effect, that the policies of the king's ministers and the unreformed Tory Parliament are conducive *"to no good purpose"*; and finally by recourse to learned cant and mystical paradox which, under the eye of those it is intended to exclude, and under the influence of the hermeneutics of suspicion, is easily converted into a parody of itself, vulnerable indeed to Coleridge's own sardonic remarks about "every talker now-a-days [who] has an *Idea;* aye, and [who] will demonstrate it too!"

Yet in placing Coleridge's peroration at the conclusion of his own review, Hazlitt takes the risk that it will in fact exceed its curt reduction to "nonsense," and appeal directly and powerfully to the interests and desires of his own readers. As Hazlitt had noted at the opening of the review, Coleridge was among the "strong minds," (7: 119) and this "specimen" of his prose is indeed a "rare rhapsody." Beyond the intended sarcasm of this last epithet, for example, lurks the exotic "other" of archetypal inspiration, recalling perhaps the dithyrambic singing of the "Abyssinian maid" that arrested the closure of the review of *Christabel.* Moreover, as Klancher demonstrates in his study, the specifically "middle class" reading audience of the nineteenth century was forming at this time around just the sort of writing exhibited in Coleridge's peroration—energetic "arguments on the powers of the mind" that impel "a florid 'poetic diction' into the very texture of argumentative prose" (52–53). Like other writers in this medium, Coleridge works in this passage at the very edges of language and syntax, demonstrating at once his own possession of the "light" so passionately invoked and inviting his readers to identify in their own minds a similar experience of "godlike" subjectivity that will become the catalyst of a new sense of intellectual and cultural authority.

A similar effect is created in the *Edinburgh* essay, but one that begins from quite different premises and ends with a strikingly different "specimen." First of all, to establish the necessary continuity with Moore's *Christabel* review, Hazlitt embellishes several of Moore's stock conceits, working them into a fresh display of journalistic "banter" designed at once to describe Coleridge's unconventional discourse and, paradoxically, to fall "a little into the style of it" (16: 100). It was Peacock, of course, who first characterized Moore's review of *Christabel* in the *Edinburgh* as a tissue of "ready cut and dried wit," a series of "excellent jokes" endlessly repeated as a substitute for true wit

(104). These jokes, we recall, include the bottomless resources of the bathos ("Forth steps Mr. Coleridge, like a giant refreshed from sleep"), the soporific effect of the work ("The lines given here smell strongly . . . of the anodyne"), and its unintelligibility ("we are wholly unable to divine the meaning of any portion of it") (Peacock 104; Reiman A: 469, 472, 471). While Hazlitt too draws on the perennial currency of such jests (particularly in his use of the word "nonsense"), his satiric strategy is to move well beyond mere iteration to entertain with inventive elaboration.

This may be illustrated by his adaptation of the fourth "joke" in Peacock's list: "that the author is insane" (104). Moore, we recall, concludes his review by describing the *Christabel* volume as "a mixture of raving and driv'ling," a vivid exaggeration of his earlier remark that "[m]uch of the art of the wild writers consists in sudden transitions—opening eagerly upon some topic, and then flying from it immediately. This indeed is known to the medical men, who not unfrequently have the care of them, as an unerring symptom" (Reiman A: 473, 470). In this way Moore retails the stock conceit, embellishing it only as far as libelous innuendo by alluding here to Coleridge's residency at Highgate with Dr. Gillman. Hazlitt, by contrast, eschews the merely personal to develop instead a series of virtuoso variations on the theme, a string of similes to describe this discursive "symptom" that are at once diverting in themselves and unexpectedly imitative of Coleridge's own practice.

> An attentive perusal of this Discourse is like watching the sails of a windmill: his thoughts and theories rise and disappear in the same manner. Clouds do not shift their places more rapidly, dreams do not drive one another out more unaccountably, than Mr. Coleridge's reasonings try in vain to "chase his fancy's rolling speed." His intended conclusions have always the start of his premises,—and they keep it: while he himself plods anxiously between the two, something like a man travelling a long, tiresome road, between two stage coaches, the one of which is gone out of sight before, and the other never comes up with him; for Mr. Coleridge himself takes care of this; and if he finds himself in danger of being overtaken, and carried to his journey's end in a common vehicle, he immediately steps aside into some friendly covert, with the Metaphysical Muse, to prevent so unwelcome a catastrophe. In his weary quest for truth, he reminds us of the mendicant pilgrims that travellers meet in the Desert, with their faces always turned towards Mecca, but who contrive never to reach the shrine of the Prophet: and he treats his opinions, as his reasons for them, as lawyers do their clients, and will never suffer them to come together lest they should join issue, and so put an end to his business. It is impossible, in short, to describe this strange rhapsody, without falling a little into the style of it. (16: 100)

With this last remark, Hazlitt allows his witty description of Coleridge's writing to double as inadvertent parody, a "falling" into Coleridge's desultory "style" that illustrates even as it satirizes. Thus he moves well beyond Moore's two-dimensional assertion of "raving and driv'ling," not only in the eclectic range of his allusions but in his willingness to complicate the strict distinction between critic and author on which Moore's satire depends. Coleridge's "strange rhapsody" is here granted a certain mesmeric power that is "impossible" to resist, while the critic's own drive for satiric closure is forestalled as he is seemingly forced to mimic Coleridge's comical delays and deferrals. Of course there is more at play here than just mimicry, as we know from the September preview, where Hazlitt's similes and appositions also "rise and disappear" and "drive one another out" quite as rapidly and unpredictably—and with the same unstoppable fecundity—as Coleridge's own thoughts and opinions are said to do. Thus we find critic and author converging unexpectedly at the level of style, as both develop a kind of "rhapsody" to fascinate their readers and enforce their authority over them.

This moment of identity—however subtle—establishes a subtext of ambivalence in Hazlitt's treatment of style in *The Statesman's Manual* that works against the grain of the *Edinburgh*'s otherwise magisterial strictures against the "Lake School." This becomes especially apparent at the end of the review, where Hazlitt once again appropriates a passage of striking lyrical intensity to serve as the conclusion to his own article. As in the *Examiner,* the ostensive aim is satiric inversion: This final "specimen" of the sermon is quoted to illustrate Coleridge's manic deviance from the norms of Enlightenment discourse. Shadowing this purpose, however, is the ironic convergence of reviewer and reviewed at the level of style. The very intensity of Coleridge's prose—whether taken on its own terms or as unwitting self-parody—inevitably enhances the readability of Hazlitt's text, and to this extent it fills the standard function of providing one of the "beauties" of the book under review. Indeed, on this occasion Hazlitt replaces his former selection of the peroration of the lay sermon proper with the "flowery meadow" passage quoted above in chapter 3, selected from what he calls the "notes" and set off from his own text with the ironically grandiose title "MR. COLERIDGE'S DESCRIPTION OF A GREEN FIELD."

At face value, of course, Hazlitt's presentation of this passage at the end of his review serves to confirm and reinforce the *Edinburgh*'s caricature of Coleridge as the ineffectual Lake poet of the "unmeaning or infantine" (to recall Moore's terms). By quoting it, moreover, Hazlitt ties together the satiric frames of the review, for this passage had already been adduced at the opening of the review as typical of Coleridge's willful blindness to pressing "matters of fact": "Instead of inquiring into the distresses of the manufacturing or agricultural districts, he . . . enters into the statistics of the garden plot under his window, and, like Falstaff, 'babbles of green fields' " (16: 100). This allusion to Falstaff also seems to echo the jest of madness, for it was on his deathbed that Falstaff "babbl'd of green fields" as he "fumble[d] with the sheets, and play[ed] with flowers, and smile[d] upon his finger's end" (*Henry V* 2.3.14–17).

Yet this allusion strikes a subtle but countervailing note of pathos. In an essay on Falstaff written just a month previously, Hazlitt describes him as "the most substantial comic character that ever was invented," in whom " 'we behold the fulness of the spirit of wit and humour,' " and with whom we are therefore "not offended but delighted" (4: 277–79). By setting off Coleridge's passage with the ironically portentous title "MR. COLERIDGE'S DESCRIPTION OF A GREEN FIELD," Hazlitt also gives it a certain idiosyncratic presence, as worthy perhaps of our indulgence as Falstaff's own "boundless luxury of . . . imagination" (4: 278).

To consider these contrasting rhetorical effects, then, the conclusion of Hazlitt's review is worth quoting in full.

> The notes are better, and but a little better, than the text. We might select, as specimens of laborious foolery, the passage in which the writer defends *second sight,* to prove that he has been unjustly accused of visionary paradox, or hints that a disbelief in ghosts and witches is no great sign of the wisdom of the age, or that in which he gives us to understand that Sir Isaac Newton was a great astrologer, or Mr. Locke no conjurer. But we prefer (for our limits are straitened) the author's description of a green field, which he prefaces by observing, that "the book of Nature has been the music of gentle and pious minds in all ages; and that it is the poetry of all human nature to read it likewise in a figurative sense, and to find therein correspondences and symbols of a spiritual nature."
>
> MR. COLERIDGE'S DESCRIPTION OF A GREEN FIELD.
>
> "I have at this moment before me, in the flowery meadow on which my eye is now reposing, one of Nature's most soothing chapters, in which there is no lamenting word, no one character of guilt or anguish. For never can I look and meditate on the vegetable creation, without a feeling similar to that with which we gaze at a beautiful infant that has fed itself asleep at its mother's bosom, and smiles at its strange dream of obscure yet happy sensations. The same tender and genial pleasure takes possession of me, and this pleasure is checked and drawn inward by the like aching melancholy, by the same whispered remonstrance, and made restless by a similar impulse of aspiration. It seems as if the soul said to herself— 'From this state' (from that of a flowery meadow) 'hast *thou* fallen! Such shouldst thou still become, thyself all permeable to a holier power! Thyself at once hidden and glorified by its own transparency, as the accidental and dividuous in this quiet and harmonious object is subjected to the life and light of Nature which shines on it, even as the transmitted power, love and wisdom of God over all fills, and shines through, Nature! But what the plant *is,* by an act not its own, and unconsciously—*that* must thou *make* thyself to *become!* must by prayer, and by a watchful and unresisting spirit, *join* at least with the preventive and assisting grace to *make* thyself, in that

light of conscience which inflameth not, and with that knowledge which puffeth not up.' "

This will do. It is well observed by Hobbes, that "it is by means of words only that a man becomes excellently wise or excellently foolish." (16: 113–14)

No doubt we are meant to infer from this final statement that Coleridge's words have rendered him "excellently foolish." Yet this formulation is surprisingly ambiguous. Falstaff himself might well be described as "excellently foolish," and (like all of Shakespeare's fools) his witty subversion of social norms lends his "foolery" the very imprint of excellent wisdom.

This ambivalence is further reinforced by the nature of the quotation itself. The passage has clearly been selected to provide self-evident continuity with Moore's caricature of the deranged somnambulist of "Kubla Khan" and "The Pains of Sleep." Of all possible excerpts from *The Statesman's Manual,* this one alone links the self-consciously lyrical ("the music of gentle and pious minds," "the poetry of all human nature") with the allegedly bathetic preoccupations of the Lake poets, such as the sleeping infant's "strange dream of obscure yet happy sensations," and Coleridge's fervent desire to become like a "plant," "all permeable to a holier power!" Yet this passage, unlike the peroration to the sermon proper quoted at the end of "Literary Notices. No. 21," does not of itself invite rebuke by any disingenuous turn from the lyric sublime to a lashing out at the *"labour of the foolish."* Quite by contrast, its theme is humility and "that knowledge which puffeth not up," and though it is certainly vulnerable to Hazlitt's charge of a retreat into mystical piety in the face of political exigency, it is nevertheless quite free of German metaphysical "cant," presenting an accessible and potentially appealing emblem of self-conscious openness to the suprarational and the numinous. As such, then, and similar to the paean to the "light" quoted in the *Examiner,* this passage might well find its way to those middle-class consumers of periodical literature who, as Klancher notes, were forming into a distinct audience at this time around a taste for such highly wrought expressions of transcendent subjectivity (51, 53).

In this way Hazlitt's appropriation of Coleridge's exercise in lyrical prose is far more complex than a merely reductive misreading as "laborious foolery." Behind the arch title and the authoritative "This will do" lies the pathos of the dying Falstaff betrayed by his erstwhile friend the king. And beyond Hobbes's stark binary of "excellently wise" and "excellently foolish" lies the possibility that within the nation's largest single reading audience there will be many middle-class readers who will make up their own minds about what Coleridge has achieved in this passage "by means of words only." Hazlitt thus concludes his review with yet another sample of Coleridge's rhapsodic style that potentially exceeds the aggressive closure of fashionable satire. In so doing, he prepares the way for the opening lines of his next article in the *Edinburgh*—a review of the *Biographia Literaria:* "There are some things readable in these volumes; and if the learned author could only have been persuaded to make them a little more conformable to their title, we have no doubt that they would have been the most popular of all his productions" (16: 115).

5

INTERROGATING THE ROMANTIC IDEOLOGY:

Hazlitt, Coleridge, and
the *"Wat Tyler* Affair"

Hazlitt's masterly critique of the *Biographia Literaria* appeared in August 1817. Yet long before this momentous encounter between the *Edinburgh Review* and Coleridge's most seminal work in prose, another, less well-known episode intervened to shape the terms of this final confrontation. This was the *"Wat Tyler* affair" of the spring of 1817: the protracted, sensational public scandal over Robert Southey's long-forgotten Jacobin play that became the unexpected catalyst of political, economic, and discursive tensions at the climax of the Distresses debate. The appearance of *Wat Tyler* (in a pirated edition) on the very day after Southey's clamant denunciation of Radicalism in the *Quarterly Review* laid bare the virulence of the Laureate's own former Radicalism in the 1790s—just as the Habeas Corpus Act was being suspended to "silence" such dissidence.[1] The resulting controversy ran the gamut of public institutions, from the House of Commons through the Court of Chancery to the burgeoning periodical press, where, in the close-printed columns of the *Examiner* and the *Courier* respectively, Hazlitt and Coleridge locked horns over "the nature and purposes of poetry itself."[2]

That this encounter between Hazlitt and Coleridge over *Wat Tyler* has remained almost completely unknown is in itself paradigmatic. Like the affair as a whole, the crucial roles played in it by these two prominent writers have been quietly ignored by a literary history dominated (in Jerome McGann's terms) "by . . . Romanticism's own self-representations" (1). Such an event, of course, represents the inverse of lyric transcendence, suggesting instead the entanglement of "Romanticism" in historically specific struggles carried on in such "ephemeral" media as anonymous newspaper reviews. One measure of the active marginalization of this event by literary scholarship lies in the number of scholarly articles that have been devoted to its issues and events: since 1817, there have been three, of which only one (published as long ago as 1941) makes any effort to go beyond *Wat Tyler* itself to the essays it generated in the periodical press.[3] Even Byron's memorialization of the affair in such canonical texts as *Don Juan* and *A Vision of Judgement* has served only to justify Southey's demotion to the status of a minor poet, allowing the more awkward details of the debate to remain conveniently uncanvassed. One such detail is the fact that Coleridge, unlike Byron, rose to Southey's defense, and undertook to prove in the government-sponsored press that both *Wat Tyler* and the laureate poems were examples of the disinterestedness of "poetic genius" and the sublime detachment of "the spirit of poetry" from all forms of political or monetary expediency (3.2: 457). Even more thoroughly obscured, of course, has been the fact that Hazlitt quickly seized on Coleridge's contradictions and, in an uncanny anticipation of "post-Romantic" criticism, performed his own critical interrogation of the "Romantic Ideology" as it was in the very process of being constructed. Answering Coleridge's Burkean rhetoric with the Paine-ite plain speech of the *Examiner,* Hazlitt summarily rejects the cult of transcendent genius, insisting instead on the inseparability of literary and political—and hence ideological—practice.

There can be little doubt, of course, that the play *Wat Tyler* illustrates just such a conjunction of the literary and the political. Written in 1794 when Southey was aflame with the anti-royalist principles of the French Revolution, its use of the fourteenth-century Peasants' Revolt as a bold allegory for Jacobin aspirations of the 1790s was so unmistakable that no one at that time would risk publishing it. In the climactic confrontation between Wat Tyler and Richard II, for example, the king asks Tyler why he chose rebellion instead of such "milder means" as petitions—because, he cozens, "The throne will always listen to petitions." To this the rebel martyr retorts:

King of England!
Petitioning for pity is most weak,
The sovereign people ought to *demand justice.*
I killed your officer, for his lewd hand
Insulted a maid's modesty; your subjects
I lead to rebel against the Lord's anointed,
Because his ministers have made him odious:
His yoke is heavy, and his burden grievous. . . .
You sit at ease in your gay palaces,
The costly banquets court your appetite,
Sweet music soothes your slumbers; we, the while,
Scarce by hard toil can earn a little food,
And sleep scarce shelter'd from the cold night wind. . . .

The Parliament for ever asks more money:
We toil and sweat for money for your taxes:
Where is the benefit, what food reap we
From all the councils of your government? . . .
What boots to us your victories, your glory?
We pay, we fight, you profit at your ease. . . .
Think you we do not feel the wrongs we suffer?
The hour of retribution is at hand.
And tyrants tremble,—mark me, King of England. (*Wat Tyler* 42–44)

For this speech, Tyler is promptly murdered by the treacherous Walworth. Such scenes rendered the play too "utopian and injudicious" even for Southey's contacts within Radical circles (Manogue 110). The printer Ridgway, for example, with whom Southey left the manuscript in 1794 when visiting him in Newgate prison, finally decided not to publish it, and the manuscript was laid aside and forgotten (Manogue 110).

Its sudden appearance in 1817 in the midst of the Habeas Corpus debate was no less politically motivated. Though the identity of the manuscript's owner in 1817 still remains a mystery,[4] his intentions (and those of the publishers Sherwood, Neeley, and Jones) were manifest: to embarrass the Laureate with the stark contrasts between this Jacobinical play and his scarcely anonymous jeremiad against "Parliamentary Reform" that had just appeared in the *Quarterly Review* (Manogue 111, 105). From the opening lines of this latter article, Southey could now be construed as unwittingly incriminating himself: "If the opinions of profligate and of mistaken men may be thought to reflect disgrace upon the nation," he begins, " . . . it might verily be said that England was never so disgraced as at this time" (16.31: 225). These disgraceful men, of course, are the writers of "Ultra-reformist" tracts, plays, and newspapers of identical sentiments with *Wat Tyler.* Southey now regards them as the very "apostles of anarchy" because they "impos[e] upon the ignorance of the multitude, flattering their errors and inflaming their passions, [and thus] exciting them to sedition and rebellion" (16.31: 226). Southey goes on to quote with disdain various such publications, including, ironically enough, a recent petition from the laborers of London.

> The resolutions from Bishopsgate assert, that the people are "goaded with an army of remorseless tax-gatherers, urged on by the cravings of a rapacious, oppressive, and imbecile administration:" they remind us that our history exhibits the patriotic sons of England as "dismissing and chastising those kings and counsellors, whose profligacy and arbitrary attempts had rendered them obnoxious;" they say that "the most profligate expenditure among the people's servants, from the lowest to the highest rank, and an unfeeling disregard of the people's wants and miseries, are among the lightest subjects of complaint." . . . They say, the said resolutioners of Bishopsgate-ward,— "We claim, we demand, and insist that we have a full constitutional voice in the House of the people." (16.31: 245–46)

The obvious parallels between this passage and Wat Tyler's demands of the king present just one of the many ways the two texts can be collated to embarrassing effect. For several weeks, then, this was the sport of Southey's political enemies, from sly allusions by the Whig Brougham in Parliament, through the Whiggish *Morning Chronicle,* to the Radical William Hone in his *Reformist's Register* (Hoadley 81). Yet as long as *Wat Tyler* remained in its handsome first edition of Sherwood, Neeley, and Jones, priced at 3s 6d, it could circulate only within the upper echelons of the book-buying public, inaccessible to such distressed communities as "the said-resolutioners of Bishopsgate-ward."

A turning point came, however, with Hazlitt's first intervention in the affair. As we saw in the last chapter, the *Examiner* was among Southey's objects of attack in his *Quarterly* article. Calling Leigh Hunt "a flagitious incendiary" (16.31: 273), Southey lumps the *Examiner* together with Cobbett's *Political Register* as reformist publications deserving the strict and immediate attention of the law (16.31: 275). Moreover, "Mr. Examiner Hunt does but blow the trumpet to usher in Mr. Orator Hunt in his tandem, with the tri-color flag before him and his servant in livery behind" (16.31: 248). The *Examiner* responded by printing large extracts of *Wat Tyler* in its edition of 9 March, which, at 10d an issue, significantly increased the availability of those passages in Southey's play most likely to excite "sedition and rebellion." These scandalous "Morceau[x]" appeared as part of Hazlitt's "Literary Notices. No. 25" in review of both *Wat Tyler* and the *Quarterly Review.* Nothing, perhaps, better illustrates the complete interpenetration of literary and political discourse at the climax of the Distresses crisis than the way this "Literary Notice" brought together for review a political essay and a dramatic poem in an article that itself would eventually be republished among Hazlitt's own *Political Essays* in 1819 (7: 168–76).

The article begins with an epigraph from Wordsworth—

"So it was when my life began,
So is it now I am a man:
So shall it be when I grow old and die.
The child's the father of the man"

—which is juxtaposed in turn with these opening lines:

According to this theory of personal continuity, the author of the Dramatic Poem, to be here noticed, is the father of Parliamentary Reform in the Quarterly Review. It is said to be a wise child that knows its own father: and we understand Mr. Southey (who is in this case reputed father and son) utterly disclaims the hypostatical union between the Quarterly Reviewer and the Dramatic Poet, and means to enter an injunction against the latter, as a bastard and imposter. (7: 168–69)

Continuing in this vein, the article becomes a pure example of the "parallelism," a genre of review-criticism which had sprung up in an age of "apostasy,"[5] and through which Hazlitt and the *Examiner* become the first to spell out in this case all the most obvious, ironic disparities between the Radical play and the reactionary review. It culminates with this breathless catalogue:

> We know no other person in whom "fierce extremes" meet with such mutual self-complacency. . . . The author of Wat Tyler was an Ultra-jacobin; the author of "Parliamentary Reform" is an Ultra-royalist; the one was a frantic demagogue; the other is a servile court-tool . . . the one saw nothing but the abuses of power; the other sees nothing but the horrors of resistance to those abuses: the one did not stop short of general anarchy; the other goes the whole length of despotism; the one vilified kings, priests, and nobles; the other vilifies the people: the one was for universal suffrage and perfect equality; the other is for seat-selling, and the increasing influence of the Crown: the one admired the preaching of John Ball; the other recommends the Suspension of Habeas Corpus, and the putting down of the *Examiner* by the sword, the dagger, or the thumb-screw; for the pen, Mr. Southey tells us, is not sufficient. (7: 170)

For Hazlitt, of course, as for other leading writers in the ascendent Opposition press, the metonymic "pen" not only *had* to be "sufficient" (confronted by a Tory majority in Parliament), but in this case actually was.

Yet in the very week this essay appeared, Parliament suspended Habeas Corpus, which may go some way to explain the intensity, as well as Paine-ite simplicity, of Hazlitt's rhetorical strategy. The device of the "parallelism" was easy to grasp, while it admitted of potentially infinite variation. The significance of its deployment here lay in two directions. On the one hand it catered to a "mode of reading" that lay outside the *Examiner*'s middle-class subscribers in the shared newspapers of the workingmen's associations, the circulating libraries, and the village inns—a readership that Cobbett was shortly to abandon for America.[6] On the other hand it was a strategy readily adapted to the needs of the outnumbered Whigs in the House of Commons. As Frank Hoadley makes clear in his 1941 article on the affair, Hazlitt's *Examiner* review inspired the next, remarkable turn of events in this controversy (83). Five days after it appeared on 14 March 1817, in the context of a heated debate over the Seditious Meetings Bill, William Smith, the Whig M.P. for Norwich, rose to speak in the House of Commons with a copy of *Wat Tyler* in one coat pocket and the latest issue of the *Quarterly* in the other. With his eye as much on the newspaper writers in the gallery as on the Tory ministers opposite, Smith inserted a cunning digression into a defense of his constituents in Norwich, duly reported the next day in all the "parliamentary reports" of the daily papers:

> The honourable member then adverted to that tergiversation of principle which the career of political individuals so often presented. He was far from supposing that a man who set out in life with the profession of certain

117

sentiments, was bound to conclude life with them. . . . But what he most detested, what most filled him with disgust, was the settled, determined malignity of a renegado. He had read in a publication (the Quarterly Review), certainly entitled to much respect from its general literary excellences, though he differed from it in its principles, a passage alluding to the recent disturbances, which passage read as follows:—"When the man of free opinions commences professor of moral and political philosophy for the benefit of the public, . . . his very breath becomes venomous, and every page which he sends abroad carries with it poison to the unsuspicious reader. . . ." With the permission of the House, he would read an extract from a poem recently published, to which, he supposed, the above writer alluded (or, at least, to productions of a similar kind), as constituting a part of the virus with which the public mind had been infected:—

> "My brethren, these are truths and weighty ones:
> Ye are all equal; nature made you so.
> Equality is your birth-right;—when I gaze
> On the proud palace, and behold one man
> In the blood-purpled robes of royalty, . . .
> I sicken, and, indignant at the sight,
> 'Blush for the patience of humanity.'" Wat Tyler.

[The honourable member] could not for a moment suppose that the same individual had written those two passages [hear, hear, hear!] but, if they were written by the same person, he should like to know . . . why no proceedings had been instituted against the author. . . . Why . . . had not those who thought it necessary to suspend the Habeas Corpus Act taken notice of this poem? Why had they not discovered the author of that seditious publication, and visited him with the penalties of the law? (*Morning Chronicle* 15 Mar. 1817; C. Southey 367–69)

Thus adapting Hazlitt's device to the high camp of the British Parliament, Smith creates an extraordinary scene that once again epitomizes the convergence of literary and political discourse at the height of the Distresses, and at the highest levels of public debate.

An even more extraordinary scene, however, was enacted just four days later in the Court of Chancery. Perhaps unique in literary history, the Laureate was here desperately seeking an injunction against one of his own works— and one that was rapidly becoming his greatest market success. With this, the commercial dimension of the *Wat Tyler* affair met and conjoined with matters of politics and literary genre. Chancery was a Court of Equity, and Southey was seeking "an accounting and surrendering of the profits [of the play], . . . the restoration of the copyright, and [an] injunction against further printing, publishing, and selling" (Manogue 111). Yet strangely enough, his injunction was denied on this very basis. To the amazement of Southey's lawyers—and to a reading public now closely following the case in the daily newspapers—the arch-conservative Lord Chancellor Eldon insisted that

"Property, not principle, was the object on which this Court decided." And precisely *because* the play had been deemed "dangerous, mischievous, and seditious," its copyright could not be protected by Chancery: "in prior cases on the same subject . . . the Court had always acted on the principle of not giving protection to the author of a work which was, or must be represented in a legal sense, as immoral or seditious." As Southey's counsel rose to object, the lord chancellor interrupted: "I must again repeat, that I am not a judge of motives or of conduct, but of property; and shall not interfere where I see I have no right. Injunction refused" (*Morning Chronicle* 19 Mar. 1817). Thus it was that by a technicality of British law, the copyright of a text "calculated to excite a spirit of open rebellion against the Sovereign" was removed, and removed just as the "Distresses of the Country" had created the largest and most receptive audience possible for such a text. Within weeks some 60,000 copies of *Wat Tyler* had been sold in a proliferation of ever cheaper editions, making it by far the greatest market success—and by far the most genuinely "popular" work—of any written by the first-generation Lake poets.[7]

At this point Coleridge joined the fray. His intervention was crucial, as it forestalled a potentially disastrous public self-defense that Southey was planning following his defeat in court. Southey had approached the *Courier* with a highly emotional "open letter" to the M.P. William Smith, but the editors of the *Courier*—seconded by Southey's closest friends—judiciously advised him to withhold it and instead allow Coleridge to take up the rhetorical cudgels. Coleridge, of course, had his own reasons for intervening in the affair. In addition to his memories of a former friendship, he was still seeking a favorable review of his *Statesman's Manual* in the *Quarterly,* not to mention his forthcoming second *Lay Sermon.*[8] Further, as Hoadley puts it, Coleridge "must have visualized himself in Southey's position, for the two had been Republicans together, Pantisocrats together, authors of *The Fall of Robespierre* together, lecturers together. Now in the eyes of the world they were Tories together" (87). Coleridge's defense of "Mr. Southey and Wat Tyler" appeared in four anonymous articles in the *Courier* over a period of two weeks at the end of March 1817.[9] Out of a number of recurring discursive and rhetorical strategies we may distinguish two general approaches that Coleridge takes to the problem: first, a broad satire of the Opposition press; and second, a deflection of the principal charge of apostasy in a defense of Southey's "poetic genius." Such "genius," in Coleridge's view, was by definition incapable of apostasy because "the nature and purposes of poetry itself" entirely transcend either political or ideological practice (*Courier* 3.2: 470).

In Coleridge's satiric counterattack on the Opposition press, we witness once again the complete interpenetration of generic, commercial, and political strategies. In these four essays, Coleridge presents a clear-sighted, if rueful, analysis of the broad patterns of political and socioeconomic change that were transforming the British social structure. He opens his first article, for example, by calling attention to the crisis of authority inherent in William Smith's use of Parliament as a tool of the media. The reporting of parliamentary debates in the daily press was still technically illegal, and this Coleridge points out by adopting, with heavy sarcasm, the discourse of reform.

> The progress of tyranny, the encroachments upon freedom during the present King's reign, have in nothing been more remarkable than in the publicity permitted to the proceedings in Parliament. . . . Since the French Revolution, the Journalists have freely commented, not always in respectful terms, on the sentiments of the speakers. All this has arisen during an age of tyranny and oppression according to the mob orators of the day. A new aera has now arrived. A Revolution has just been attempted in England; and Parliament is selected as the fit place for proving the inconsistency of the public Journalists! A noble task! . . . Since a Quarterly Reviewer has thus been courageously unmasked, we shall soon find the inconsistency of Weekly Reviewers also demonstrated; and in time the daily press may come under the rod. . . . A dignified task! Hitherto Journalists have endeavoured to place Members of Parliament in the wrong, according to their way of thinking; but now Members of Parliament are to turn the tables, and prove the Journalists in error! . . . Sunk will be the Parliament, elevated the Journalists! Such is the implied confession of the ascendency of the press made by that enlightened statesman and loyal patriot, Mr. William Smith. We thank him for this homage to our calling. (*Courier* 3.2: 449–50)

Though with bitter regret, Coleridge correctly identifies the advent of a "new aera" in the distribution of cultural authority within the bourgeois public sphere that has emerged from the postwar political crisis. With or without parliamentary reform, "the ascendency of the press" has engineered a new form of political agency in the shape of "public opinion," which is now having a tangible impact on the conduct of parliamentary debate.

What Coleridge also perceives here is that the reading audiences of the Opposition press now extended well beyond the boundaries of the bourgeois public sphere. In this case, with or without the universal suffrage demanded by popular Radicalism, the agency of the press was shaping public opinion among those Coleridge describes as "the deluded multitude out of doors, the dupes of incendiary demagogues" (3.2: 450). And the *Wat Tyler* affair has brought these changes into horrifyingly sharp focus. "Is it not strange," inquires Coleridge regarding Smith's quotation of *Wat Tyler* in Parliamentary debate, "that he should have selected a passage which appeared to him more particularly calculated to have an effect on the lower orders at the present time, when, by so doing, he must have known, that he should be the means of dispersing it in the course of a week, not only where the *Wat Tyler* would never have come, but in every alehouse and village over the whole United Kingdom?" (3.2: 472). The irony here, of course, is that Coleridge is availing himself of precisely the same influential medium to which William Smith has paid "homage," an irony evident in Coleridge's admission of "compunction" at joining the struggle over *Wat Tyler* and in so doing assisting William Smith in "advertising and thus exciting public curiosity about a silly, yet poisonous book" (3.2: 453).

The implied difference, of course, is that such newspapers as the *Courier*, tacitly underwritten by the Tory ministry, constitute a legitimate forum for the exercise of journalistic authority. Like Southey's article in the *Quarterly* (advertised here as "the best exposition of the present state of the country which has yet appeared"), they are of a fundamentally distinct moral as well as discursive character (3.2: 454). Coleridge endeavors to make this point— through an elaborate parody of the Opposition press—in his third essay in the series, which he presents as an article that has supposedly been rejected by the fictitious "Westminster or Parliamentary Review" on account of its "style and principles" (3.2: 466). Unfortunately, Coleridge's control of the satiric mode is less than sure, for in an essay intended to distinguish itself by its superior "style and principles," he resorts to the very ad hominem mudslinging that he otherwise professes to deplore—in passages that even his first editor, his daughter Sara Coleridge, could not bring herself to reprint (3.2: 467–68n. 9). William Smith, for example, is characterized as

> grave and solid from his infancy, like that most *useful* of domestic animals, which, even as a *piggie*, never runs but with some foreseen and prudent motive, whether it be to the mast, the grains, or the wash-tub; and at no time a slave to the present moment, never grunts over the acorns before him without a *scheming* squint, and a segment at least of its wise little eye, cast toward those on one side, which his neighbour is enjoying, or may be about to enjoy. (3.2: 469)

In general, however, Coleridge is successful in distinguishing his essays stylistically by overt signs of learnedness and erudition; the use of recondite puns, etymologies, and mythological allusions; and the elaborately subordinated syntax associated with Edmund Burke. The result is a prose that defines its reading audience by offsetting the material accessibility of the newspaper with a style discursively inaccessible to all but the relatively small circle of university educated gentlemen and "men of letters." The best example is found in Coleridge's most direct attack on Hazlitt himself. Alluding to Smith's adoption of the debating strategies of the *Examiner*, Coleridge notes that "It might be a service to certain persons who let themselves be used as conducting-pipes of slander pumped up from the cellars and poison-vaults of roguery, if we hinted at the *etymological* appropriateness of the term *diabolical* as applied to this transaction" (3.2: 454). After a remarkably convoluted series of puns on these terms, he continues:

> It is some small proof of our previous respect for Mr. W. S., that we were actually surprised at his condescending to *sing base* to the Hunts, Hazlitts, and Cobbetts in this asinine Io Triumphe of detraction. The exultation is pardonable in *them*. For what can be more natural than for

such creatures to fling out and wax wanton proud on the *supposed* discovery, that a man of Southey's genius and high rank in Literature, had
once thought like themselves? It was in truth no small honour to *them,*
that even the boy Southey, even at his private writing desk, should have
but *sported* (and that in a Dramatis Personae consisting of Rioters and
Mob-Preachers) with provocatives, labelled, perhaps, but never administered
to the same low appetites, for which in right prosing *earnest,* and in the
full vigour of their incapacity, *they* have been so long the public purvey-
ors? (3.2: 455)

Here the horizontal struggle for authority between middle-class men of letters
is recast as a vertical struggle between those of a "high rank in Literature"—
exemplified by Southey but including the present writer and even William
Smith—and such nonuniversity educated "creatures" of the "cellars and
poison-vaults of roguery" as the "Hunts, Hazlitts, and Cobbetts," whose "low
appetites" confuse the mere sporting with "provocatives" at one's "private
writing desk" with the actual administration of effective opiates to the masses.

This caricature of the reformist press is taken one step further in a brilliant
piece of mythopoeia designed to reinforce Southey's "high rank in Literature"
by casting it as the sublime transcendence of Apollo himself.

We might fancy, that as a long-eared virtuoso is said to have found in a bed
of thistles the flute of Apollo, left behind by him, when he ascended to his
own natural place to sit henceforward with all the Muses around him instead
of the ragged cattle of Admetus; so one of his descendants of the present
day, snuffing at a forgotten Pan-pipe of Southey's "made of *green* corn," had
rendered it vocal. What wonder, if delighted at hearing the blast of his own
nostrils modulated, so sweetly he "nosed the element" in triumph, *sawing* the
air in one long-continued bravura without accompaniment, till not an Ass in
the whole neighborhood but left mumbling its prickly fare to bray in chorus.
(3.2: 455–56)

Here *Wat Tyler* is no longer political "poison" but rather the forgotten "Pan-
pipe" of a once-bucolic Laureate who has since achieved the apotheosis that
has lifted him to his "proper place" among the Muses, far from the "prickly
fare" of political struggle. It is a sign of Coleridge's own metamorphosis of
"rank" that he feels free here to place the same ass's head on the Radicals of
the present day that the *Anti-Jacobin Review* had unceremoniously bestowed
on Southey and himself—back in the pantisocratic days when the laureateship
would have hardly been the site where they would have located the "natural
place" of Apollo and the Muses.[10]

This allusion also serves as a transition from Coleridge's satire on the
Opposition press to his defense of Southey's "poetic genius." In general,
Coleridge's procedure is to deflect the charge of apostasy by displacing the
discourse of politics, here with mythological allusion and elsewhere with the
discourses of ethics and religion. "Sinners make the best Saints," for example,

is the moral of one lengthy passage (3.2: 451). But more important for our purposes is his central exculpation of *Wat Tyler* itself.

> Had we been ignorant of the author's name, [posits Coleridge] and known only that the *Wat Tyler* had been written at the first dawn of the French Revolution . . . we fully believe that the following would have been our conclusion. The writer, we should say, was a very young man of warm feelings and active fancy, full of glorious visions concerning the possibilities of human nature, because his lofty, imaginative, and *innocent* spirit "had mistaken its own virtues for the average character of mankind." We should have seen that the vivid, yet indistinct images, in which he had painted to himself the evils of war and the hardships of the poor, proved that neither the forms or the feelings were the result of real observation. The product of the Poet's own fancy, they were impregnated, therefore, with that pleasurable fervour which is experienced in all energetic exertions of intellectual power.—But as to any serious wish, akin to reality; as to any real persons or events designed or expected; we should think it just as wise, and just as charitable, to believe that Quevedo or Dante would have been glad to realise the horrid phantoms and torments of imaginary oppressors, whom *they* beheld in the Infernal Regions—*i.e.* on the slides of their own magic lanterns. (3.2: 459)

Here Apollo among the cattle of Admetus is exchanged for a "young man" who "had mistaken his own virtues and powers for the average character of mankind." This, then, is the "Poet," whose "lofty, imaginative, and *innocent* spirit" is fundamentally detached from "real persons or events designed or expected" or even "real observation." Employing a remarkably mechanical model for the imagination in the newly invented "magic lanterns" (Johnson 152–54), Coleridge represents Southey's play as the result not of hopes for a republican revolution but of an entirely private and ecstatic union of the "products of the . . . fancy" with the "pleasurable fervour . . . of intellectual power."

If this is the case, then it follows that such a private drama of desire is susceptible to misuse by those who are neither poets nor intellectuals. To assist the less gifted of his *Courier* readers in this dilemma, Coleridge offers two possible approaches to *Wat Tyler*. Read with an educated appreciation for irony, it is merely an "admirable burlesque of the pompous extravagances of the demagogues of the day" or, better, it is a moral tale of chivalry, arising from Southey's attachment to Spenser and "the indignation, which . . . the outrage on Wat Tyler's Daughter had kindled in him" (3.2: 453, 460). At most it is a piece "designed to be read by imagined oppressors, not by the oppressed" (3.2: 458). But when misdirected beyond the boundaries of its appropriate reading audience to those incapable of deciphering these subtleties, it becomes a "poisonous book" that may be "used to the very worst purposes among the ignorant, distressed of the lower class" (3.2: 453). The charge of apostasy as well as sedition is thus deflected from the disinterestedness of poetic genius onto the politically interested use of this manuscript as an instrument of persuasion at a moment of national crisis: "Not the thoughts or the feelings as generalities (and the Poet's characters, the historic not less than the factitious in *name,* as well as in reality, are mere personifications of general laws), but the misapplication of them to particular times and persons, for immediate purposes—not the *writing* but the deliberate *publication,* constitutes the criminality" (3.2: 471). We can discern in this defense something of the dichotomy between symbol and allegory, between the rebel Wat Tyler as a "mere personification of [a] general law," transcending history and ideology, and "the misapplication" of this symbol as an allegory for "particular times and persons, for immediate purposes."

Coleridge's line of argument here depends heavily on overlooking the fact that Southey himself had tried very hard indeed to have *Wat Tyler* published in 1794. Even this, however, could be put down to Southey's youth at the time, for in the end the entire controversy over his supposed apostasy boils down, in Coleridge's view, to a "compleat ignorance of the whole form, growth and character of a Poet's mind, in early youth and during the first *growing pains* of poetic genius, and its essential difference from the minds of those . . . in whom money is an innate idea" (3.2: 469). The Whig William Smith is Coleridge's example of such a philistine, and after the rather crude caricature of the politician-capitalist as a *"piggie"* (quoted above), he continues:

> We contend that such fortunate persons are not calculated to be judges of states of being utterly alien from their own; nor can they conceive how entirely a young Poet, in all his poetic moments, lives in an *ideal* world—how remote, both from his own intentions and from the nature and purposes of poetry itself, is any *direct* influence on the actions of men. On the sub-stratum of their general feelings he is to act by general truths, general emotions—the grandeur of liberty, compassion for the oppressed, indignation against the oppressors, are as natural to him, when these are his subject, as fidelity, loyalty, the majesty of law, and devotion, even to the death, for friend, or King, or Country, are, in his next Poem, perhaps. (3.2: 470–71)

This is the core of Coleridge's defense, and it represents an early formative moment in what we now call the Romantic Ideology. The forceful conjunction of literary and political practice, symbolized by the introduction of *Wat Tyler* into Parliament, forces Coleridge into making explicit the "essential differ-ence" between the "Poet" and the politician, as well as between "the nature and purposes of poetry itself" on the one hand, and any activity designed to have a *"direct* influence on the actions of men" on the other. The poet and his poetry inhabit an *"ideal"* world that is grounded in such "general truths, general emotions" that, with perfect indifference, he can move from poetic subject to poetic subject among such ahistorical polarities as "indignation against . . . oppressors" and "devotion, even to the death for . . . King or Country."

For this reason, then, even the Laureate's pension and annual butt of sack can be construed as a symbol of "honour" rather than "love of gain"

(3.2: 452). After all, as Coleridge quite correctly points out, Southey could make "thousands, where he makes hundreds" if only he had become a "Journalist in London" instead of the reclusive Laureate. Nevertheless, Southey's "honour" does have certain ideological implications, and far from avoiding these, Coleridge embraces them with Burkean fervor.

> Those who hate the Government in Church and State, naturally enough wish to make all public offices disgraceful; and, in particular, they attempt to render those ridiculous which are merely of an elegant nature, and ornamental to the Crown. Mr. Southey has the courage to hold one of these, evidently for the sake of honour, not from the love of gain, and it is this which exasperates his opponents. . . . [F]or galled they are to the quick, by seeing men of great talents, extensive information, experience in the world, by the world esteemed, proud of the trappings of Royalty. Such occurrences are fatal to their views. They spread a grace around the Throne, they inspire a reverence for it; they contributed to preserve that sacred awe which was the other day in St. James's Park, trodden down by the hoofs of the Swinish multitude. (3.2: 452)

The ragged cattle of Admetus and the asses of the Radical press have been here transmuted into a far more insidious, and numerous, "creature." According to this writer for the *Courier* at least, it would seem that at a time when the Regent's carriage is vulnerable to the attacks of this "swinish multitude," the "Throne" becomes indeed the "proper place" for the Muses of poetic genius to assist in preserving "that sacred awe" for an institution that since the defeat of the French Revolution has been restored to apparently universal "legitimacy."

Needless to say, Hazlitt had a somewhat different view of the matter. And in whàt would have been a widely anticipated article titled "The Courier and 'The Wat Tyler,'" he set out to make this abundantly clear. Appearing in the *Examiner* of 30 March 1817, immediately after the third of Coleridge's essays was published, this article was not part of the "Literary Notices" series, though it begins with the same admixture of literary, political, and satiric strategies:

> Doth not the appetite alter? A man loves the meat in his youth, that he cannot endure in his age. Shall quips and sentences, and these paper bullets of the brain awe a man from the career of his humour? —*Much Ado about Nothing.*

> Instead of applying for an injunction against *Wat Tyler,* Mr. Southey would do well to apply for an injunction against Mr. Coleridge, who has undertaken his defense in *The Courier.* If he can escape from the ominous patronage of that gentlemen's pen, he has nothing to fear from his own. (7: 176)

With this, Hazlitt delivers one of his own well-aimed "paper bullets." The opening quip from Shakespeare manages to cut through the intensity of the entire controversy, while nevertheless registering its displaced violence. If indeed "paper bullets" are the official ordinance in this war of words, then success will go to those whose pens are most "sufficient." To this end, Hazlitt adopts the shorthand of Coleridge's "ominous patronage," conjuring for his *Examiner* readers the entire matrix of obfuscation and contradiction satirized in previous reviews, as well as the witty image of Southey forced to seek a second injunction just to stanch the flow of what is elsewhere in the article dubbed Coleridge's "maudlin methodistical casuistry" (7: 178).

Yet if there is to be discursive violence in this affair, it can be traced, in Hazlitt's view, to Southey himself.

> The best thing for Mr. Southey (if we might be allowed to advise) would be for his friends to say nothing about him, and for him to say nothing about other people. We have nothing to do with Mr. Southey "the man," or even with Mr. Southey the apostate; but we have something to do with Mr. Southey the spy and informer. Is it not a little strange, that while this gentleman is getting an injunction against himself as the author of *Wat Tyler,* he is recommending gagging bills against us, and the making up by force for his deficiency in argument! (7: 177)

Against the authoritarian "force" of censorship and repression, Hazlitt and the *Examiner* wield the more democratic weapon of superior rhetoric. At the same time, in response to the violent polarization of political debate, a subtle shift has taken place in the *Examiner*'s self-positioning. To reinforce its discursive authority, it now assumes the moral high ground of moderation:

> What are we to think of a man who is "now a flagitious incendiary," (to use the epithets which Mr. Southey applies to the Editor of the *Examiner*) "a palliator of murder, insurrection, and treason," and anon a pensioned scribbler of court poetry and court politics? . . . Mr. Coleridge indeed steps in to the assistance of his friend in this dilemma, and says (unsaying all that he says besides) that the ultra-jacobinical opinions advanced in *Wat Tyler* were "more an honour to the writer's heart than an imputation on his understanding?" Be it so. The Editor of this Paper will, we dare say, agree to this statement from disinterested motives, (for he is not answerable for any ultra-jacobinical opinions) as we suppose Mr. Southey will accede to it from mere self-love. . . . Why then not extend the same charitable interpretation to those who have held a middle course between his opposite extremes? We are sure that to be thought *a little less wise and virtuous* than that celebrated person thinks himself, would content the ambition of any moderate man. (7: 177)

Thus the *Examiner* lays claim to a politics of "a middle course between . . . opposite extremes." The "Editor of this Paper"—and his literary reviewer— can safely distance themselves from any discomfiting "answerab[ility]" for "ultra-jacobinical opinions," and this in turn guarantees the moral authority with which they can contest the violent intolerance of "court politics." This rhetoric of the "middle" nevertheless bears with it the metaphoric potential to be recast as a rhetoric of class, by which "any moderate man" might distinguish himself in turn from "lower" and "upper."

In the meantime, however, the pivot upon which Southey's apostasy—and, by implication, that of his defender—turns is the familiar binary of past and present. To this end, Hazlitt's principal point of attack in this review is the emphasis Coleridge places on "the boy Southey" as the author of *Wat Tyler,* a rhetorical exaggeration by which Coleridge imputes a similar immaturity in all those who continue, like the readers of the *Examiner,* to subscribe to "the cause of liberty." Hazlitt's answer is to adopt the plainest style of public debate, enumerating what he analyses as Coleridge's principle "assumptions" and providing in each case an answer ranging from the witty to the Juvenalian. An instance of the latter is the second assumption in the series:

> 2. *That Mr. Southey was a mere boy when he wrote* Wat Tyler, *and entertained Jacobin opinions: that being a child, he felt as a child, and thought slavery, superstition, war, famine, bloodshed, taxes, bribery and corruption, rotten boroughs, places, and pensions, shocking things; but that now he is become a man, he has put away childish things, and thinks there is nothing so delightful as slavery, superstition, war, famine, bloodshed, taxes, bribery and corruption, rotten boroughs, places and pensions, and particularly, his own.* (7: 181)

Coleridge's reliance on a dichotomy between immaturity and wisdom to account for the difference between *Wat Tyler* and the *Quarterly Review* is discovered by Hazlitt not only to underwrite a status quo of injustice but to discredit by implication all the other achievements of revolutionary Romanticism:

> *Answer.* Yet Mr. Coleridge tells us that when [Mr. Southey] wrote *Wat Tyler,* he was a man of genius and learning. That Mr. Southey was a wise man when he wrote this poem, we do not pretend: that he has ever been so, is more than we know. This we do know, and it is worth attending to; that all that Mr. Southey has done best in poetry, he did before he changed his political creed; that *all* that Mr. Coleridge ever did in poetry, as the *Ancient Mariner, Christabel,* the *Three Graves,* his Poems and his Tragedy, he had written, when, according to his own account, he must have been a very ignorant, idle, thoughtless, person; that much the greater part of what Mr. Wordsworth has done best in poetry was done about the same period; and if what these persons have done in poetry, in indulging the "pleasing fervour of a lively imagination," gives no weight to their political opinions at the time they did it, what they have done since in science or philosophy to establish their authority, is more than we know. All the authority that they have as poets and men of genius must be thrown into the scale of Revolution and Reform. Their Jacobin principles gave rise to their Jacobin poetry. Since they gave up the first, their poetical powers have flagged, and been comparatively or wholly "in a state of suspended animation." Their genius, their style, their versification, every thing down to their spelling, was revolutionary. . . . Poet-laureates are courtiers by profession, but we say that poets are naturally Jacobins. (7: 181–82)

Here, then, is an alternative ideology of Romanticism, one that holds poetic practice in general to be an inseparable function of "political opinion"
and locates Romantic discourse in particular within a politics of resistance.
"Authority" can consist only in an evident continuity of principle within the
various discursive contexts a given author will engage.

The irony for Hazlitt—and what gives this essay (despite its resolute
certainties) an undertone of regret—is the fact that in the very "romanticism"
of poetic genius lies what seems to be a fatal defect of character.

> All the poets of the present day have been [Jacobins], with a single exception,
> which it would be invidious to mention. If they have not continued so, this
> only shews the instability of their characters, and that their natural generosity
> and romantic enthusiasm, "their lofty, imaginative, and innocent spirits,"
> have not been proof against the incessant, unwearied, importunities of vulgar
> ambition. (7: 182)

The result is the spectacle of co-opted genius, which Hazlitt describes with a
striking counter-mythologization of Southey's apotheosis.

> Poor Bob Southey! How they laugh at him! What are the abuse and contumely
> we are in the habit of bestowing on him, compared with the cordial contempt,
> the flickering sneers, that play round the lips of his new-fangled friends, when
> they see the "Man of Humanity" decked out in the trappings of his prostitution,
> and feel the rankling venom of their hearts soothed by the flattering reflection
> that virtue and genius are marketable commodities? (7: 179)

Along with this image of silken malice comes the equally disturbing recognition that poetry is no less entangled in the exchange of "commodities" than it
is in the politics of distress.

Yet the stark commodification of "virtue and genius," though regret-
table enough, is nothing as compared with its rationalization. This Hazlitt
locates in Coleridge's unusual depiction of the poetic imagination as a "magic
lantern," in which he reads a dangerous disjunction between mental reality
and lived history.

> 5. Mr. Coleridge sums up his opinion of the ultimate design and secret origin
> of "the *Wat Tyler*" in these remarkable words:—"We should have seen that
> the vivid, yet indistinct images in which he had painted the evils of war and
> the hardships of the poor, proved that neither the forms nor the feelings were
> the result of real observation. The product of the poet's own fancy, they"
> —[*viz.* the evils of war and the hardships of the poor]—"were impregnated,
> therefore, with *that pleasurable fervour which is experienced in all energetic
> exertion of intellectual power.* But as to any serious wish, akin to reality,"
> [that is, to remove these evils] "as to any real persons or events designed or
> expected, we should think it just as wise and just as charitable, to believe
> that Quevedo or Dante would have been glad to realise the horrid phantoms
> and torments of *imaginary* oppressors, whom they beheld in the infernal
> regions—*i.e.* on the slides of their own magic lantern."

Answer. The slides of the guillotine, excited (as we have been told) the same pleasurable fervour in Mr. Southey's mind: and Mr. Coleridge seems to insinuate, that the 5,800,000 lives which have been lost to prove mankind the property of kings, by divine right, have been lost "on the slides of a magic lantern"; the evils of war, like all other actual evils, being "the products of a fervid imagination." So much for the sincerity of poetry.

Audrey. Is not poetry a true thing?

Touchstone. No.

Would these gentlemen persuade us that there is nothing evil in the universe but what exists in their own imagination, but what is the product of their fervid fancy? That the world is full of nothing but their egotism, their vanity, and their hypocrisy? The world is *sick* of their egotism, their vanity, and their hypocrisy. (7: 184)

With this uncompromising gesture, Hazlitt attempts to nullify the authority of the nascent ideology of Romanticism, with its attendant cult of poetic genius. The disinterested "imagination" Hazlitt reads as a mask for a solipsistic and even cynical detachment from "any serious wish, akin to reality," a "hypocrisy" that is the moral opposite of "sincerity." As a result, the poet's claim to represent in the "products of [his] fancy" an intuition of universal truth is deconstructed as the absurd claim to construct reality itself, an ideology that claims to transcend ideology.

Of course when such an ideology is indeed marketable, and enlisted to "spread a grace" around social injustice, then the results, from Hazlitt's point of view at least, are at once macabre and apocalyptic. Where Coleridge saw the "swinish multitude," Hazlitt sees the grim pageant of superannuated tyranny.

In courtly malice and servility, Mr. Southey has outdone Herodias's daughter. He marches into Chancery "with his own head in a charger," as an offering to Royal delicacy. He plucks out the heart of Liberty within him, and mangles his own breast to stifle every natural sentiment left there: and yet Mr. Coleridge would persuade us that this stuffed figure, this wretched phantom, is the living man. The finery of birth-day suits has dazzled his senses, so that he has "no speculation in those eyes that he does glare with"; yet Mr. Coleridge would persuade us that this is the clear-sighted politician. Famine stares him in the face, and he looks upon her with lack-lustre eye. Despotism hovers over him, and he says, "Come, let me clutch thee." He drinks the cup of human misery, and thinks it is a cup of sack. . . . And they would persuade us that this non-entity is somebody—"the chief dread of Jacobins and Jacobinism, or quacks and quackery." If so, Jacobins and Jacobinism have not much to fear; and Mr. Coleridge may publish as many Lay-sermons as he pleases.[11] (7: 185–86)

With this stark allegory, we are given the central scene of the *Wat Tyler* affair, the strange spectacle of a prominent author struggling in Chancery to suppress his own most popular work. Coleridge read this act as an appropriate response to the "criminality" of publishing, without authorization, a private manuscript that had been intended to remain only on the "slides of [Southey's] own magic lantern." Hazlitt reads it as the grotesque suicide of revolutionary Romanticism as it transforms itself from an ideology of "Liberty" and "natural sentiment" into an ideology of putative transcendence and spurious autonomy, of "imagination" and "genius."

In either case, this scene represents a pivotal moment in the making of what we now refer to as the Romantic Ideology. Four months later, the seminal *Biographia Literaria* would finally appear, in which Coleridge selects Wordsworth and Shakespeare as more plausible illustrations of his "philosophical criticism." Almost simultaneously Hazlitt would publish his *Characters of Shakespeare's Plays,* in which would reappear his essay on Coriolanus composed at the height of public rioting in December 1816. Here, and by way of epilogue to this affair, Hazlitt reflects on the "nature of purposes of poetry," radically qualifying his claim that "poets are naturally Jacobins" and suggesting that, for him at least, the Jacobin Romantic may well have been what Wordsworth calls "the gleam / The light that never was / on sea or land."

> The cause of the people is indeed but little calculated as a subject for poetry: it admits of rhetoric, which goes into argument and explanation, but it presents no immediate or distinct images to the mind, "no jutting frieze, buttress, or coigne of vantage" for poetry "to make its pendant bed and procreant cradle in." The language of poetry naturally falls in with the language of power. . . . [Poetry] is everything by excess. . . . It shows its head turretted, crowned, and crested. Its front is gilt and blood-stained. . . . It has its altars and its victims, sacrifices, human sacrifices. Kings, priests, nobles are its train-bearers, tyrants and slaves its executioners.—"Carnage is its daughter." Poetry is right-royal. (4: 214)

6

HISTORY AND PARTICULAR FACTS:

Hazlitt's Review of
the *Biographia Literaria*

While the confrontation between Hazlitt and Coleridge in the pages of the *Examiner* and the *Courier* brought into sharp focus the political, economic, and discursive issues raised by the *Wat Tyler* affair, the affair itself continued to command public attention for another two months of 1817. In April Southey published his *Letter to William Smith,* rekindling the flames of controversy with the bold claim that *Wat Tyler* was not in fact seditious (C. Southey 372). Described by Hoadley as "an autobiography written in tears" (89), this pamphlet sold out four editions by the end of the year and attracted a series of fierce rebuttals from the Opposition press, including Hazlitt's three-part "Literary Notice" in the *Examiner* in April (7: 186–208), and Jeffrey's mercilessly detailed analysis in the *Edinburgh Review* in May (28: 151–74).

One of the most important consequences of this protracted controversy—and one that has (again) gone completely unnoticed by literary history—is that it established the context of discursive and ideological struggle in which Coleridge's *Biographia Literaria* was first published and first read. As is now well known, the *Biographia* was composed and even printed as early as 1815, but due to a series of complications it had lain idle for almost two years.[1] Now, in the midst of the *Wat Tyler* affair—and during the final, most acrimonious, phase of the Distresses crisis—Coleridge found himself in a position to see his long delayed book through to publication. To bring his "literary life and opinions" up to date, he composed a new concluding chapter describing the years 1816 and 1817, and though it does not mention the *Wat Tyler* affair specifically, this chapter clearly bears the imprint of its disputatious tone and style. Like Southey's *Letter,* it is a bitterly recriminatory account of the reception of *Christabel* and *The Statesman's Manual,* bringing to an emphatic head the critique of anonymous review-criticism that runs throughout the *Biographia.* As we saw at the outset, Hazlitt is all but named here as the epitome of "personal enmity behind the mask of anonymous criticism," while Jeffrey is similarly arraigned with "indignant contempt" as his "employer and suborner" (7.2: 239, 242). By throwing down this gauntlet, Coleridge asks, in effect, that his entire book be read as a deliberate intervention in the volatile public debates of 1817, thus adding increased polemical vigor to such elements as his "principles in Politics," his pointed encomium of Robert Southey, his factious review of Maturin's *Bertram,* and his concern to define (and model) the cultural function of "absolute genius" (7.1: 5, 31). In this way, too, then, chapter 24 of the *Biographia* sets up the final and most culturally resonant contest for cultural authority between Hazlitt and Coleridge during the Distresses crisis. The confrontation between the two anonymous writers for the *Examiner* and the *Courier* was now recast as a full-scale struggle between the *Edinburgh Review* and the author of a book that was to become the most seminal text in English Romantic criticism.[2]

The *Wat Tyler* affair, then, provides an indispensable context in which to rehistoricize the *Biographia Literaria.* Our best guide to such a rereading lies in the book's first and most immediately influential critique: Hazlitt's full-length review-essay in the *Edinburgh Review.* The significance of this review is recognized even by literary historians who have not fully taken into account its determinant contexts in public debate. Walter Jackson Bate, for example, in his introduction to the Bollingen edition of the *Biographia,* identifies Hazlitt's article as one of the two most important reviews of the book, the other being John Wilson's satire in *Blackwood's Magazine*—an article Bate regards as notable only for its "indiscriminate . . . savagery" (lxv). By contrast, Hazlitt's review, though "headily perverse in places," is distinguished by its "verve and gusto." In Bate's view, moreover, this article, "by the greatest English critic of the period except for Coleridge himself, not only typifies what many of the reviewers seemed to have felt and lacked the talent and confidence to say, but it is also a prototype of most of the adverse criticism of the *Biographia* from Coleridge's time to our own" (lxvi). Bate thus asserts a double significance for this review, a significance now further clarified by a recognition of its rootedness in the controversies of the Distresses period. First, because Hazlitt had already largely formulated his critique of Coleridge's Romantic idealism in the struggle over *Wat Tyler,* he is able easily to "typif[y] what many of the reviewers seemed to have felt and lacked the talent and confidence to say." Second, as in all of his reviews of Coleridge's works during this period, Hazlitt invokes an Enlightenment ideology of empiricist "common sense," in conjunction with a particular emphasis in this review on the norm of "history and particular facts" (16: 118), to produce a "prototype" of the various materialist and historicist rereadings of this seminal text in our own day. Indeed, what Bate reads as "headily perverse" in this review is in fact Hazlitt's uncompromising insistence on the entanglement of the *Biographia* in a historically specific context of political and ideological struggle, a context that Coleridge's book—and especially its concluding chapter—so skillfully and attractively elides.[3]

Hazlitt takes the theme of his review from a highlighted passage in Coleridge's account of his school days, in which the author affably admits that *"at a very premature age, even before my fifteenth year, I had bewildered myself in metaphysicks, and in theological controversy. Nothing else pleased me. History, and particular facts, lost all interest in my mind"* (16: 117; Hazlitt's emphasis). Such an admission, of course, plays directly into the public image of the "bewildered" metaphysician either comically or culpably abstracted from material reality—an image that Coleridge otherwise claims to resist, and which Hazlitt is now able to recapitulate with practiced compression.

> Mr. Coleridge has ever since [his fifteenth year], from the combined forces of poetic levity and metaphysic bathos, been trying to fly, not in the air, but under ground—playing at hawk and buzzard between sense and nonsense,— floating or sinking in fine Kantian categories, in a state of suspended anima- tion 'twixt dreaming and awake,—quitting the plain ground of "history and particular facts" for the first butterfly theory, fancy-bred from the maggots of his brain—going up in an air-balloon filled with fetid gas from the writings of Jacob Behmen and the mystics, and coming down in a parachute made of the soiled and fashionable leaves of the Morning Post,—promising us an account of the intellectual System of the Universe, and putting us off with a reference to a promised dissertation on the Logos, introductory to an intended commentary on the entire Gospel of St John. (16: 118)

Though perhaps "headily perverse," this piece of satiric banter serves to orient its readers to the third in the *Edinburgh*'s series of reviews on the Gothic poet of "suspended animation," and the lay preacher of "Kantian categories." Yet Hazlitt's particular interest here in measuring such attributes against the "plain ground of 'history and particular facts' " is clearly a product of the intervening *Wat Tyler* debate, which was focused on the relationship between historical "truth" and the cultural authority of poetic "genius."

Hazlitt thus treats the *Biographia* as a public reiteration and development of the ideas Coleridge had already expressed anonymously in the *Courier*. Turning from satire to analysis, he continues:

> [Mr. Coleridge] tells us, with a degree of *naïveté* not usual for him, that, "even before his fifteenth year, history and particular facts had lost all interest in his mind." Yet, so little is he himself aware of the influence which this feeling still continues to exert over his mind, and of the way in which it has mixed itself up in his philosophical faith, that he afterwards makes it the test and definition of a sound understanding and true genius, that "the mind is affected by thoughts,

rather than by things; and only then feels the *requisite* interest even for the most important events and accidents, when by means of meditation they have passed into *thoughts.*" p. [7.1: 31]. We do not see, after this, what right Mr. C. has to complain of those who say that he is neither the most literal nor logical of mortals. . . . If it is the proper business of the philosopher to dream over theories, and to neglect or gloss over facts, to fit them to his theories or conscience; we confess we know of few writers, ancient or modern, who have come nearer to the perfection of this character than the author before us. (16: 118)

This final hyperbole is once again the inverted sign of respect: like the "post-Romantic" criticism of our own day, Hazlitt and the *Edinburgh* are willing to register the significance of the *Biographia* as a clear epitomization of the ideology of transcendence, in which to "dream over theories" becomes a way to "gloss over facts"—in which pure intellect appears to transcend the claims of a stubbornly historicist empiricism.

Coleridge's "perfection of this character" is measured against the norm of "history and particular facts" in a number of ways in the review that follows. First, Hazlitt takes on "the school of politics of which Mr Burke [is] at the head" in order to present a politicized counter-narrative to Coleridge's "Literary Life" that he calls the "*true* history of our reformed Antijacobin poets" (16: 133, 138; emphasis added). Taking as his cue Coleridge's tribute to Edmund Burke in chapter 10 and his defense of Robert Southey in chapter 3 (7.1: 191–2; 7.1: 55–56), Hazlitt rewrites Coleridge's subtle claims to "consistency" as the repressed narrative of "apostasy," a narrative "gloss[ed] over" by members of the Burkean "school" through the art of the "Apology" and the disconcerting power of their richly metaphorical style. This leads Hazlitt in the end to pursue on behalf of the *Edinburgh* a significantly new emphasis in his view of the relationship between literary and political practice. In the conclusion of the review, he claims to abandon any belief in a trustworthy conjunction of poetry and politics, declaring himself in ironic agreement with Coleridge that poets "live in an ideal world of their own; and it would be, perhaps, as well if they were confined to it" (16: 137).

Meanwhile, the norm of "history and particular facts" is used to turn back Coleridge's assault on the authority of review-criticism within the literary marketplace. In the review's most striking discursive feature, Coleridge's specific charges against the *Edinburgh* are answered with the unprecedented gesture of a long, closely printed footnote signed by Francis Jeffrey, in which he responds in propria persona to those "averments in points of fact" he deems to be of a "personal and injurious nature" (Reiman A: 492; Jackson 314). Though Jeffrey's self-defense here is ironically akin in genre to both Southey's *Letter* and the *Biographia* itself, Jeffrey claims a higher moral ground by adopting the skillfully unemotional style of the attorney-at-law, and by proving himself unexpectedly willing to doff the "mask" of anonymity in order "to answer [Coleridge] distinctly, and in the first person" (Reiman A: 492). While

134

the "public honour" of the *Edinburgh* is being thus vindicated by its editor, Hazlitt turns to challenge the rival authority of Coleridge's "philosophical criticism," first by dismissing its philosophical underpinnings as the "wilful and monstrous absurdity" of Kantian metaphysics (16: 123), and then by turning to historical precedents within British literature to ground his own counter-definitions of "the essence of poetry," invoking Milton and Shakespeare to refute the hubristic innovations of self-declared "genius" (16: 135–36).

Finally, and in these circumstances most surprisingly, the norm of "history and particular facts" lies behind the review's clearly positive evaluation of certain aspects of genre and style in the *Biographia*. Hazlitt, as we have seen, had already introduced a note of undecidability into his treatment of style in *The Statesman's Manual,* but this had remained at best a subtle overtone offsetting the *Edinburgh's* otherwise unmitigated rejection of *Christabel.* Here, however, the *Biographia* is treated with unusual restraint, largely because Coleridge's "poetic levity and metaphysic bathos" is balanced in this instance by a welcome turn to biography and "narrative" (16: 125). "There are some things readable in these volumes," the review begins, "and if the learned author could only have been persuaded to make them a little more conformable to their title, we have no doubt that they would have been the most popular of all his productions" (16: 115). If Coleridge, that is, had delivered only the "Biographical Sketches" announced in his title, he would have achieved an immediate cultural authority that is denied other generic elements of his book such as Burkean politics and German metaphysics. As we shall see, this public privileging of biography reflects an emergent alternative to Coleridge's bid to transcend history in general and the Distresses in particular. Where Coleridge stresses the timeless search for "universal principles," the *Edinburgh* promotes a new aestheticization of history that serves the interests of a reading audience defined on the one hand by its actual immunity to the distresses of scarcity and oppression, and on the other by its shared memories, at once bitter and lyrical, of revolution and its aftermath.

Yet it was not until the 1820s that such a reading audience would be fully consolidated by the art of nostalgia. As long as the shadow of the Distresses lay over public discourse, middle-class narratives of revolution and post-revolution would be acrimoniously divided along the fault line separating "consistency" from "apostasy." As Hazlitt goes on to note in his opening remarks, the *Biographia,* though "readable" in places, is "[u]nfortuneately . . . not so properly an account of [Mr. Coleridge's] Life and Opinions, as an Apology for them" (16: 115). Coleridge's turn from biography to "Apology," whether in describing his own career or that of such symbolic surrogates as Burke and Southey, signifies for Hazlitt the need to deny a narrative of self-contradiction in response to radical change, leading to a loss of "sincerity"—and hence authority. Coleridge's foremost strategy in this regard is to refer beyond history to a discourse of unchanging "principles" that underwrite the necessary evolution of merely provisional "opinions" (7.1: 190). Undoubtedly his boldest illustration of this process lies in his tribute, in chapter 10, to the political integrity of Edmund Burke—a figure who, for the Whigs at least, fully epitomized the phenomenon of self-conscious "apostasy." The recent *Wat Tyler* debates give this illustration additional prominence because of the link Coleridge makes in it between Burke's putative "consistency" and his widespread discursive influence. As Hazlitt describes it:

> [In the tenth chapter of his literary autobiography,] Mr. C. takes occasion to eulogize the writings of Mr. Burke, and observes, that "as our very signboards give evidence that there has been a Titian in the world, so the essays and leading paragraphs of our journals are so many remembrances of Edmund Burke." This is modest and natural we suppose for a newspaper editor: But our learned author is desirous of carrying the parallel a little further,—and assures us, that nobody can doubt of Burke's consistency. "Let the scholar," says our biographer, "who doubts this assertion, refer only to the speeches and writings of Edmund Burke at the commencement of the American war, and compare them with his speeches and writings at the commencement of the French Revolution. He will find the principles exactly the same, and the deductions the same—but the practical inferences almost opposite in the one case from those drawn in the other, yet in both equally legitimate and confirmed by the results." (16: 130)

The assertion of Burke's "consistency," precisely because it is subject to "doubt," turns biography into "Apology," producing Coleridge's characteristic distinction between unchanging "principles" and radically opposed "practical inferences." Moreover, this consistency is supplemented in Burke's case by a uniformity of stylistic excellence that makes him the "Titian" of political prose.

As Burke is clearly intended by Coleridge to symbolize his own claims to political consistency (if not of literary influence), and as Burke, rather than Coleridge, was a figure of greater and more lastingly notorious political profile among the Whig readers of the *Edinburgh,* Hazlitt is given scope to devote five full pages of his review to commentary on this passage. This part of the review, moreover, was later extracted to appear in both the *Champion* and Hazlitt's *Political Essays* of 1819 under the title "The Character of Mr. Burke." His approach to this "character" is twofold, complicated by the fact that both Hazlitt and his readers actually agreed with Coleridge's assessment of Burke's stylistic achievement. Thus Hazlitt concedes that "Burke's literary talents were, after all, his chief excellence" and proceeds to include in his analysis a detailed appreciation of the sublime "force" of his style, using Pope's words in the end to declare that Burke is "Never so sure our rapture to create, / As when he treads the brink of all we hate" (16: 133–34). Nevertheless, and for this very reason, the influence of what Hazlitt calls "the school of politics, of which Burke is at the head" must be vigorously contested with every resource of argument and countervailing force of style. In so doing, what might otherwise appear a disproportionate and even "headily perverse" digression in a review of Coleridge's *Biographia* is in fact Hazlitt's opportunity to restate many of the ideas originally introduced in his *Examiner* articles on Coleridge during the *Wat Tyler* affair—but now in a journalistic context of decisive cultural influence. Most interesting for our purposes is the way the paradigmatic figure of Burke produces an ironic reversal of the positions assumed by Coleridge and Hazlitt on the relationship between literary and political practice. Where Coleridge sees in Burke a desirably potent conjunction of political authority and verbal art, Hazlitt is led by this same perception to conclude that "Reason and imagination are both excellent things; but perhaps these two provinces ought to be kept more distinct than they have lately been" (16: 137).

This is because, when measured against the norm of "history and particular facts," Burke (like Coleridge) is discovered to be "a man of fine fancy and subtle reflection; but not of sound and practical judgement—nor of high or rigid principles" (16: 131–32). The story of his career presents the violent self-alienation of apostasy:

> It is not without reluctance that we speak of the vices and infirmities of such a mind as Burke's: But the poison of high example has by far the widest range of destruction; and, for the sake of public honour and individual integrity, we think it right to say, that however it may be defended upon other grounds, the political career of that eminent individual has no title to the praise of consistency. Mr Burke, the opponent of the American war—and Mr Burke, the opponent of the French Revolution, are not the same person, but opposite persons—not opposite persons only, but deadly enemies. (16: 130)

Burke's "high example," which Coleridge defends "on other grounds," in fact embodies and disseminates self-contradictions that not only vitiate "individual integrity" but come to symbolize—and even foster—the internecine divisions of the British public sphere. To expose these contradictions, Hazlitt once again takes up the role of Thomas Paine, deploying "plain facts and principles" in a style that relies on the simple, cumulative power of the "parallelism."

> In the American war, [Mr. Burke] constantly spoke of the rights of the people as inherent, and inalienable: after the French Revolution, he began by treating them with the chicanery of a sophist, and ended by raving at them with the fury of a maniac. In the former case, he held out the duty of resistance to oppression, as the palladium, and the only ultimate resource, of natural liberty; in the latter, he scouted, prejudged, vilified and nicknamed, all resistance in the abstract, as a foul and unnatural union of rebellion and sacrilege. In the one case, to answer the purposes of faction, he made it out, that the people are always in the right; in the other, to answer different ends, he made it out that they are always in the wrong—lunatics in the hand of their royal keepers, patients in the sick wards of an hospital, or felons in the condemned cells of a prison. . . . In the one, he insulted kings personally, as among the lowest and worst of mankind; in the other, he held them up to the imagination of his readers as sacred abstractions. In the one case, he was a partisan of the

137

people, to court popularity; in the other, to gain the favour of the Court, he became the apologist of all courtly abuses. (16: 130–31)

It is passages like this that explain Hazlitt's inclusion of this "character" in his *Political Essays* of 1819. In a seemingly endless catalogue of reversals (of which only a selection is cited here), Hazlitt is able to encapsulate the history of change during the period narrated by the *Biographia,* and to insist, in this case, on its reincorporation into Coleridge's narrative.

Yet while this catalogue provides, in Hazlitt's view, "ample proofs of inconsistency" in Burke's political career, what remains consistent across these oppositions is Burke's skillful appeal to "the imagination of his readers," and in particular his seminal use of metaphor. This is the phenomenon of Burke's "style," in which "he gives loose reins to his imagination, and follows it as far as the language will carry him." In this way, Burke's "whole theory of government" was constructed "not on rational, but on picturesque and fanciful principles": "Facts or consequences never stood in the way of this speculative politician. He fitted them to his preconceived theories, instead of conforming his theories to them. They were the playthings of his style, the sport of his fancy. They were the straws of which his imagination made a blaze, and were consumed, like straws, in the blaze they had served to kindle" (16: 132–33). Ultimately, then, the sublime power of Burke's "imagination" is the source of his authority: "[H]e always aims at overpowering rather than at pleasing; and consequently sacrifices beauty and grandeur to force and vividness. He invariably has a task to perform, a positive purpose to execute, an effect to produce. His only object therefore is to strike hard, and in the right place" (16: 134). Needless to say, such "literary talents" become "a dangerous engine in the hands of power, which is always eager to make use of the most plausible pretexts to cover the most fatal designs" (16: 132). Indeed, all that stands in the way of this formidable conjunction of literary and political power is what Hazlitt described in a previous review as "the exercise of public opinion," a form of criticism that, for "the sake of public honour and individual integrity," is willing to remain fully consistent with its roots in Enlightenment ideology:

> [I]f we can once get rid of the restraints of common sense and honesty, we may easily prove, by plausible words, that liberty and slavery, peace and war, plenty and famine, are matters of perfect indifference. This is the school of politics of which Mr. Burke was at the head; and it is perhaps to his example in this respect, that we owe the prevailing tone of many of those newspaper paragraphs, that Mr Coleridge thinks so invaluable an accession to our political philosophy. (16: 133)

As we have seen, Hazlitt reads this "indifference" to the lived history of repression and distress in Coleridge's own most recent "paragraphs" in the *Courier* defending the practices of the Laureate. Alongside the narrative of apostasy, then, emerges another, less obvious, and therefore more insidious narrative:

the continuous, and seemingly inevitable co-optation of "imagination" by the forces of oppression.

Even by the late summer of 1817, there was no more notorious instance of such co-optation than the author of *Wat Tyler,* the laureate odes, and the leading essays of the *Quarterly Review.* For this reason, Coleridge's defense of Southey's moral integrity in chapter 3 of the *Biographia* stands out with the same symbolic prominence as his tribute to Burke—a prominence, however, which has remained invisible to later critics who have disregarded its defining context in public debate. Coleridge himself, when he wrote this passage on Southey in 1815, could not have imagined the profile it would assume when delivered into the political arena of 1817, yet it is similar enough to his anonymous essays in the *Courier* to constitute a public restatement of those views. Certainly this is the way Hazlitt reads this chapter, treating it like the passage on Burke as a displaced statement of Coleridge's own political loyalties. Once again Hazlitt seizes on elements of rhetorical excess and strategic indirection in Coleridge's praise of the Laureate, in this case his uncomfortably fulsome encomium of Southey's "personal, domestic, and literary habits."

> Some people say, that Mr. Southey has deserted the cause of liberty: Mr. Cole-ridge tells us, that he has not separated from his wife. They say, that he has changed his opinions: Mr. Coleridge says, that he keeps his appointments; and has even invented a new word, *reliability,* to express his exemplariness in this particular. It is also objected, that the worthy Laureate was as extravagant in his early writings, as he is virulent in his present ones: Mr. Coleridge answers, that he is an early riser, and not a late sitter up. It is further alleged, that he is arrogant and shallow in political discussion, and clamours for vengeance in a cowardly and intemperate tone: Mr. Coleridge assures us, that he eats, drinks, and sleeps moderately. It is said that he must either have been very hasty in taking up his first opinions, or very unjustifiable in abandoning them for their contraries; and Mr. Coleridge observes, that Mr. Southey exhibits, in his own person and family, all the regularity and praiseworthy punctuality of an eight-day clock. (16: 118, 120–21)

With this witty accumulation of displacements, all quite faithful to Coleridge's text, Hazlitt reiterates the narrative of Southey's apostasy within the public sphere that is avoided by Coleridge's celebration of his consistency within the private sphere. At the same time, Hazlitt's strict concentration on matters of public concern works to ironize Coleridge's own practice, exposing his turn to private "character" as merely the tendentious inversion of the "personal enmity" with which he charges "anonymous criticism" in the *Biographia* (7.2: 239).

This strategy is reinforced in Hazlitt's treatment of the long, strangely revealing footnote attached to the encomium of Southey. In this note Coleridge frankly admits to a "debt of justice" that has "impelled" him to eulogize his friend, and he proceeds to offer, as a "specimen" of the unjust allegations of anonymous criticism, a slanderous remark from the *Beauties of the Anti-jacobin* written in the 1790s, in which Coleridge himself was said to have "*left his poor children fatherless, and his wife destitute. Ex his disce his friends, Lamb and Southey*" (16: 119; italics in original [7.1: 67n]). Other critics, notably *Blackwood's Magazine* and Coleridge's later biographers, have read in this footnote the submerged pressure of Coleridge's private "debt" to Southey for taking in his abandoned family. Hazlitt, however, decorously confines himself to exposing another narrative of much greater import to the "Reading Public." After searching through all the years for an appropriately damaging "specimen" of anonymous criticism, Coleridge chooses one that serves only to highlight the disreputable practices of the *government*-sponsored press, and in particular the very editors for whom Southey now writes in the *Quarterly Review.* Aware himself of this difficulty, Coleridge is forced to conclude with the awkward query, "Is it surprising that many good men remained longer than they perhaps otherwise would have done, adverse to a party which encouraged and openly rewarded the authors of such atrocious calumnies?" (7.1: 67n). Hazlitt retorts:

> With us, we confess the wonder does not lie there:—all that surprises us is, that the objects of these atrocious calumnies were *ever* reconciled to the authors of them;—for the calumniators were the party itself. The Cannings, the Giffords, the Freres, have never made any apology for the abuse which they then heaped upon every nominal friend of freedom; and yet Mr. Coleridge thinks it necessary to apologize in the name of all good men, for having remained so long adverse to a party which recruited upon such a bounty; and seems not obscurely to intimate that they had such effectual means of propagating their slanders against those good men who differed with them, that most of the latter found there was no other way of keeping their good name but by giving up their principles, and joining in the same venal cry against all those who did not become apostates or converts, ministerial Editors, and "laurel-honouring Laureates" like themselves! (16: 119)

Thus the art of Coleridge's "Apology" is firmly linked once again to the narrative of apostasy, vitiating all claims to steadfastness of "principle." At the same time, the practice of "personal enmity behind the mask of anonymous criticism" is identified with the policies of the ruling party whose cultural authority is entirely a function of its unprincipled powers of coercion.

Yet Hazlitt's own subtle compromises with the pressure of editorial politics are evident when he turns from Burke and Southey to consider the political career of Coleridge himself. Here once again Hazlitt must conform to the *Edinburgh*'s view of Coleridge as politically inconsequential, turning down the ample opportunity offered by the *Biographia* to press home the charge of apostasy. Instead he relies on strategies of implication and indirection ironically comparable to Coleridge's own. Southey, for example, is said to have "chimed in" with Coleridge "both in poetry and politics, in verse and prose, in Jacobinism and Antijacobinism, any time these twenty years" (16: 121); Coleridge is said (in a footnote) to be "out of the Pantisocratic or Lake school" (16: 128n 1); and he is called a "disappointed demagogue" at the end of the review (16: 138). But when the story of Coleridge's politically nonconformist newspaper the *Watchman* is quoted at length, and when at the end of this account Coleridge boldly challenges his dissenting friends from the 1790s to "bear witness for [him], how opposite, even then, [his] principles were to those of Jacobinism, or even Democracy," Hazlitt visibly retreats from a full rebuttal:

> We shall not stop at present to dispute with Mr. Coleridge, how far the principles of the *Watchman,* and the *Conciones ad Populam* were or were not akin to those of the Jacobins. His style, in general, admits of a convenient latitude of interpretation. But we think we are quite safe in asserting, that they were still more opposite to those of the Anti-Jacobins, and the party to which he admits he has gone over. (16: 129)

One wonders how such a passage might have been taken up in the *Examiner* on behalf of such "readers" as "SEMPER EGO AUDITOR." Writing for the *Edinburgh,* however, Hazlitt allows Coleridge a "convenient latitude of interpretation" in spite of Coleridge's own unique movement from ardent pantisocrat to Tory apologist. As when *The Statesman's Manual* was said by the *Edinburgh* to have "no leaning any way," the *Biographia* is here allowed only a marginally less ambivalent "leaning to the side of power" by comparison with such high profile representatives of "the party itself" as Burke and Southey.

Even at the very conclusion of the review, where the political entanglements of the *Biographia* are vigorously reiterated, Coleridge himself is subsumed within a larger category of writers called "our reformed Antijacobin poets," a category more closely modeled on the practices of the Laureate than on the author of *Christabel.* Moreover, to denounce such poets with appropriate finality, Hazlitt must appear to renounce any residual belief in the "sincerity" of poetry, and thus any belief in the possibility of a positive conjunction of literary and political practice. Where he was able to claim in *The Examiner* that "poets are naturally Jacobins," he now concludes his review of Coleridge on behalf of the *Edinburgh* with the following observation, "of a very plain and practical nature, . . . forced upon us by the whole tenor of the extraordinary history before us."

> —Reason and imagination are both excellent things; but perhaps their provinces ought to be kept more distinct than they have lately been. . . . We would not, with Plato, absolutely banish poets from the commonwealth; but we really think they should meddle as little with its practical administration as may be. They live in an ideal world of their own; and it would be, perhaps, as well if they were confined to it. Their flights and fancies are delightful to themselves and to everybody else; but they make strange work with matters

of fact; and, if they were allowed to act in public affairs, would soon turn the world upside down. (16: 137)

With self-conscious irony indicated by his use of Coleridge's own phraseology from the *Courier* ("they live in an ideal world of their own"), Hazlitt arrives at the same conclusion as was there "forced" upon the Laureate's apologist—but for precisely the opposite reasons. Where Coleridge had to argue for the political innocence of *Wat Tyler,* Hazlitt is arguing here for the ideological complicity of poets who claim to "live in an ideal world of their own," but who follow the "high example" of Burke in allowing their "flights and fancies" to "make strange work with matters of fact."[4]

To enforce this point, Hazlitt recapitulates "the true history of our reformed Antijacobin poets" in a fierce, final burst of invective. "As romantic in their servility as in their independence," he asserts, such poets "require only to be distinguished, and are not scrupulous as to the means of distinction" (16: 137). In generating the necessary intensity of style to refute such "romantic[s]" conclusively, however, Hazlitt is led into a telling relativization of the claims of "the people," shaped at once by the gentrified politics of the *Edinburgh* and by the all-pervasive influence of Burke himself. Following the rhetorical logic of self-contradictory extremes, the apostate poets are now said to "oscillate . . . from one absurdity to another": whether as "Jacobins or Antijacobins—outrageous advocates for anarchy and licentiousness, or flaming apostles of persecution—[they] expiate the follies of their youth by the heartless vices of their advancing age" (16: 137). Thus from the putative political neutrality of the *Edinburgh,* each phase in the career of such writers is now regarded as equally absurd, meaning that the ideals of Radicalism are transformed for stylistic effect into "anarchy and licentiousness" and "the follies of . . . youth." Moreover, having kindled this blaze of invective, Hazlitt's final caricature of such "follies" ironically bears the imprint of Burke himself in its recourse to the metaphor of "poisons."

> In their days of innovation, indeed, the philosophers crept at their heels like hounds, while they darted on their distant quarry like hawks; stooping always to the lowest game; eagerly snuffing up the most tainted and rankest scents; feeding their vanity with the notion of the strength of their digestion of poisons, and most ostentatiously avowing what ever would most effectually startle the prejudices of others. Preposterously seeking for the stimulus of novelty in truth, and the eclat of theatrical exhibition in pure reason, it is no wonder that these persons at last became disgusted with their own pursuits, and that, in consequence of the violence of the change, the most inveterate prejudices and uncharitable sentiments have rushed in to fill up the *vacuum* produced by the previous annihilation of common sense, wisdom, and humanity. (16: 137–38)

Like the "middle ground" staked out by the *Examiner,* the "common sense, wisdom, and humanity" that guarantees the political authority of the *Edin-*

burgh comes in the end to identify itself with a middle position between the "poisons" of Radicalism and the "inveterate prejudices" of reaction, a position measurably distinct from that of Hazlitt's other "political essays" of the period.[5] In this difference is concealed the subtler "apostasy" of anonymity. In order to achieve the necessary cultural authority decisively to contest Coleridge's political allegiances, Hazlitt must temporarily "stand away" from his own "good name," colluding with the inevitably partisan ideological allegiances of high-level corporate journalism.

Perhaps in no other article of the *Edinburgh Review* are the issues of anonymity and editorial presence more vividly foregrounded than in this review of the *Biographia Literaria.* Jeffrey's ceremonial doffing of the "mask of anonymity" in the footnote that dominates the center of the review is virtually unprecedented in the periodical writing of the time. It demonstrates, among other things, that if the *Edinburgh* refused Coleridge any authority within the political arena, it took his views on the authority of anonymous criticism within the literary marketplace very seriously indeed. Though Jeffrey's footnote is designed in part to demystify the practice of anonymity, it nevertheless emerges from a point in the text where the plural "we" covers a complex interchange of critical voices, in the transition from Hazlitt's analysis of Burke (later claimed under his own name among his *Political Essays*) to the matter of Jeffrey's "former remarks" on Wordsworth:

> Mr. C. enters next into a copious discussion of the merits of his friend Mr. Wordsworth's poetry,—which we do not think very remarkable either for clearness or candour; but as a great part of it is occupied with specific in-culpations of our former remarks on that ingenious author, it would savour too much of mere controversy or recrimination, if we were to indulge ourselves with any observations on the subject. Where we are parties to any dispute, and consequently to be regarded as incapable of giving an *impartial* account of our adversary's argument, we shall not pretend to give any account of it at all;* and therefore, . . . [we] shall pass over all this part of the work before us, by merely remarking . . . [etc.]. (16: 134)

Readers of the *Edinburgh* would already be quite aware by the sign of style that Jeffrey was not the principal reviewer of the *Biographia,* yet he has clearly taken over the critical voice in this passage, throwing into instructive uncertainty for later scholars the exact point at which Hazlitt's "own" views reemerge in the discussion of poetic diction that follows. Even the opening gestures of Jeffrey's footnote continue to conflate the identities of editor and essayist in the collective terms "Review" and "Reviewer."

> *If Mr. C. had confined himself to matters of argument, or to statements contained in the Review, we should have added no note to this passage, but left him in quiet possession of the last word on the critical question he has thought fit to resume. But as he has been pleased to make several averments in points of fact, touching the personal conduct and motives of his Reviewer,

we must be indulged with a few words to correct the errors into which he has fallen. (Reiman A: 492; Jackson 314)

Thus the anonymous "Review" reasserts its integrity, equating its criticism with that which is public and available, in contrast once again with Coleridge's inappropriate recourse to the "personal." To emphasize this point, Jeffrey begins in the third person, itemizing in the form of an impersonal affidavit each one of the "averments in points of fact" made in the *Biographia* regarding "the principal conductor of this Review"—including, of course, those made in chapter 24 about the "employer and suborner" of the critics of *Christabel* and *The Statesman's Manual* (Reiman A: 492; Jackson 315).

Responding to this most serious affront, Jeffrey drops the mask of anonymity in a unique and unusual interchange of third- and first-person identities: "These are the charges against the principal conductor of this Review; to which, in order to avoid all equivocation, that individual begs leave to answer distinctly, and in the first person, as follows. I do not know that I need say anything in answer to the *first* imputation . . . [etc.]" (Reiman A: 492, 315). The "answer" that follows, like Southey's *Letter* and even the *Biographia* itself, appeals earnestly to the jury of public opinion, yet Jeffrey's legal training equips him to manage this genre of apologia in the manner of a defense attorney, skillfully subordinating what is necessarily "painful" in a display of outraged moral sensibilities to the stark evidence of "history and particular facts." This approach is epitomized in his concluding remarks on *The Statesman's Manual.*

> As to the review of the Lay Sermon, I have only to say, in one word, that I never employed or suborned any body to abuse or extol it or any other publication. I do not so much as know or conjecture what Mr C. alludes to as a malignant lampoon or review by anticipation, which he says had previously appeared somewhere else. I never saw nor heard of such a publication.[6] Nay, I was not even aware of the existence of the Lay Sermon itself, when a review of it was offered me by a gentleman in whose judgment and talents I had great confidence, but whom I certainly never suspected, and do not suspect at this moment, of having any personal or partial feelings of any kind towards its author. I therefore accepted his offer, and printed his review, with some retrenchments and verbal alterations, just as I was setting off, in a great hurry, for London, on professional business, in January last.
>
> It is painful, and perhaps ridiculous, to write so much about one's self; but I would rather submit to this ridicule than to the imputations which Mr C. has permitted himself to make on me—or even the consciousness of having made these rash and injurious imputations.
>
> F. J. (Reiman A: 494; Jackson 318)

The authority of the role thus constructed by such a defense is precisely the opposite of that sought by the "Romantic" poet within the literary marketplace. Jeffrey presents himself as a brisk and efficient man of "professional business" for whom the convention of anonymity, far from being a mask for the "personal or partial," is instead the sign of a decorous subordination of "one's self" to more important public tasks and interests, a turning away from the "painful, and perhaps ridiculous" concentration on one's own "Life and Opinions" to accommodate the greater demands of *public* opinion.

To meet such demands, of course, Jeffrey must rely on the "judgment and talents" of such writers as Hazlitt, who "at this moment" is conducting, in the main body of the review, the *Edinburgh*'s response to the less "rash and injurious" aspects of Coleridge's "philosophical criticism." Hazlitt's own philosophical training, if not his experience as a writer of "Literary Notices," makes him particularly well suited to contest Coleridge's authority within the literary marketplace. He is able, for example, to present specific objections to Coleridge's views on the history of rationalist philosophy, before mounting a distinctly Humean riposte to modern German metaphysics. In Hazlitt's view, it is Hobbes not Descartes who lies behind what he calls "the modern system of philosophy."

> That Hobbes was in fact the original inventor of the doctrine of Association, and of the modern system of philosophy in general, is a matter of fact and history; as to which, we are surprised that Mr C. should profess any doubt, and which we had gratified ourselves by illustrating by a series of citations from his greater works,—which nothing but a sense of the prevailing indifference to such discussions prevents us from laying before our readers. (16: 123)

The norm of "fact and history" is reinvoked to govern philosophical as well as political debate, though we note in this instance it is quickly subordinated to the more powerful norm of public taste and interest. Yet even "prevailing indifference" to a discussion of British empiricism does not prevent Hazlitt from devoting a full page of the review to a brusque summary of German idealism, which he describes as "absurdities that have not even the merit of being amusing" (16: 124). This critique of Kant is significant, however, both as a register of contemporary British opinion, and as a fair "prototype," to borrow Bate's words, "of most of the adverse criticism of [Kant] from Coleridge's time to our own" (introduction, *Biographia* lxvi). Not surprisingly, it is Hume's skepticism that undergirds Hazlitt's analysis.

> If [Kant] cannot make good an inference upon acknowledged premises, or known methods of reasoning, he coolly refers the whole to a new class of ideas, and the operation of some unknown faculty, which he has invented for the purpose, and which he assures you *must* exist,—because there is no other proof of it. . . . For example, he sets out with urging the indispensable necessity of answering Hume's argument on the origin of our ideas of cause and effect; and because he can find no answer to this argument, in the experimental philosophy, he affirms, that this idea *must be* "a self-evident truth, contained in the first forms or categories of the understanding;" that is, the thing must be as he would have it, whether it is so or not. (16: 123–24)

Hazlitt, of course, has his eye in this passage on Coleridge's own (re)invention of the "imagination" as a mental faculty fundamentally distinct from the "fancy." Like Kant vis-à-vis Hume on the idea of cause and effect, Coleridge overcomes the strict rationalist limitations of associationism by redefining the "IMAGINATION" as a faculty that partakes of the "infinite" and the "*vital*"— "the living Power and prime Agent of all human Perception"—while reducing the "fancy" to a mere "mode of Memory" with "no other counters to play with but fixities and definites" that "*as* objects, are essentially fixed and dead" (7.1: 304–5).

Yet, unlike the majority of literary critics since, Hazlitt does not treat Coleridge's distinction between fancy and imagination in any detail—after all, he notes wryly, "Mr C. has suppressed his Disquisition on the Imagination as unintelligible" (16: 138).[7] Instead he is concerned with the sort of cultural authority to which Coleridge aspires in making such a distinction, especially evident in his anxiety to establish clear proprietary rights to it. Like Kant's insistence that "the thing must be as he would have it, whether it is so or not," Coleridge's claim to originality in defining the imagination serves only to foreground the inherent arbitrariness of such a definition. Hazlitt nicknames Kant "the German oracle," and similarly Coleridge is seen to supplement the role of poet-prophet with a desire for definitive intellectual authority. The result is Hazlitt's most memorable depiction of the *Biographia*.

> With chap. IV. begins the formidable ascent of the mountainous and barren ridge of clouds piled on precipices and precipices on clouds, from the top of which the author deludes us with a view of the Promised Land that divides the regions of Fancy from those of the Imagination, and extends through 200 pages with various inequalities and declensions to the end of the volume. The object of this long-winding metaphysical march, which resembles a patriarchal journey, is to point out and settle the true grounds of Mr Wordsworth's claim to originality as a poet; which, if we rightly understand the deduction, turns out to be, that there is nothing peculiar about him; and that his poetry, in so far as it is good for anything at all, is just like any other good poetry. (16: 121–22)

Even the most sympathetic reader of the *Biographia* will recognize the wit—and the uncanny accuracy—of this image of Coleridge as the latter-day patriarch of the "Promised Land" of Romanticism. In a superb balance of the sublime and the bathetic, of frank admiration for the grandeur of Coleridge's design and harsh insight into the delusion of its fulfillment, Hazlitt deconstructs the "grounding" of literary criticism in transcendental philosophy as at once illusory and unnecessary.

By contrast, what Hazlitt and the *Edinburgh* offer instead is designed to be both practical and historical. Far from the inaccessible and uncertain heights of Coleridge's "philosophical criticism," the *Edinburgh* grounds the authority of its anonymous criticism in observations on the literary practices of the most widely read British poets, principally Milton and Shakespeare. Here again Hazlitt was well-equipped as a critic to answer the challenge presented by the *Biographia:* having just published *Characters of Shakespeare's Plays,* he was now preparing a public lecture series on the English poets.[8] He invokes Milton to authorize an epigrammatic counter-definition of "the essence of poetry," and in the variations on the theme that follow we overhear Hazlitt rehearsing the first of his lectures, now widely disseminated under the title "On Poetry in General."

> Mr Coleridge bewilders himself sadly in endeavouring to determine in what the essence of poetry consists;—Milton, we think, has told it in a single line—
> ——"Thoughts that voluntary move
> Harmonious numbers."

> Poetry is the music of language, expressing the music of the mind. Whenever any object takes such a hold on the mind as to make us dwell upon it, and brood over it, melting the heart in love, or kindling it to a sentiment of admiration;—whenever a movement of imagination or passion is impressed on the mind, by which it seeks to prolong and repeat the emotion, to bring all other objects into accord with it, and to give the same movement of harmony, sustained and continuous, to the sounds that express it,—this is poetry. The musical in sound is the sustained and continuous; the musical in thought and feeling is the sustained and continuous also. Whenever articulation passes naturally into intonation, this is the beginning of poetry. There is no natural harmony in the ordinary combinations of significant sounds: the language of prose is not the language of music, or of *passion:* and it is to supply this inherent defect in the mechanism of language—to make the sound an echo to the sense, when the sense becomes a sort of echo to itself—to mingle the tide of verse, "the golden cadences of poesy," with the tide of feeling, flowing, and murmuring as it flows—or to take the imagination off its feet, and spread its wings where it may indulge its own impulses, without being stopped or perplexed by the ordinary abruptnesses, or discordant flats and sharps of prose—that poetry was invented. (16: 136; see also 5: 11–12)

Where Coleridge asks "What is poetry?" and then recurs to a discourse of abstract "faculties" in the mind of "poetic genius," Hazlitt uses Milton's metaphor of music to devise an answer ultimately rooted in both sensory experience and the materiality of the poetic signifier. Indeed, cutting across the distinction between poetry and prose here is the "music" of Hazlitt's own phrasing, with its rhythmic patterns of repetition and alliteration, and the contrasting onomatopoeic effects of "murmuring" and "discordant flats and sharps." Yet according to the logic of the review as a whole, it is only poetry and not prose that was invented "to take the imagination off its feet, and spread its wings where it may indulge its own impulses." We saw how Burke "gives loose reigns to his imagination, and follows it as far as the

147

language will carry him," but this led to Hazlitt's urgent call for a new distinction between "Reason and imagination." In this definition of poetry, by contrast, "Reason and imagination" may safely part ways in a politically neutral distinction between the representational and nonrepresentational arts, between the rational and the affective.

Yet the lingering political inflection of the *Edinburgh*'s literary criticism is evident in the related discussion of "poetic diction." Here, in response to what Coleridge calls the "long continued controversy concerning the true nature of poetic diction" (7.1: 5), and despite Jeffrey's decorous vow to abstain from any notice of the poet whose writings were at the center of this controversy, the *Edinburgh* indulges in some parting remarks on "Mr Wordsworth's ingenious project of confining the language of poetry to that which is chiefly in use among the lower orders of society" (16: 134–35). With the claim that "the truth and common sense of the thing [is] so obvious, and, we apprehend, so generally acknowledged, that nothing but a pitiful affectation of singularity could have raised a controversy on the subject," the *Edinburgh* proceeds to sketch a simple triadic hierarchy of poetic "styles" clearly based on the metaphor of class (16: 135).[9] At one extreme is a poetry "made up of "*slang* phrases"—"words associated only with mean and vulgar ideas"—that corresponds to Wordsworth's ill-advised championing of the "language" of "the lower orders." At the other extreme lies what Wordsworth stigmatized as "*poetic diction*," but which is here described as the "ornamented or coloured style" that is "connected only with the most pleasing and elegant associations," and "made up of words . . . warmed by the glow of genius, purified by the breath of time, . . . that varnish *over* the trite and commonplace, and lend a gorgeous robe to the forms of fancy" (16: 135–36; emphasis added). Most tellingly, however, both of these styles—the "vulgar" and the "elegant"— are in turn said to "differ essentially from the *middle or natural style,* which is a mere transparent medium of the thoughts, neither degrading nor setting them off by any adventitious qualities of its own, but leaving them to make their own impression, by the force of truth and nature" (16: 135; emphasis added). The discourse of the "middle," then, fulfils the Enlightenment ideal of clear linguistic transparency, and thus accedes to the cultural authority associated with "the force of truth and nature." While this "middle" style may be compared to the position taken up by the *Edinburgh* between the "poisons" of Radicalism and the "inveterate prejudices" of reaction, it is nevertheless marked by an attractive inclusiveness. This is "a simple and familiar language, common to almost all ranks, and intelligible through many ages"; and because it is "best fitted for the direct expression of strong sense and deep passion," it is "consequently . . . the language of the best poetry as well as of the best prose" (16: 135). Unlike "*poetic diction*," then, which is an exclusively poetic style and which thus "has to lend a borrowed, and, in some sort, meretricious lustre to outward objects," the "common or natural style is the truly dramatic style, that in which [the writer] can best give the impassioned, unborrowed, unaffected thoughts of others" (16: 135). Not surprisingly, the exemplar of this style is Shakespeare, whose "dialogues of Othello and Lear furnish the most striking instances of plain, point-blank speaking, or of the real language of nature and of passion" (16: 135).

This *"middle, or natural style,"* in short, is the discourse of such middle-class men of letters as Hazlitt, Jeffrey, Wordsworth and Coleridge, and the example of Shakespeare provides not only a fixed point of reference in British literary history, but also a potential locus of consensus across many lines of political and literary dispute. Another locus of consensus is evident in the *Edinburgh*'s unexpectedly positive evaluation of certain aspects of Coleridge's prose style in the *Biographia,* an evaluation linked to the ascendency of (auto)biographical narrative in the literary marketplace. Here we find the norm of "history and particular facts" provides a point of stylistic and generic convergence for both anonymous critic and garrulous author. The same market demand that makes "some things readable" in Coleridge's *Biographia* encourages Hazlitt to ensure, through generous quotation, that "there are some things readable" in his own review as well (16: 115). He certainly wastes no time in this regard. The opening paragraph of the review leads directly into one of the two longest quotations of the entire article with this remark: "There are, in fact, only two or three passages in the work which relate to the details of the author's life, such as the account of his school-education, and of his setting up the *Watchman* newspaper. We shall make sure of the first of these curious documents, before we completely lose ourselves in the multiplicity of his speculative opinions" (16: 115). To "make sure" is a telling phrase in this context. Contrasted with "lose ourselves," it aligns the "curious" appeal of autobiography—the "details of the author's life"—with the discourse of "history and particular facts." By moving quickly into a long passage in the voice of Coleridge's autobiographical persona, Hazlitt can "make sure" of the reader's interest in his own review, appealing at once to the demand for the factual and the aesthetically entertaining. This in turn points to a deeper practicality in Hazlitt's use of such quotations. By remaining anonymous, he himself is not free to indulge in anecdote; his commitment to the plural "we" constrains him to rely on Coleridge to bring personal presence to his text. In a curious chiasmus, Coleridge is enfolded in the communal "we," while his speaking "I" is employed to narrate the story of many: the history of a generation and a class during the revolutionary period.

This subtlety, of course, remains entirely implicit, not unlike Hazlitt's quotation of the "friends in youth" passage in his *Examiner* review of *Christabel.* Moreover, this account of Coleridge's school days is invaded, as we have seen, by the italicization of Coleridge's self-mocking attachment "*at a very premature age*" to "*metaphysicks,*" laying the ground in the comments that follow for the operative distinction between Coleridge's "philosophical faith" and the sane touchstone of "history and particular facts." Yet running counter to this argument, the sheer length of Hazlitt's quotation allows Coleridge the

149

opportunity to seek his own readership by demonstrating his own subscription to proto-positivist discourse. For example, the long tale of the headmaster of Christ's Hospital is told to credit that venerable tyrant with having inculcated principles of literary criticism based on "grounds of plain sense, and universal logic" (Howe 16: 115; Coburn 7.1: 9). Rev. Bowyer taught that "Poetry, even that of the loftiest, and, seemingly, that of the wildest odes, had a logic of its own as strict as that of science" (16: 115–16; 7.1: 9). Further, Coleridge himself mocks his own metaphysics as a "mental disease" and lampoons his interest in it as a bathetic "delving in the unwholesome quicksilver mines of metaphysic depths" (16: 117; 7.1: 17).

Coleridge is thus granted a persona new to the *Edinburgh*'s criticism of him, the table-talker of genial good sense, deploying what he calls elsewhere in the *Biographia* the trope of *"risu honesto,"* or the "honest laughter" of emblematic caricature (7.1: 26), here invoked with either foolish or decorous good nature at his own expense. This, for example, is the master-trope of the account of "setting up the *Watchman* newspaper," the subject of Hazlitt's other lengthy quotation. This passage is offered to his readers as a kind of respite after the thankless task of demolishing Kantian metaphysics. Thus, as a gesture of good will, he explains that

> Out of regard for Mr C. as well as our readers, we give our longest extract from this narrative part of the work—which is more likely to be popular than any other part—and is, on the whole, more pleasingly written. We cannot say much, indeed, for either the wit or the soundness of judgment it displays. But it is an easy, gossiping, garrulous account of youthful adventures—by a man sufficiently fond of talking of himself, and sufficiently disposed to magnify small matters into ideal importance. (16: 125)

While Coleridge is ritually censured for the (by now) familiar improprieties of unsound judgment, clumsy wit, egotism, and distorted perception, this very context of judgment throws into relief Hazlitt's contrasting approbation of his achievement as an autobiographer. Particularly noteworthy is the description here of the stylistic elements that go into "popular" biographical narrative. This is the *"middle, or natural style,"* governed on the one hand by the norm of "history and particular facts," and on the other by a growing demand, in the aftermath of "distress," for the "pleasing." The result is "an easy, gossiping, garrulous account of youthful adventures," a standard of social discourse in which can be glimpsed a language of possible consensus, a *"conversational"* style (as Hazlitt was later to describe it) that may transcend the partisan conflicts of the middle class (8: 333).

The class inflection of this discourse is more than evident in one of the "youthful adventures" related by Coleridge and quoted—without comment or interjection—by Hazlitt. This is the story of the "the tallow-chandler," in which the trope of *"risu honesto"* is produced not only by Coleridge's own self-caricature but by a structure of contrasts between the highly literate and loquacious author and his minimally educated interlocutor. Full of "youthful" idealism, Coleridge canvasses the industrial Midlands in search of subscribers to his newspaper, and is introduced to a prospective reader.

> I commenced an harangue of half an hour to Phileleutheros the tallow-chandler, varying my notes through the whole gamut of eloquence, from the ratiocinative to the declamatory, and in the latter, from the pathetic to the indignant. I argued, I described, I promised, I prophesied; and, beginning with the captivity of nations, I ended with the near approach of the millennium; finishing the whole with some of my own verses, describing that glorious state, out of the *Religious Musings.*
> —"Such delights,
> As float to earth, permitted visitants!
> When in some hour of solemn jubilee
> The massive gates of Paradise are thrown
> Wide open: and forth come in fragments wild
> Sweet echoes of unearthly melodies,
> And odours snatch'd from beds of amaranth,
> And they that from the crystal river of life
> Spring up on freshen'd wings, ambrosial gales!"
> (Howe 16: 126–27; Coburn 7.1: 181)

In this, of course, we overhear once again the lyric preacher of "Truth and Genius" described by "SEMPER EGO AUDITOR" in the pulpit at Shrewsbury. Yet where "AUDITOR" aimed to lay bare the bitter narrative of apostasy for the *Examiner,* this quotation of Coleridge's own self-mocking reminiscence suggests such a narrative only by the most indirect implication. Presented without commentary in the pages of the *Edinburgh,* it serves instead as a source of amusement for *all* men of letters who are willing to stand away momentarily from the repressed knowledge that education has made it possible to produce rhetoric at will—rhetoric whose Burkean hyperbole is the sign of its possible disjunction from any "rational" referent.

Coleridge's self-caricature is counterbalanced by a grotesque cartoon of the tallow chandler that evokes the stark otherness of the laboring and artisan classes.

> He was a tall, dingy man, in whom length was so predominant over breadth, that he might almost have been borrowed for a foundry poker. O that face! . . . I have it before me at this moment. The lank, black, twine-like hair, *pingui-nitescent,* cut in a straight line along the black stubble of his thin gunpow-der eyebrows, that looked like a scorched *after-math* from a last week's shaving . . . while the countenance, lank, dark, very *hard,* and with strong perpendicular furrows, gave me a dim notion of some one looking at me through a *used* gridiron, all soot, grease, and iron! (16: 126; 7.1: 180–81)

This grim product of industrialization is given a dialect and preoccupations meant to contrast with those of the eloquent author.

And what, Sir! (he said, after a short pause) might the cost be? *Only* four-pence, (O! how I felt the anti-climax, the abysmal bathos of that *four-pence!*) *only four-pence, Sir, each Number, to be published on every eighth day.* That comes to a deal of money at the end of a year. And how much did you say there was to be for the money? *Thirty-two pages, Sir! large octavo, closely printed.* Thirty and two pages? Bless me; why, except what I does in a family way on the Sabbath, that's more than I ever read, Sir! all the year round. I am as great a one as any man in Brummagem, Sir! for liberty, and truth, and all them sort of things; but as to this, (no offence, I hope, Sir!) I must beg to be excused. (16: 127; 7.1: 181–82)

At this all middle-class writers for the reading public close ranks and laugh, for here is a man bluntly impervious to all eloquence but that of "Brummagem" demagogues and the Bible. Here too the autobiographer has condescended to approach the very outer borders of the domain of public discourse, a domain which gentlemen of all political stripes, however violently they may contest it, hold nevertheless in common. Perhaps Hazlitt includes this sketch because it is the "true history" of Coleridge at his political best, in eloquent negotiation with the social "other"—in this case a Dissenting "Phileleutheros" (or lover of freedom). Moreover, this is the closest that Coleridge's autobiography can come to Hazlitt's own, as well as to that of all those liberal readers of the *Edinburgh* ever touched by the "youthful adventures" associated with revolution.

Yet as long as the shadow of the Distresses lay over public discourse, the difference between Coleridge's aims in telling this story and the *Edinburgh*'s aims in reprinting it would remain in evidence. Coleridge seeks to distance himself and his readers with laughter from the utter futility of mingling idealism with any attempt to have "*direct* influence on the actions of men" (3.2: 470). The *Edinburgh,* by contrast, aims to consolidate a middle-class readership by catering to a new taste for the art of nostalgia, while at the same time nullifying the authority of Coleridge's opinions in politics, philosophy, and literature, and even naming him in the final paragraph of the review, with reference to this passage, a "disappointed demagogue."

Notwithstanding this aim, however, the moment of middle-class consensus that opens up briefly in the quotation of these passages looks forward to a decade of bourgeois prosperity in which the painful narratives of apology and apostasy are seemingly transcended by an aestheticization of history and memory: of lived "history" and personal "facts" packaged in an "easy, gossipping, garrulous" style.

7

BRUTUS'S LOVE TO CAESAR:

Hazlitt's Writings
on Coleridge, 1818–1819

Hazlitt was to characterize the 1820s as "an age of talkers, and not of doers" (11: 28), and something of this ultimate triumph of conversation over activism is foreshadowed in the popularity of public lectures in 1818—a year of "declining alarm" between the crisis of 1816–17 and the year of Peterloo (Evans 21). Unlike the 1820s, however, political tensions in 1818 were merely abated, not crushed, a temporary quiescence produced by the suspension of Habeas Corpus and a good crop year. The fact, then, that both Hazlitt and Coleridge turned simultaneously to public lecturing in the early months of 1818—and for several weeks held forth on the very same nights—is a coincidence explained in part by larger cultural trends, even as it presents a striking extension of their contest for cultural authority into an alternate (and only partially depoliticized) medium. Not surprisingly, this turn to lecturing has been traditionally regarded as a (welcome) retreat on the part of these two critics from the maelstrom of partisan politics to "the serenity of the lecture desk" and to talk of pure literature (Baker 252). Yet Hazlitt's last review of Coleridge during the Regency—a rarely noticed article on "Mr. Coleridge's Lectures" in John Hunt's political weekly the *Yellow Dwarf*—clearly proves otherwise. This review, in turn, sets the tone for the remarks on Coleridge that conclude Hazlitt's own lecture series "on the English Poets" several weeks later. And with the return of "alarm" in 1819, Hazlitt would go back to his reviews of Coleridge during the crisis of 1816–17, retitle many of them

Political Essays, and republish them under his own name at the climax of postwar distress.

Although Hazlitt's last review of Coleridge does not appear in *Political Essays,* it serves (like those that do) to disturb a received impression of transcendence—in this case, that Coleridge's and Hazlitt's 1818 lectures rise above the historical relativity of Regency politics to offer enduring statements about "the nature of poetry itself." One evident source of this tradition is the fact that Coleridge's lecture series on "The Principles of Judgement, Culture, and European Literature" was presented at an institution (the London Philosophical Society) that pointedly disallowed any topics relating to "Theology and Politics" (5.2: 25). Similarly, though Hazlitt was under no such constraint at the Surrey Institution, his biographers describe his turn to lecturing in 1818 as an attempt to launch "a new career" as a literary critic, leaving behind the uncertainties of freelance journalism to capitalize on the success of *Characters of Shakespeare's Plays* (now reaching a second edition). This version of events, however, overlooks a parallel and equally important project: Hazlitt's "brief but fruitful collaboration" with John Hunt in producing the new weekly political journal, the *Yellow Dwarf* (Greenberg 434). It is a fact rarely noticed that in the same five months that Hazlitt was delivering, redelivering, and then publishing his famous *Lectures on the English Poets,* he had become "the leading spirit" of the *Yellow Dwarf,* taking on the role of "its most frequent and expansive contributor" (Greenberg 437). Several of the energetic articles he prepared for this paper would eventually appear as *Political Essays,* including such classics of political prose as "On Court Influence," "On the Clerical Character," and, most famously, "What is the People?" Far from turning away from interventionist journalism, then, Hazlitt in fact embarks on a double career in 1818 as both a "talker" and a "doer," balancing "the serenity of the lecture-desk" with the agency of the press to give his "political force . . . a new medium of appeal" (Blunden 146).

Most important for our purposes, it was from within this new medium that Hazlitt launched his final Regency article on Coleridge, a review of his rival's first lecture at the London Philosophical Society. This was designed to prove that Coleridge too, despite the constraints of his host society, had scarcely abandoned politics in talking about "Judgement, Culture, and European Literature." Hazlitt himself, of course, did not attend Coleridge's talk—he was delivering his own lecture that night across the Thames at the Surrey Institution. His article, therefore, takes the familiar form of a review of a review, a journalistic riposte to a brief, enthusiastic endorsement of Coleridge's lectures that had appeared five days earlier in the *Courier.* This review-text is reprinted at the outset of his article:

> On Friday evening, Mr. Coleridge gave his first Lecture on Shakspeare to a numerous and genteel audience. He stated the permanent objects Shakspeare had in view in drawing his characters, and how obviously he disregarded

those that were of a transitory nature. The character of *Caliban,* as an original and caricature of Jacobinism, so fully illustrated at Paris during the French Revolution, he described in a vigorous and lively manner, exciting repeated bursts of applause. . . . [H]e said, wherever Shakspeare had drawn a character addicted to sneering, and contempt for the merits of others, that character was sure to be a villain. Vanity, envy, and malice, were its certain accompaniments: too prudent to praise itself, it fed its concentrated egotism by sarcasm and lowering others. This is but a poor description of the very glowing language, ample detail, and profound thought, Mr. Coleridge displayed on this topic, which produced a thunder of applause.—*Courier,* Feb. 9. (19: 206)

This cheery puff of Coleridge's anti-Jacobin poetics affords Hazlitt a familiar opening for journalistic wit. On this occasion he seizes on the contradiction between Coleridge's unchallenged use of *The Tempest* as political allegory and his actual mandate as a lecturer at the London Philosophical Society, announced in a prospectus which Hazlitt has (typically) obtained—and retained—for just such an opportunity.

Mr. Coleridge, in his prospectus, modestly observed, that the attending his course of Lectures on Poetry . . . would enable any grown gentleman to talk on all subjects of polite conversation, except religion and politics. By the above extract, and from what we have heard, it should appear that Mr. Coleridge has gone beyond his engagement, and given his grown gentlemen a slice of religion and politics in the same dish with his account of the Dark Ages. Not like a lady who puts her mind into the postscript, Mr. C. does that first which he promised last. (19: 206–7)

We note that Hazlitt makes no pretense here of actually having attended the lecture: this article responds to the *Courier* as much as it does to Coleridge, and to a review whose praise alone would be enough to politicize Coleridge's lecture by association, whether or not the lecturer had "produced a thunder of applause" by going "beyond his engagement."

But Coleridge did go beyond his engagement, and what lies behind the intensity of Hazlitt's response on this occasion is the very invisibility of Coleridge's remarks as "political" within a growing reactionary hegemony. While the review that follows is certainly driven in part by direct market-place competition—one lecturer undermining the authority of his closest competitor—its primary function as an article in the *Yellow Dwarf* is manifestly political. It intervenes to keep visible the signs of repression in culture at large, in this case by exposing the way a respected lecturer has tailored his remarks on Shakespeare to fit the unexamined anti-Jacobin prejudices of the lecture-going public. Hazlitt's approach is three-fold: he offers a counter-reading of *The Tempest* that reduces to absurdity its use as a political allegory; he offsets the "thunder of applause" with the voice of a heckler; and he questions Coleridge's moral authority in the marketplace for criticism, first by alluding to his reviews of *Bertram* as evidence of Coleridge's ironic

155

affinity with the character of "vanity, envy, and malice" that he ascribes to his "Jacobin" opponents, and then by interpreting Coleridge's attempt to appear fashionably anti-Jacobin as a curious extension of his former liberalism, a "magnanimity" that would embrace even the bane of his own principles in order to secure applause, and in so doing empty the contents of his otherwise "capacious mind" of any certain authority (19: 209).

Hazlitt's reductio ad absurdum of the political appropriation of Caliban is, among other things, a lesson in historical relativity. Hazlitt seems at first to anticipate a post-colonial reading: "Caliban is so far from being a prototype of modern Jacobinism, that he is strictly the legitimate sovereign of the isle, and Prospero and the rest are usurpers, who have ousted him from his hereditary jurisdiction by superiority of talent and knowledge. 'This island's mine, by Sycorax my mother;' and he complains bitterly of the artifices used by his new friends to cajole him out of it" (19: 207). Of course, "legitimate sovereign" is the key term that for Hazlitt in 1818 connotes not an instance of colonial oppression but rather a counter-demonization of Caliban that wryly recasts Prospero in the role of the ultimate Jacobin philosophe—Napoleon:

> [Caliban] is the Louis XVIII. of the enchanted island in *The Tempest:* and Dr. Stoddart would be able to prove by the civil law, that he had the same right to keep possession of it, "independently of his conduct or merits, as Mr. Coke has to his estate at Holkam." Even his affront to the daughter of the upstart philosopher Prospero, could not be brought to bar his succession to the natural sovereignty of his dominions. His boast that "he had peopled else this isle with Calibans," is very proper and dignified in such a person; for it is evident that the right line would be supplanted in failure of his issue; and that the superior beauty and accomplishments of Ferdinand and Miranda could no more be opposed to the legitimate claims of this deformed and loathsome monster, than the beauty and intellect of the Buonaparte family can be opposed to the bloated and ricketty minds and bodies of the Bourbons, cast, as they are, in the true *Jus Divinum* mould! This is gross. Why does Mr. Coleridge provoke us to write as great nonsense as he talks? (19: 207)

At the risk once again of collapsing the opposition between reviewer and reviewed at the level of style, Hazlitt produces "nonsense" to disturb the complacency with which the patrons of the supposedly apolitical London Philosophical Society—not to mention the openly partisan *Courier*—greet Coleridge's tendentious reading of Shakespeare. Without such shock tactics, we may infer, Coleridge's political reference would go completely unnoticed.

To underscore this role for his review (and by extension for the *Yellow Dwarf* as a whole), Hazlitt projects the voice of a heckler into the "repeated bursts of applause" excited by Coleridge's lecture: "We are sorry to hear, that on one occasion Mr. C. was interrupted in a tirade upon this favourite topic [the Jacobinical 'envy of superior genius and virtue' at the time of the French Revolution] . . . by a person calling out in good broad Scotch,

'But you once praised that Revolution, Mr. Coleridge!'" (19: 208). Records do not show whether this colorful interruption actually took place, but the voice of the *Yellow Dwarf* serves the same purpose within the arena of London journalism, delivering as harsh and uncompromising an indictment of Coleridge's apostasy as ever appeared in Hazlitt's *Examiner* reviews.

> The worst is, that Mr. Coleridge praised that Revolution when it was triumphant, going on "conquering and to conquer," as it was thought; and now that it has fallen, this man of mighty mind,—of gigantic genius, and superiority to interested motives and mob-sycophancy, insults over it,— tramples on the carcase,—kicks it with his asinine hoofs, and brays a long, loud, dreary, doleful bravura over it. Of what the Jacobins were in 1793, this person has a right to speak, both from experience and observation. The worst he can say of them is, he was one of the set. (19: 208)

To support this claim, Hazlitt once again recurs to grim paradox: Coleridge's former Jacobinism is revealed in his affinity with the very character of "vanity, envy, and malice" he attributes to Shakespeare's "original and caricature of Jacobinism," Caliban. As proof, Hazlitt makes a similar point to one that has been made in our own time by Hayter in "Coleridge, Maturin's *Bertram,* and Drury Lane": that Coleridge's anonymous reviews of Maturin's *Bertram* in 1816, republished in 1817 as chapter 23 of the *Biographia Literaria,* undermine the validity of his moral indictment of anonymous review-criticism elsewhere in that book. Coleridge's horrified rejection of *Bertram* as an example of "modern jacobinical drama" shows him fully capable of politically motivated anonymous criticism (7.2: 221). And the possibility that this criticism was inspired in part by bitterness—occasioned by Drury Lane's rejection of his own play *Zapolya* and the subsequent success of *Bertram*— accentuates for Hazlitt the irony of Coleridge's ascription of "envy and malice" to "jacobins" alone.

More important than this, however, is Hazlitt's larger point that in catering to the unexamined anti-Jacobinism of the London Philosophical Society, Coleridge represents "a terrible petrification of religion, genius, and the love of liberty" (19: 210). What is new in this instance is a foreshadowing of Hazlitt's final modification of this indictment in 1825, when he recognizes with hindsight that Coleridge's willingness to embrace "all opinions" brings with it an elusiveness of mind that makes him ultimately impossible to co-opt. Thus we encounter, on the one hand, the familiar picture of Coleridge's mystification of his genius through self-contradiction.

> The reason . . . why Mr. Coleridge is not what he might be, is, that he would be thought what he is not. His motto is, to be nothing or everything. . . . He would glitter in the sunshine of public favour and yet he would cast no shadow. . . . His capacious mind has room for all opinions, both those which he believes and those which he does not. He thinks he shews the greatest

magnanimity when he shews the greatest contempt of his own principles, past, present, and future. (19: 209–10)

Yet this hemorrhaging of authority in a compulsive "magnanimity" of mind has its hidden advantages. Thus we encounter, on the other hand, the pressure of Hazlitt's underlying respect for—and even identity with—the object of his criticism in a series of rhetorical questions that depict a man immune to "party" or "sect."

> Would anyone catch him in the trammels of a sect? Would any one make him swear to the dogmas of a party? . . . Would the Presbyterians try to hook him in?—he knows better than Socinus or old John Knox. Would the Established Church receive him at her wide portals?—he carries too great a weight of the Fathers and school divinity at his back. Would the Whigs patronise him?—he is too straitened in antiquated notions and traditional prejudices. Would the Tories take him in?—he is too liberal, enlightened, and transcendental for them. Would principle bind him?—he shuffles out of it, as a clog upon his freedom of thought. . . . Would interest lay dirty hands upon him?—he jockies her too by some fetch or conundrum, borrowed from the great clerks of the so-called Dark Ages. (19: 210)

In a final paradox, Coleridge's weakness for qualification and deferral becomes his greatest strength. Beyond the tragedy of his inevitable rejection by each of the intellectual formations of his day lies the certainly that "interest" will be unable to "lay dirty hands upon him." This is a foreglimpse of Hazlitt's parting image of Coleridge in *The Spirit of the Age,* in which he is pictured having successfully resisted co-optation by tyranny, "pitching his tent upon the barren waste" outside "Shiraz' walls"—the "city of refuge" that has absorbed his sinecured friends Wordsworth and Southey. The only difference in 1818 is that there remains the remote possibility that Coleridge might recover his former, and infinitely more substantial, integrity and authority, and it is the role of the *Yellow Dwarf* and its "leading spirit" to promote this possibility: "You see him now squat like a toad at the ear of the *Courier;* and oh! that we could rouse him up once more into an archangel's shape" (19: 210).

This challenge sets the tone for Hazlitt's closing remarks on Coleridge at the end of his own lecture series several weeks later. Unlike his rival at the London Philosophical Society, Hazlitt was free to discuss political topics at the Surrey Institution,[1] and, especially in this final lecture "On the Living Poets," he aims for a "becoming frankness" when taking up "the Lake school of poetry," making no attempt "to screen either its revolutionary or renegado extravagances" (5: 161). This is certainly true when he turns in the end to Coleridge: "It remains that I should say a few words of Mr. Coleridge; and there is no one who has a better right to say what he thinks of him than I have. 'Is there here any dear friend of Caesar? To him I say, that Brutus's love to Caesar was no less than his' " (5: 166). With this striking analogy from Shakespeare, Hazlitt sums up his relationship with Coleridge and the motivation behind his entire series of reviews over the previous two years. While the image of "Brutus's love" might seem at first to ratify the theme of treacherous, "personal" betrayal that has since dominated our understanding of these reviews, we note that Hazlitt has chosen Brutus, not Iago, to depict his role as Coleridge's critic, thus figuring his challenge to the cultural authority of his erstwhile mentor not as one of "motiveless malignity" (Baker 356) but rather as one of public, political, and historical necessity—an action undertaken in reluctant response to his antagonist's own, prior betrayal of republican ideals. In the commentary that follows, Hazlitt draws on his writings in the *Examiner* to reinforce this political analogy, quoting once again the "friends in youth" passage from *Christabel* as an implicit allegory of political alienation and division, and adducing such poems as "Fire, Famine and Slaughter" from the period of Coleridge's republicanism as examples of "high poetical enthusiasm and strong political feeling" (5: 166).

The *Wat Tyler* affair had taught that such a conjunction of "high poetical enthusiasm" with "the *good cause*" of emancipatory politics was at best unstable and at worst a complete illusion. Hazlitt, moreover, had been challenged by Coleridge's writings—and his tergiversation—to construct his own positive definition of poetry that would account at once for its social value and its tendency to conform to "the language of power" (4: 214). One element of this counter-definition we have already come across in the review of the *Biographia:* Hazlitt's emphasis on the materiality of the poetic signifier (as we would now put it). Contrasted with prose, poetry "make[s] the sound an echo to the sense"; it "suppl[ies] the inherent defect of harmony in the customary mechanism of language"; and thus "Poetry is the music of language, answering to the music of the mind" (16: 136; 5: 12). Hazlitt expands on this "music of the mind" in his opening lecture ("On Poetry in General"), where he begins by addressing the "subject-matter" of poetry. Here the Romantic metaphor of music is grafted onto such Enlightenment universals as "the mind of man" to thoroughly democratize the poetic impulse. "Man is a poetical animal," Hazlitt declares, and "there is no thought or feeling that can have entered into the mind of man, which he would be eager to communicate to others, or which they would listen to with delight, that is not a fit subject for poetry" (5: 2). With this, Hazlitt directly contests the elitist tendencies of Coleridge's definition in the *Biographia,* where the question "What is poetry?" is immediately referred to the question "what is a poet?" which in turn is figured as "a distinction resulting from the poetic genius itself" (7.2: 15). Hazlitt, by contrast, with no similar need to mystify his own authority as a "poetic genius," recurs instead to the inclusive first-person plural of anonymous criticism: "the flame of the passions, communicated to the imagination, reveals to us, as with a flash of lightning, the inmost recesses of thought, and penetrates our whole being" (5: 3).

Most interesting for our purposes is the way Hazlitt's concept of poetry is further qualified in his commentary on Coleridge's *Ancient Mariner.* No doubt with the recently published *Sibylline Leaves* in mind (where the *Ancient Mariner* appeared enhanced for the first time by its prose gloss), Hazlitt begins with an assessment well corroborated by posterity. This poem, he claims, is Coleridge's "most remarkable performance, and the only one that [he] could point out to any one as giving an adequate idea of [Coleridge's] natural powers" (5: 166). Yet, as in the review of *Christabel,* this judgment is immediately qualified by Hazlitt's implicit recurrence to the norm of "history and particular facts," against which he measures Coleridge's willingness to construct a world of pure—and ultimately enigmatic—vision, into which the "glittering eye" and importunate grip of the mariner-poet is our only guide (*Poetical Works* 187). "[His Ancient Mariner], Hazlitt continues, "is high German, however, and in it he seems to 'conceive of poetry but as a drunken dream, reckless, careless, and heedless, of past, present, and to come' " (5: 166). For Hazlitt, then, while the "subject-matter" of poetry may well range across the entire spectrum of "thought and feeling" in "the mind of man," the poet, to earn the approbation of the public, must nevertheless remain heedful of "past, present, and to come"—must retain, that is, some vestige of responsibility to historical cause and effect, and (by implication) to the ongoing process of human enlightenment. Thus Hazlitt continues to contest a Romanticism of visionary withdrawal that produces only the idiosyncratic "dream" of genius—a lyric discourse that, in Coleridge's own words, is not at all designed to have "any *direct* influence on the actions of men" (3.2: 471).

To conclude his 1818 lecture, Hazlitt draws on such writings as his preview of *The Statesman's Manual* and the "AUDITOR" letter to construct a coda for his Regency criticism of Coleridge that at the same time anticipates his writings on him in the 1820s. While acknowledging to the crowded auditorium that Coleridge is "the only person I ever knew who answered to the idea of a man of genius," Hazlitt nevertheless roots his own species of Romantic bardolatry within a strongly politicized dichotomy of past and present.

> [Mr. Coleridge] was the first poet I ever knew. His genius at that time had angelic wings, and fed on manna. . . . In his descriptions, you then saw the progress of human happiness and liberty in bright and never-ending succession, like the steps of Jacob's ladder, with airy shapes ascending and descending, and with the voice of God at the top of the ladder. And shall I, who heard him then, listen to him now? Not I! . . . That spell is broke; that time is gone for ever; that voice is heard no more: but still the recollection comes rushing by with thoughts of long-past years, and rings in my ears with never-dying sound. (5: 167)

The key word here is "liberty," and it would remain the operative theme in Hazlitt's two most "familiar" reworkings of this passage: "My First Acquaintance With Poets" (1823), and the essay "Mr. Coleridge" from *The Spirit of the Age* (1825).

In the meantime, however, the immediate outcome of this contest for cultural authority may be measured in the rough ledgers of the literary marketplace in 1818. Hazlitt's skill as a periodical reviewer had laid the groundwork for his sudden success as a public lecturer, and when his first series filled the "ample hall" of the Surrey Institution "to the very ceiling,"[2] he was encouraged to repeat it a few weeks later at the very epicenter of reformist politics, the Crown and Anchor tavern, before publishing it as *Lectures on the English Poets*. Meanwhile, Coleridge's lectures, though equally well-attended, were neither repeated nor published, perhaps because, in Henry Crabb Robinson's view, they contained "much obscurity . . . and not a little cant and commonplace" (qtd. in Jones, *Hazlitt* 283). On the strength of Hazlitt's success, his *Characters of Shakespeare's Plays* passed easily into a second edition, while the *Biographia Literaria* did not, nor did either of Coleridge's two lay sermons, his *Sibylline Leaves* (1817), or the new three-volume *Friend* (1818). By June 1818, Hazlitt was ensconced as one of the nation's "two most eminent speculators on literary topics."[3] The other such eminent speculator was not thought to be Coleridge, however, but the editor of the *Edinburgh Review*.

Perhaps our best indication that the "Notices" and reviews which produced this effect were written out of public rather than merely "personal" concerns lies in the fact that Hazlitt republished the majority of them in August 1819, at the very height of a second and even more severe national crisis. Thus the intensity of focus on Coleridge and his works in 1816–17 reappears at a moment of equally intense sociopolitical upheaval. It is no coincidence that the publication of Hazlitt's *Political Essays* by the Radical William Hone preceded the Peterloo massacre by just two days. In Evans's words, "the political temperature in the summer of 1819 was higher than ever," and "fears of a breakdown of public order, which some construed as preparation for rebellion," were already "rife" when "Orator" Hunt accepted the invitation to address the fateful meeting in St. Peter's Fields at Manchester (23). This watershed event of the postwar era, however, did not bring the "heroic age of popular Radicalism" immediately to an end (Thompson 603). On the contrary, Hazlitt's *Essays* had four more months to circulate in a context of extreme public turmoil, as the martyrdom of peaceable reformists at Manchester galvanized the Opposition press and the Whigs in Parliament, briefly transforming what Hazlitt calls the "*good cause*" into a truly "national cause" (7: 129; Evans 23). Inevitably, however, this cause was silenced in December 1819 by the "Six Acts"—or rather, it was sent so far underground by these "Gagging Acts" (as they were then popularly known) that it would not reemerge for another full decade.

Of the seven reviews written during the Distresses of 1816–17, Hazlitt selected five for republication in his *Political Essays:* three *Examiner* articles on *The Statesman's Manual,* the article on Coleridge's *Wat Tyler* essays in the *Courier,* and the passage on Burke from his *Edinburgh* review of the

Biographia. As noted at the end of chapter 2 above, Hazlitt's republication of these reviews, under his own name and in August 1819, significantly altered their orientation within the discursive environments identified in this study. Appearing now under the unifying rubric of *Political Essays,* they are given thematic coherence by the prefatory essay explaining Hazlitt's "hatred of tyranny and . . . its tools," and his view that tyranny is propagated as much by "poets with their pens" as by "kings" with their "swords" (7: 7, 10). Published, moreover, from the house of William Hone, these essays are now directed well beyond the boundaries of the middle-class readerships of the *Examiner* and the *Edinburgh* toward the "radical" audience first gathered by Cobbett, and then taken over by Hone and his *Reformist's Register* when Cobbett fled to America in 1817 (Thompson 639–40). This volume represents Hazlitt's equivalent, in effect, to Coleridge's unwritten third lay sermon. In this context, the letter from "SEMPER EGO AUDITOR" at the center of the volume takes on greater prominence for its personification of an activist "of clerkly acquirements"—a reader, that is, whose Latinate pseudonym is the sign of his refusal of the position of merely passive "auditor" ("Must I be always a listener only?") (Rudd 3). In his letter this persona dramatizes the process of becoming one who actively audits—or calls to account—both poets and kings, thus joining the dialectical process by which public opinion is formed.

At the same time, of course, the writerly skill with which this process is dramatized is reclaimed by Hazlitt himself on this occasion as he drops the mask of pseudonymity. This change is instructively ambivalent in its implications. If there is anything "personal" about these *Essays,* it is Hazlitt's willingness now to sign his own name to them, to mortgage his newfound cultural authority as a literary critic for unequivocal solidarity with the movement for reform at this crucial juncture in its evolution. Now as a bold "asserter of the people's rights" (7: 10), Hazlitt positions himself as "one of the ablest and most eloquent critics of the nation,"[4] exchanging the trope of anonymity for the ethos of individual courage in the very teeth of reactionary alarm. However, by invoking the cultural authority that has accrued to his name, Hazlitt abandons the rhetorical advantage implicit in anonymity as a self-effacing enactment of "the intellect of the people" (7: 269), and he sets up in its place an equally implicit hierarchy of (active) author and (passive) auditor. As we saw, for example, in the footnote added to the preview of *The Statesman's Manual,* we find Hazlitt now advertising the skill with which he once marshaled the dissembling strategies of anonymous criticism, "profess[ing] to criticize" a book that (at the time) had not yet appeared in print (7: 114n. 1).

For a political satirist to drop the mask of anonymity was to invite the counterattack of political satire. Hazlitt's new prominence as a literary critic in 1818 had already made him the target of the ministerial press, and these *Political Essays* merely confirmed the need for governmental writers to abate his influence. In a series of articles throughout 1818 and 1819, beginning with a libelous attack in *Blackwood's* (based on Lake School gossip about

Hazlitt's private character)[5] and continuing with three reviews in the *Quarterly* of the *Round Table, Characters of Shakespeare's Plays,* and *Lectures on the English Poets,*[6] Hazlitt was stigmatized as a lascivious, unlettered "cockney" (*Blackwood's*) adept only in "the trade of sedition" (*Quarterly* 18: 466). Now, in response to the *Political Essays,* he is reviled by the *Quarterly* as a mere "insect of the moral world" (22: 158) whose "powers of mischief hardly extend beyond the making of some dirt and some noise"—yet an "insect," we note, which the *Quarterly* must nevertheless spend considerable effort "to fasten . . . down upon a sheet of paper with [its] other specimens" (22: 163). Shortly after this review, Parliament took similar measures against the art of dissident satire as a whole, and with the repressive "Six Acts" it ushered in the quietist 1820s—a new era "of talkers, and not of doers" (11: 28).

Hazlitt's eight reviews of Coleridge during the Distresses period represent an intensity of focus on his erstwhile mentor unmatched in the remainder of his long and prolific writing career. Such compression has made these reviews seem aberrant to traditional literary history, a "deplorable" but passing outburst of spleen rooted in personal—even "motiveless"—malignity, and quite dispensable, therefore, to our understanding of their subject matter (Baker 356). *Contest for Cultural Authority,* by contrast, finds in this very concentration of public statements an indispensable core of criticism focused on one of the key figures in the making of the "Romantic Ideology," essential alike to our understanding of the writings of Coleridge and Hazlitt, and of the brief period in which these reviews appeared in public newspapers and journals. Nor, in the end, are these reviews anomalous. Despite the pressures of conformity, Hazlitt's political vision—his commitment to "the cause of civil and religious liberty" (17: 110)—remained consistent throughout his entire oeuvre, up to and including his final, monolithic *Life of Napoleon* (1828–30).[1]

Though the "Gagging Acts" of 1819 necessarily muted the intensity with which this vision is expressed, the central drama of "liberty" oppressed by "tyranny" continues to animate his writings throughout the 1820s, not least in his two most famous essays on Coleridge, "My First Acquaintance With Poets" (1823) and the chapter on "Mr. Coleridge" in *The Spirit of the Age* (1825). As we saw at the outset, the adjustment of rhetorical register in these essays has been traditionally interpreted as a process of growth to maturity:

Hazlitt's "most mature manner of treating revolutionary and radical themes," says Ruddick (248), consists of a successful—and implicitly desirable—"internalization of radical energies" (243). What was "harsh, impetuous, [and] paradoxical" in such articles as the "AUDITOR" letter (253) is displaced by a "joy-suffused rediscovery of the past, rapturous from beginning to end" in such essays as "My First Acquaintance With Poets" (251). Yet, as we have seen from the *Wat Tyler* affair, this model of political maturation is endorsed by Coleridge, but emphatically rejected by Hazlitt, who traces it to the tendentious rationalization of apostasy rather than to its frank exposure. Indeed, Cook has described this model as an "influential myth of maturity" by which "a growth to maturity is a growth to conservatism" (introduction xiii); as such, we can recognize it as one of "Romanticism's" own most powerful "self-representations" (McGann 1). When applied to a reading of Hazlitt's 1823 essay, for example, it involves overlooking the fact that the unsold copies of *Political Essays* were reissued in 1822 as a "second edition" just months before the publication of "My First Acquaintance With Poets" (7: 2)—indicating, among other things, that Hazlitt expected his "AUDITOR" letter to be read as a parallel version rather than as a "primitive draft" of his memories of Coleridge in the 1790s (Jones, "First Flight" 36).

The difference between these two texts, then, must be accounted for in other terms. Politically, of course, the difference is defined by Peterloo. In 1817 Hazlitt wrote as an activist with hope that the interventions of an ascendent Opposition press would enforce change through the democratic pressure of popular opinion. In 1823 he writes without hope, "repining but resigned" (as he describes his father in the essay [17: 110])—resigned to the ascendency of a reactionary press anxious to preserve a status quo that has delivered accelerating prosperity to a reading public dominated by an equally ascendent middle class. With political change outlawed, the literary tastes of what Klancher defines as the "middle class" reading audience are now fully oriented toward those genres of discourse best designed to consolidate its identity and authority over its emergent counterpart in "mass" (rather than "radical") culture (Klancher 47–53). We have already encountered two such genres of the "middle" style: first, those "arguments on the powers of the mind" that impel "a florid 'poetic diction' into the very texture of argumentative prose" (Klancher 51, 53); and second, what Hazlitt identified as the "easy, gossiping, garrulous account of youthful adventures" that draws bourgeois readers together in shared memories of a Romantic age of activism and its aftermath—an age now regarded as either safely or tragically distanced by time and change (16: 125). The differences between Hazlitt's essays of 1817 and 1823 may also be defined in commercial terms as an adept reflection of this shift in public taste from satiric banter to gregarious "table-talk" on the part of a writer still making his living on the very pulse of periodical fashion. Hazlitt's generic solution is to graft a Wordsworthian or Rousseauist lyric nostalgia onto an ironic (because often implicit) narrative of political betrayal

166

and defeat, and the result is an epiphany of plenitude rooted in historical time rather than in timeless "vision." Yet Hazlitt's generic compromise also involves an often overlooked element of continuity with his *Political Essays* of the Regency. These were subtitled "With Sketches of Public Characters," and in both "My First Acquaintance With Poets" and later in "Mr. Coleridge" from *The Spirit of the Age: Or, Contemporary Portraits,* something of the witty cartoonist persists.[2] Indeed, like the much maligned preview of *The Statesman's Manual,* there are now (once again) no review-texts to hand, and thus Coleridge's talking (not his doing) must substitute as source of both admiration and despair.

An accurate reading of "My First Acquaintance With Poets" must also take into account the embattled circumstances of its publication in the *Liberal,* a rhetorical context easily overlooked—or downplayed[3]—by latter-day readers of the anthologized essay. Hazlitt himself, it should be noted, never anthologized "My First Acquaintance With Poets," as he might easily have done by republishing it in the later, Paris edition of *Table Talk* (1825) or in *The Plain Speaker* (1826). In other words, he never disengaged this essay from its original discursive context, and this context, on closer inspection, we find to be one of dramatically renewed political, commercial, and generic struggle. The title of the *Liberal* alone indicates as much. Under the hegemony of political reaction, such a rubric was deliberately provocative, and doubly so coming from an editorial collective (Byron, Shelley, and Leigh Hunt) that had been stigmatized as "the Satanic School" by Southey in his preface to "The Vision of Judgement" (1821). In Elledge's account, the short-lived *Liberal* "set the London literary scene boiling and seething[,] first in expectation of it, then over its contents, and briefly in its wake" (221). The first number contained an unexpurgated version of Byron's satire of "The Vision of Judgement," which earned the publisher John Hunt a swift indictment for seditious libel. Its second number accompanied a revised edition of Byron's "Vision of Judgement" that now included his combative "preface" to the satire, clarifying his object of attack as the Poet Laureate, not the king, and in the process reopening all the issues of the *Wat Tyler* affair. In its third number appeared "My First Acquaintance With Poets," alongside an "Advertisement" by Leigh Hunt designed to bait rather than mollify the reactionary press on the widening "Vision of Judgement" scandal (*Liberal* 2: v–viii). For its first readers, then, Hazlitt's reference to this scandal in the essay itself would serve to ground it clearly in the same rhetorical contrast of past and present that animated the "AUDITOR" letter of 1817. On this occasion, Coleridge's description (back in the 1790s) of "the third heaven, of which he had had a dream" is now said to be "very different from Mr. Southey's Vision of Judgment, and also from that other Vision of Judgment, which Mr. Murray, the Secretary of the Bridge-street Junto, has taken into his especial keeping!" (17: 115). Here, then, in place of the contrast between Coleridge's two sermons of 1798 and 1816 we are given the difference between Coleridge's "dream" of the 1790s and

Southey's "Vision" of 1821—and between this "dream" and Byron's daring satire in the *Liberal*. This contrast would serve in turn as a thematic catalyst for references elsewhere in the essay to Coleridge as a "wayward enthusiast" whose very habit of "shifting from one side of the path to the other" was an undetected sign in the 1790s of a future "instability of purpose or involuntary change of principle" (17: 112–13).

Heightening the contrast between past and present in the 1823 essay is the larger context of political reaction, dating to Peterloo but epitomized in the swift indictment of John Hunt as well as in the well-publicized discord fomented among the journal's editors by John Murray (Elledge 224)—not to mention in the imminent and inevitable collapse of the *Liberal* itself. Against this backdrop of the present-day betrayal and persecution of "liberty," Hazlitt paints the bright portrait of Coleridge's liberalism in the 1790s, the very intensity of which may be read as a rhetorical exaggeration designed to throw into correspondingly poignant and ironic contrast the loss of this "genius" to the failing cause of liberty in the 1820s. Within the essay itself, moreover, this contrast is supplemented by Hazlitt's introduction of his own father as a character foil for the young Coleridge.

> It was curious to observe the contrast between him and my father, who was a veteran in the cause. . . . [My father] had been relegated to an obscure village . . . far from the talk he loved, the talk about disputed texts of Scripture and the cause of civil and religious liberty. Here he passed his days, repining but resigned. . . .
>
> No two individuals were ever more unlike than were the host and his guest. A poet was to my father a sort of non-descript: yet whatever added grace to the Unitarian cause was to him welcome. He could hardly have been more surprised or pleased, if our visitor had worn wings. Indeed, his thoughts had wings; and as the silken sounds rustled around our little wainscoted parlour, my father threw back his spectacles over his forehead . . . and a smile of delight beamed across his rugged cordial face, to think that Truth had found a new ally in Fancy! (17: 110–11)

Like his son in later years, the elder Hazlitt's pleasure in this new alliance was short-lived. The very next morning, "Fancy" was to break ranks with "Truth" when Coleridge accepted the Wedgewood annuity; "instead of . . . being the pastor of a Dissenting congregation at Shrewsbury, he was henceforth to inhabit the Hill of Parnassus, to be a shepherd on the Delectable Mountains!" (17: 112). Literary history has exulted over this turn in Coleridge's career, and has read in Hazlitt's depiction of it a similarly approving dichotomy of prosaic "pastor" and poetic "shepherd." We nevertheless overhear the politically inflected irony of this contrast, equivalent to the opposition of "reality" and "dream" in the review of *Christabel,* and aligned in this essay with the opposition between the career of the elder Hazlitt and the "wayward" poet. As Stanley Jones puts it:

Whereas in 1817 Coleridge's volte-face was shown by the contradiction between what he himself once said and what he was now saying, in 1823 the same point . . . is implicitly but far more effectively clinched in the profounder contrast, exemplary on a human and existential and not merely abstract level, between one man who has shifted his ground with the passing of years and another who had remained all his life as immovable as a rock. The Rev. William Hazlitt is here portrayed as a humbly heroic figure who sustained in the moral history of his time, together with his equally obscure fellow-pastors Rowe of Shrewsbury and Jenkins of Whitchurch, that "line of communication by which the flame of civil and religious liberty was kept alive, and nourished its smouldering fires unquenchable." (17: 107; "First Flight" 37)

Jones quotes here the second of the two points in this essay where Hazlitt clarifies what he intended by the "*good cause*" in his account of the Shrewsbury sermon. It is "the cause of civil and religious liberty," and in both texts, we recall, this cause is pitted against "the brand of JUS DIVINUM" (17: 109)—an agent of tyranny later described in *The Spirit of the Age* as "the murderous practices of the hag, Legitimacy" (11: 34).

Thus Hazlitt's most frequently anthologized essay on Coleridge presents a parallel rather than a "more mature" version of his politics during the Distresses crisis. This is true of the generic features of the essay as well. While Hazlitt has acceded to changes in literary fashion by combining the lyric epiphany of the Shrewsbury sermon passage with "an easy, gossiping, garrulous account of [his] youthful adventures" in Wem and Nether Stowey, he has also incorporated into this generic fusion the (satiric) "sketch of a public character" that forms one of the key ingredients of his *Political Essays*— and later of *The Spirit of the Age*. In perhaps the most famous description of Coleridge in the canon, Hazlitt presents a witty phrenological portrait that directly recalls his bantering preview of *The Statesman's Manual* in its graphic rendering of Coleridge's "nose."

His forehead was broad and high, light as if built of ivory, with large projecting eyebrows, and his eyes rolling beneath them like a sea with darkened lustre. "A certain tender bloom his face o'erspread," a purple tinge as we see it in the pale thoughtful complexions of the Spanish portrait-painters, Murillo and Velasquez. His mouth was gross, voluptuous, open, eloquent; his chin good-humoured and round; but his nose, the rudder of the face, the index of the will, was small, feeble, nothing—like what he has done. It might seem that the genius of this face as [if] from a height surveyed and projected him (with sufficient capacity and huge aspiration) into the world unknown of thought and imagination, with nothing to support or guide his veering purpose, as if Columbus had launched his adventurous course for the New World in a scallop, without oars or compass. So at least I comment on it after the event. (17: 109)

169

From the sublime forehead to the bathetic nose, from Columbus to the tossing "scallop, without oars or compass," we are given the same set of satiric contrasts as those between the "eagle dallying with the wind" and Coleridge's treacherous "balloon" in the 1817 letter, or between Coleridge's "talk" and his "attempt[s]" to write in the 1816 preview. Once again, too, Hazlitt grounds the essay efficiently in the present, balancing the entire, loquacious account of Coleridge's remarkable powers against the terse referent "what he has done," which in 1823 still remains, in his view, "small, feeble, nothing."

Further complicating matters of style and genre in this essay is Hazlitt's direct thematization of them, and in particular his identification of the origins of his own discursive facility in what Jones calls "the thaumaturgic splendour" of Coleridge's conversation ("First Flight" 37). Where in Hazlitt's Regency reviews of Coleridge the convergence of satirist and subject at the level of style was tentative and ironic ("It is impossible, in short, to describe this strange rhapsody without falling a little into the style of it" [16: 100]), in the age of "table-talk" this identity is now overt and acknowledged, and its source celebrated in quasi-mythological terms.

> As we passed along between W——m and Shrewsbury, . . . a sound was in my ears as of a Siren's song; I was stunned, startled with it, as from a deep sleep; but I had no notion then that I should ever be able to express my admiration to others in motley imagery and quaint allusion, till the light of his genius shone into my soul, like the sun's rays glittering in the puddles of the road. I was at that time dumb, inarticulate, helpless, like a worm by the wayside, crushed, bleeding, lifeless; but now, bursting from the deadly bands that bound them
>
> "With Styx nine times round them,"
>
> my ideas float on winged words, and as they expand their plumes, catch the golden light of other years. My soul has indeed remained in its original bondage, dark, obscure, with longings infinite and unsatisfied; . . . but that my understanding also did not remain dumb and brutish, or at length found a language to express itself, I owe to Coleridge. (17: 107)

From what has gone before, we can read in the contrast now developed between the "bondage" of Hazlitt's soul and the eloquence of his "understanding" the contrast between political defeat and commercial viability in an age of "talkers, and not of doers." We note that the language of "motley imagery" and "quaint allusion" that Coleridge is said to have inspired in him is of value now only to "catch the golden light of other years," to celebrate, in other words, the brief—and possibly illusory—convergence of "Truth" and "Fancy" in "the year 1798." While literary history has welcomed this turn to reminiscence in Hazlitt's writing and incorporated it into a narrative of generic development—the ascendency of Romantic biography and "joy-suffused" lyricism over "harsh, impetuous, paradoxical" satire—it has done so only at the cost of overlooking the (political) tragedy that underlies it.

Moreover, this narrative of development, with its affinities to the "influential myth of maturity," is once again soundly rejected by Hazlitt himself in another reflection on the question of style. "I can write fast enough now," he remarks, after describing his frustrations composing his first work, his *Essay on the Principles of Human Action.* But then he asks, "Am I better than I was then? Oh no! One truth discovered, one pang of regret at not being able to express it, is better than all the fluency and flippancy in the world. Would that I could go back to what I then was!" (17: 114). With this, Hazlitt reduces the essay style for which he is most valued—his "most mature" mode of the 1820s—to mere "fluency and flippancy," thus subordinating both what he has acquired from Coleridge and what he has since *required* to contest his mentor's authority to the radical inarticulateness that attends the direct apprehension of "truth." This movement, of course, is not unlike that of Wordsworth in the "Intimations Ode," or even of Coleridge himself in "Dejection: an Ode," yet with the difference that the "truth" once apprehended by Hazlitt is not one that authorizes individual "genius" and "the growth of a poet's mind" but rather one that serves the "cause of civil and religious liberty" by proving "*the Natural Disinterestedness of the Human Mind*" (17: 114).

Yet it was "fluency and flippancy" that sold periodicals and books in "an age of talkers," and while Coleridge continued to hold forth at Highgate, becoming something of a pre-Victorian sage for his legendary powers of "conversation," Hazlitt continued to make a living by combining "the *literary* and the *conversational*" in the medium of print (8: 333). Thus it is that Hazlitt's most securely canonized work, *The Spirit of the Age,* has as its centerpiece a "Contemporary Portrait" of Coleridge as "the most impressive talker of his age" (11: 1, 30), and contains as its most striking stylistic innovation an 840-word sentence designed at once to celebrate and parody this unstoppable phenomenon (11: 32–34). In this balance of sincerity and irony, Hazlitt summarizes his entire collection of writings on Coleridge, from the unwieldy "capacity" of this genius found in the review of *Christabel* (19: 32), through the narrative of apostasy in the Distresses reviews, to the politicized summary of Coleridge's poetical achievement in the 1818 lecture, and to the use of a character foil—this time "Mr. Godwin"—to illustrate Coleridge's unique dissipation of his "capacity."

Indeed, the recurrent theme of Hazlitt's final essay on Coleridge is taken from the opening lines of his first review: the paradox that "from an excess of capacity, [Mr. Coleridge] does little or nothing" (19: 32). The only difference between the review of *Christabel* and *The Spirit of the Age* is that by 1825 Coleridge's very uniqueness in this regard suggests—again paradoxically— a general cultural trend. For if "the present is an age of talkers, and not of doers," Hazlitt explains, it is because "We are so far advanced in the Arts and Sciences, that we live in retrospect and doat on past achievements. The accumulation of knowledge has been so great, that we are lost in wonder at the height it has reached, instead of attempting to climb or add to it; while the variety of objects distracts and dazzles the looker-on" (11: 29). Epitomizing this latter-day phenomenon, Coleridge has " 'a mind reflecting ages past,' " in which there is "hardly a speculation . . . left on record from the earliest time, but it is loosely folded up in [his] memory, like a rich, but somewhat tattered piece of tapestry" (11: 29). Like the "age" as a whole, then, "Mr. Coleridge is too rich in intellectual wealth, to need to task himself to any drudgery: he has only to draw the sliders of his imagination, and a thousand subjects expand before him, startling him with their brilliancy, or losing themselves in endless obscurity" (11: 30).

This image of Coleridge playing with the "sliders of his imagination" offers one clue to the complex tone that infuses this portrait of plenitude. Having encountered this image in the context of the *Wat Tyler* affair, we can register more precisely the irony with which Coleridge's own simile of the magic lantern is once again taken up to reduce visionary Romanticism to mere solipsistic bemusement with the gadget of the "imagination." Yet at the same time, when Hazlitt follows up this image with the comment that such a mind "thinks as it were aloud, and babbles in its dreams!," what might otherwise appear a blunt indictment is tempered by our recollection of another image from the Distresses period: of Coleridge as the dying Falstaff "babbl[ing] of green fields" (16: 100). As before, then, the bitterest irony is crossed by sympathetic pathos as well as Hazlitt's own characteristic insight. For if indeed "[p]ersons of greatest capacity are often those, who for this very reason do the least" (as Hazlitt now restates the wry paradox), then it is because such persons "prefer the contemplation of all that is, or has been, or can be, to the making a coil about doing what, when done, is no better than vanity" (11: 30).

One effect of Hazlitt's generalization of the character-type is to modify the extent to which Coleridge can be held responsible for his failure to perform up to "capacity" on behalf of the "*good cause*." This effect is borne out in turn by Hazlitt's lengthening perspective on the narrative of apostasy. The narrative itself, to be sure, is rehearsed every bit as vividly and emphatically as it ever was in the *Political Essays*. By 1825, however, it had become apparent that Coleridge, unlike Southey or Wordsworth, was not about to accept any of the "places or pensions" proffered by "the hag, Legitimacy" (11: 37, 34). Like them, still, his achievement as an author is limited to the era of his political resistance: "All that he has done of moment, he had done twenty years ago," when "he hailed the rising orb of liberty . . . and had kindled his affections at the blaze of the French Revolution" (11: 30, 34). Certainly, too, Coleridge's very "capacity" must still be regarded as a political liability: " 'Frailty, thy name is *Genius*!'—What is become of this mighty heap of hope, of thought, of learning, and humanity? It has ended in swallowing doses of oblivion and in writing paragraphs in the *Courier.*—Such, and so little, is the mind of man!" (11: 34). With such "paragraphs in the *Courier*" in mind, moreover, Coleridge is once again arraigned for having "turned on the pivot of a subtle casuistry to the *unclean side*" (11: 34). Yet by contrast with his fellow Lake poets, he is at least one whose

> discursive reason would not let him trammel himself into a poet-laureate or stamp-distributor, and he stopped, ere he quite passed that well-known "bourne from whence no traveller returns"—and so has sunk into torpid, uneasy repose, tantalized by useless resources, haunted by vain imaginings, his lips idly moving, but his heart for ever still, or, as the shattered chords vibrate of themselves, making melancholy music to the ear of memory! Such is the fate of genius in an age, when in the unequal contest with sovereign wrong, every man is ground to powder who is not either a born slave, or who does not willingly and at once offer up the yearnings of humanity and the dictates of reason as a welcome sacrifice to besotted prejudice and loathsome power. (11: 34)

We note that the fundamental struggle between liberty and tyranny remains unaltered here. Coleridge's role in this struggle has been subtly refigured, however, with greater emphasis now on the dying Falstaff, perhaps, than on the sovereign Caesar—on Coleridge as the hapless victim rather than the fully co-opted agent of tyranny. The poignancy of this portrait is redoubled by the fact that Hazlitt is now describing his own "fate" as well as that of Coleridge in an era of "sovereign wrong." Like Coleridge, he too has been "ground to powder" for refusing to "offer up the yearnings of humanity and the dictates of reason" to the cultural imperatives of "loathsome power." In commercial terms, for example, the continued assault on Hazlitt's reputation by the Tory press had forced him to publish the first edition of *Spirit of the Age* anonymously, until its success allowed a second edition later in the year under his own name (11: 2). This convergence of critic and subject under a regime of "besotted prejudice" is once again reflected in a final identity at the level of style: both writers, in this view, are reduced to making "melancholy music to the ear of memory."

Yet when Hazlitt turns to treat "Mr. Coleridge's productions" in more detail, the imprint of their struggle for authority clearly remains. Drawing heavily on his 1818 lecture, Hazlitt once again praises Coleridge's poetry from the era of his republicanism, quoting "his affecting Sonnet to the author of the Robbers" and again isolating the *Ancient Mariner* as Coleridge's most preeminent work. Here, we note, he revises his assessment to align it better with the theme of Coleridge's "capacity": "Let whatever other objections be made to it, [this poem] is unquestionably a work of genius—of wild, irregular, overwhelming imagination, and has that rich, varied movement in the verse, which gives a distant idea of the lofty or changeful tones of Mr. Coleridge's voice" (11: 35). No longer a "drunken dream," the *Ancient Mariner* is nevertheless "wild, irregular, [and] overwhelming," the first of these epithets being the key word in the controversy over *Christabel,* just as "overwhelming" recalls the way the earlier poem was said to throw the critic's faculties "into a state of metaphysical suspense and theoretical imbecility" (19: 33). The phrase "changeful tones" is also more than just a compliment on Coleridge's elocution; it doubles as a further index of his instability of character. Certainly it is this negative side effect of his "capacity" that lies behind the final, stinging rebuke of Coleridge's prose.

> If our author's poetry is inferior to his conversation, his prose is utterly abortive. Hardly a gleam is to be found in it of the brilliancy and richness of those stores of thought and language that he pours out incessantly, when they are lost like drops of water in the ground. The principal work, in which he has attempted to embody his general view of things, is the FRIEND, of which, though it contains some noble passages and fine trains of thought, prolixity and obscurity are the most frequent characteristics. (11: 35)

It is Coleridge's prose, after all, that bears his turn "on the pivot of a subtle casuistry to the *unclean side*" (11: 34), and in these astringent comments we revisit the terms in which *The Statesman's Manual,* the *Courier* essays, and the *Biographia* were contested during the Distresses. The word "casuistry," for example, recalls the "maudlin Methodistical casuistry" with which Coleridge was said to defend Southey during the *Wat Tyler* affair (7: 178), and this word is in turn a variation on the key term "cant" used to depict the German metaphysics through which Coleridge effected his retreat from politics into pure vision (7: 135). By such strategies of prose, in Hazlitt's view, Coleridge's "excess of capacity" has been aborted—or, worse, transformed into its grim parody, "prolixity and obscurity."

To summarize the multiple elements of this portrait, Hazlitt makes use of another character-foil, this time William Godwin, author of the anarchist manifesto *Political Justice* and the Jacobin allegory *Caleb Williams.*

> No two persons can be conceived more opposite in character or genius than the subject of the present and of the preceding sketch. Mr. Godwin, with less natural capacity, and with fewer acquired advantages, by concentrating his mind on some given object, and doing what he had to do with all his might, has accomplished much, and will leave more than one monument of a powerful intellect behind him; Mr. Coleridge, by dissipating his, and dallying with every subject by turns, has done little or nothing to justify to the world or to posterity, the high opinion which all who have ever heard him converse, or known him intimately, with one accord entertain of him. (11: 35–36)

Like the opposition of "Truth" and "Fancy" in the 1823 essay, Godwin presents an example of the successful concentration of "capacity," however modest, in contrast to Coleridge's dissipation of his "excess." Though left unstated, the politics of this contrast would also have been readily evident to Hazlitt's first readers, if nowhere else than in Hazlitt's view that Godwin "has accomplished much." Like the elder Hazlitt, who tenaciously upheld "the flame of civil and religious liberty" (17: 107), Godwin symbolizes an unwavering commitment to "abstract reason" and the radical implications of "universal benevolence" (11: 18–19), easily contrasted with Coleridge's desultory "dallying" with both the "*good*" and the "*unclean side.*" Yet in each case these former champions of the "*good cause*" have suffered a tragic fall amounting almost to premature death. Godwin (not unlike Hazlitt's father) has been cast into utter obscurity by the age's "dastard submission to prejudice and to the fashion of the day," leaving him "to all intents and purposes dead and buried" (11: 16–17). Coleridge, meanwhile, by attempting to follow these same turns of fashion and prejudice, has become "the greatest talker" in "an age of talkers," and for this very reason he has been induced to lay aside his pen "for the stare of an idler," becoming a grotesque parody of his potential with "lips idly moving, but his heart for ever still" (11: 30, 34).

Hazlitt's original version of this essay ends with his comparison of Godwin and Coleridge, leaving its political applications largely implicit. These, however, he clearly wished to clarify and reinforce, for in another edition of *Spirit of the Age* published shortly after in Paris, he added a new, final paragraph to the essay that was retained in the second (signed) English edition of 1825 as well as in all subsequent ones. This final paragraph constitutes, in effect, Hazlitt's last addition to *The Spirit of the Age* as a whole. As such it reflects both the importance he attached to the portrait of Coleridge in particular, and his ongoing concern to situate that portrait within the larger narrative of revolution and reaction defined by his *Political Essays.* Here, then, is Hazlitt's own, resounding coda to the body of criticism taken up in this study.

> It was a misfortune to any man of talent to be born in the latter end of the last century. Genius stopped the way of Legitimacy, and therefore it was to be abated, crushed, or set aside as a nuisance. The spirit of the monarchy was at variance with the spirit of the age. The flame of liberty, the light of intellect was to be extinguished with the sword—or with slander, whose edge is sharper than the sword. The war between power and reason was carried on by the first of these abroad—by the last at home. No quarter was given (then or now) by the Government-critics, the authorised censors of the press, to those who followed the dictates of independence, who listened to the voice of the tempter, Fancy. Instead of gathering fruits and flowers, immortal fruits and amaranthine flowers, they soon found themselves beset not only by a host of prejudices, but assailed with all the engines of power, by nicknames, by lies, by all the arts of malice, interest, and hypocrisy, without the possibility of their defending themselves "from the pelting of the pitiless storm," that poured down upon them from the strong-holds of corruption and authority. The philosophers, the dry abstract reasoners, submitted to this reverse pretty well, and armed themselves with patience "as with triple steel" to bear discomfiture, persecution, and disgrace. But the poets, the creatures of sympathy, could not stand the frowns of both kings and people. They did not like to be shut out when places and pensions, when the critic's praises,

and the laurel-wreath were about to be distributed. They did not stomach being *sent to Coventry,* and Mr. Coleridge sounded a retreat for them by the help of casuistry, and a musical voice.—"His words were hollow, but they pleased the ear" of his friends of the Lake School, who turned back disgusted and panic-stricken from the dry desert of unpopularity, like Hassan the camel driver,

> "And curs'd the hour, and curs'd the luckless day,
> When first from Shiraz' walls they bent their way."

They are safely inclosed there, but Mr. Coleridge did not enter with them; pitching his tent upon the barren waste without, and having no abiding place nor city of refuge. (11: 37–38)

With this, Hazlitt updates the narrative of revolution and "retreat" to the year 1825, and Coleridge's pivotal role within it. Here we are taken back to "AUDITOR"'s aborted quest for "immortal fruits and amaranthine flowers," and forward to a new and final image of Coleridge shut out from the walls of "Shiraz," at once unwilling to "trammel himself into a poet-laureate or stamp-distributor" (11: 34) and constitutionally incapable of focusing his prodigious "capacity"—even on the project of rationalizing tyranny.

For Hazlitt, as always, the tragedy here lies in the "barren waste," a reflection of Coleridge's refusal of meaningful political agency disguised now as a kind of Romantic otherworldliness. In a previous age, however, "Genius stopped the way of Legitimacy," creating the illusion that an alliance between "the light of intellect" and "the tempter, Fancy" would bring millennial force to bear in the archetypal "war between power and reason." Not surprisingly, only the "dry abstract reasoners" like Godwin (and the veterans of Dissent like the elder Hazlitt) could withstand the inevitable "pitiless storm" of reaction. As for the poets, the very conditions that made their poetry possible—their "sympathy" with *all* "the thoughts and feelings of man"—also made it possible for them to romanticize "corruption and authority." Here especially Coleridge played the crucial role of supplementing the "musical voice" of poetry with the "casuistry" of Transcendental Idealism. Thus he "sounded a retreat" for the poets of the age, leaving behind in his prose the legacy of an ideology that seeks to transcend ideology.

Hazlitt himself, meanwhile, in such passages as this, continues to uphold "the flame of liberty" into the very midst of the reactionary 1820s, unwilling to accept the equally "barren" obscurity of a Godwin or a provincial Dissenter. Here once again he sounds the note of an alternative Romanticism of resistance, carrying into the very drawing rooms of the "age of talkers" this ongoing "war between power and reason." By adding this paragraph to his second edition of *The Spirit of the Age,* his latest masterpiece of "fluency and flippancy" is identified in tone and theme—as well as in name—with his *Political Essays,* reworking its "Sketches of Public Characters" into "Contemporary Portraits" and declaring once again in no uncertain terms the author's "hatred of tyranny, and [his] contempt for its tools." Thus he ensures that the narrative of apostasy is registered as an indispensable feature of "the spirit of the age."

With the hindsight of cultural history, of course, we can now see Coleridge safely ensconced within "Shiraz' walls" of academic posterity. Even Hazlitt, insofar as he is thought to be "the most representative critic in English romanticism," has been given limited asylum within this "city of refuge" (Bate, introduction, *Criticism* 282). Yet his *Political Essays* have been "set aside as a nuisance," despite their obvious affinities with his more securely canonized works and despite the fact that Hazlitt himself would rank these among his most important contributions to "the spirit of the age." Certainly in the critique of Coleridge at their very center, he takes on a far more important role than that of mere supplement and acolyte to Coleridge's "genius" in the annus mirabilis of British Romanticism. Instead he is the vigilant chronicler of the "retreat" of that Romanticism—under Coleridge's banner—from the "cause of civil and religious liberty" to a myth of "maturity," from the "mind of man" to "the visions of recluse genius," from the plural and the public to a solitary lyric "dream."

NOTES

Introduction

1. Walter Jackson Bate declares that Hazlitt is "the greatest English critic of the period except for Coleridge himself" (introduction, *Biographia* lxvi), and according to Thomas McFarland, he "may be the finest pure critic of literature that English culture has brought forth" (57).

2. The years 1815–19 comprise a period of more or less continuous distress and crisis, but the years 1816–17 were particularly acute, as the euphoria of Waterloo gave way to an unprecedented collapse of the coal, iron, and textile industries. In addition, widespread agricultural foreclosures in early 1816 led to what Parliament then named "the Distresses of the Country," even as the unusually wet summer of 1816 ruined crops all over Europe, creating what Post has called "the last great subsistence crisis in the Western world"; White, *Waterloo to Peterloo* passim; Thompson 603–40; Evans 7–27; Woodward 62–65, and Post passim.

3. See Belsey's standard definition of the "Theory and Practice" of "cultural history," Klancher's seminal application of this methodology to the period in question, and Chandler's landmark study of the origins of such periodized treatments of "the spirit of the age" in Romantic historicism itself.

4. See Habermas passim, and Eagleton 8–9 and passim, on the eighteenth-century "public sphere."

5. See Barker-Benfield on the eighteenth-century "culture of sensibility." See also Coburn's edition of the *Collected Works of Samuel Taylor Coleridge*, 7.1: 38; 7.2: 15, 19–28 on "POETIC GENIUS" (7.2: 132). Unless otherwise indicated, all references to Coleridge's writings will be by volume and page number of the Coburn edition.

6. McFarland's influential study is a case in point: "Hazlitt's Struggle with Coleridge" is ultimately explained as a case of Bloomian anxiety—"it was psychologically necessary for Hazlitt to turn against Coleridge to become his own man intellectually" (82). The reviews of Coleridge, meanwhile, he quotes only once—to illustrate a flaw in style (67).

7. *Letters*, 4: 668; see also *Letters* 4: 669–70, 685–86, 692–93, 699–701, 716.

8. See Schneider, and also Coburn, "Who Killed *Christabel?*," for convincing evidence that Thomas Moore (not Hazlitt) wrote the *Edinburgh*'s notorious satire of *Christabel*.

9. The influence of Coleridge's most important editors and biographers cannot be underestimated in this process. Griggs, for example, writing in 1959, reduces these reviews to a "veritable campaign of hate" (668); Jackson presents a subtler view, but nevertheless remarks that "the treatment of Coleridge's writing during this period [the years 1816 and 1817] is one of the sorriest performances in the history of reviewing . . . [and] William Hazlitt played a disproportionately large part in the hostilities" (introduction 9, 10).

10. "Hazlitt and Jeffrey," *Blackwood's Magazine* (June 1818: 303). Hazlitt's very eminence induced a campaign of satire against him in the same magazine, beginning in August 1818.

11. Unless otherwise indicated, all references to Hazlitt's works will be by volume and page number in Howe's edition, *The Complete Works of William Hazlitt*.

12. Severe food shortages throughout the winter had quickly turned an economic crisis into a political one. The huge "Spa Fields" meetings in November and December (one of which erupted in violent rioting and arrests), and the arrival in London of reformist delegates from all over England to the "Crown & Anchor Convention" (scheduled to coincide with the reopening of Parliament) created an atmosphere of intensified confrontation and crisis.

13. Unless otherwise indicated, all italics or emphases in quotations are understood to be in the original.

Chapter 1

1. "Literary Notices. No. 1," *Examiner* 2 June 1816: 348–49; *Works* 19: 32–34; Reiman A: 530–32.

2. "The Riots," *Examiner* 26 May 1816: 328–29.

3. Qtd. by *Examiner* in "The Riots," 26 May 1816: 329.

4. [untitled editorial], *Times* 30 May 1816.

5. Though Griggs (4: 634) gives 25 May as the publication date for the book, Jones records 10 May (*Hazlitt* 222–23), and the volume is indeed advertised as "published this day" in the *Morning Chronicle* on that date. Moreover, as noted in the introduction, the *Champion* review, which appeared 26 May, suggests a public discussion of the book that had lasted longer than a mere twenty-four hours.

6. *Letters* 4: 917–18. As we have already seen, however, the early *Champion* review makes clear that public discussion of the poem included from the very outset the possibility that Geraldine was a man: "Is *Lady Geraldine* a sorceress? or a vampire? or a man? or what is she, or he, or it?" (Reiman A: 268).

7. See also 4: 670, 735; and see Beer for a useful summary of Coleridge's "highly-coloured" counter-rumors, including an unpublished annotation in a copy of *Christabel* given to his son Derwent.

8. See *Letters* 5: 162, for example, where Coleridge asserts that the *Christabel* volume "fell almost dead-born from the press."

9. Schneider's 1955 article ("The Unknown Reviewer of *Cristabel*") proved controversial, but it was followed in 1962 by her "Tom Moore and the *Edinburgh* Review of *Christabel*," and was further corroborated in 1965 by Coburn, in "Who Killed *Christabel?*"

10. See Blunden passim, and Wallins 150–51. On the liberal politics implied by the *Examiner*'s status as a Sunday newspaper, see Morison 227–35, and Aspinall, *Politics* 13–16.

11. See Jones, *Hazlitt* 106–12, for an excellent account of this practice and of Hazlitt's early apprenticeship in it.

12. *Morning Chronicle* 10 May 1816.

13. Howe notes the personal allegory, but only in his notes to Hazlitt's *Lectures on the English Poets* (5: 399)

14. Aspinall, in "The Social Status of Journalists at the Beginning of the Nineteenth Century," describes the prevailing "assumption that no one connected with the newspaper Press was fit for the society of gentlemen" (217).

15. *Edinburgh Review* 21 (July 1813): 299; qtd. in Janowitz, 21.

Chapter 2

1. Coleridge's advertisement appeared in mid-August 1816; by late September (two weeks after Hazlitt's review), Coleridge records in a letter that the announced work was still only in draft form: "I attempted to dictate a something that is coming out" (*Letters* 4: 673).

2. Howe quotes Crabb Robinson's diary: "14 October:——I read to the party Hazlitt's article against Coleridge and an equally admirable notice of Owen of Lanark's View of Society. . . . William Taylor had never before heard any of Hazlitt's compositions. He declared these to be masterpieces of banter" (190).

3. R. J. White, editor of the *Lay Sermons* for the definitive Coburn edition of Coleridge's *Works* (vol. 6), elides the entire issue of Coleridge's premature advertisement of *The Statesman's Manual,* quoting only his reference to it in a letter (*Letters* 4: 672), while dismissing Hazlitt's "crass malevolence" in writing a purely "anticipatory review" (introduction xxxviii–xxxix and xxxixn. 1).

4. The three editions of the *Christabel* volume in 1816 would have totaled approximately 2,250 copies, while the combined circulation of the *Times* and the *Courier* was approximately 12,000 (Erdman 54).

5. Three new reviews of the *Christabel* volume were in circulation in early August: the *British Review* for July invokes "the moral muse" to deplore Coleridge's adherence to "Lord Byron's tainted muse" and advises him to undertake "the frequent, and perpetual perusal of the word of God" (Reiman A: 240–41); the *Scourge* for July sees the volume as part of a conspiracy "to undermine the foundations of taste and common sense" (Reiman A: 865); while the *Anti-Jacobin Review* claims the volume excites nothing but "astonishment and disgust" (Reiman A: 23).

6. "Distresses of the Poor," *Examiner* 4 Aug. 1816: 482–85. This article is a verbatim report of the meeting, analogous to the parliamentary reports printed during active parliamentary sessions.

7. In the *Times* of 15 August, for example, some seventy names are listed, beginning with those contributing over £100; "the Amount of Subscriptions already advertised" totaled over £30,000.

8. "Distresses of the Country," *Edinburgh Review* 27 (June 1816): 255–56. This edition first appeared on 9 August ("Published this Day," *Morning Chronicle* 9 Aug. 1816).

9. Coleridge's advertisement first appeared three days after the *Edinburgh* review was published, on 12 August.

10. Ongoing reports of the trial in the *Examiner,* for example, included a verbatim report of the judge's address on 30 June and culminated in a detailed account of the mass execution on 7 July.

11. "In a few days will be published, price 2s, THE REMEDY; or, Thoughts on the Present Distresses, in a Letter to a Public Editor. . . . 'The above pamphlet, as its title imports, proposes a Remedy the most effective, suitable to the present unparalleled deplorable state of the times' " (*Times* 20 Aug. 1816).

12. "This day is published, price 1d or 9d. per dozen, for distribution, A WARNING TO ENGLAND, on its present alarming situation . . ." (*Times* 29 Aug. 1816).

13. Written by the Poet Laureate Robert Southey, who at this time emerged as a leading political essayist for the *Quarterly Review* (5: 29 [April 1816]). This edition, like the June edition of the *Edinburgh,* appeared belatedly in August (Shine 55).

14. The circulation of the *Examiner* at this time was between 7,000 (1812) and 3,000 (1821)—perhaps around 3,500 copies per week—by comparison with approximately 6,000 daily

for both the *Times* and the *Courier,* and approximately 13,000 quarterly for the *Edinburgh* and the *Quarterly* (Wallins 151; Erdman 54n. 3, and Jones, *Hazlitt* 146n. 43).

15. "Literary Notices. No. 2" (16 June 1816: 379–80) and "3" (30 June 1816: 411–12) comprise a two-part review of the "Report of the Select Committee of the House of Commons on the Elgin Marbles" in which the political issues surrounding the appropriation of the marbles are directly addressed. "Literary Notices. No. 4" (7 July: 426–28) and "5" (14 July: 441–43) take aim at Robert Southey and his strenuous epithalamion "The Lay of the Laureate," composed for the marriage of Princess Charlotte. This double article was the first of the "Literary Notices" later to be republished as *Political Essays* (7: 85–97). It focuses intensely on Southey's political apostasy—"It is the first time that ever a Reformist was made a Poet-Laureate," notes Hazlitt—and the result, significantly enough, is "a Methodist sermon turned into doggerel verse" (7: 86–87). The second article vigorously assaults the poem's celebration of "Legitimacy" (or "the doctrine of 'divine right' "), which Hazlitt describes as "that detestable doctrine, which in England first tottered and fell headless to the ground with the martyred Charles; which we kicked out with his son James, and kicked twice back with two Pretenders"; and which would, "with all the sanctions of religion and morality, sacrifice the blood of millions to the least of its prejudices," but which nevertheless still "rears its bloated hideous form to brave the will of a whole people" (7: 93).

16. The epigraphs, of course, are equally appropriate to Hazlitt's own essay, epitomizing his "remedy" for the "Distresses," which is divided into four points, "as if we were writing a Lay-Sermon":

I. To Take off One-fifth from all Incomes paid by the Public Amounting to above a Hundred a Year, or to Tax all such incomes One-fifth. . . .

II. To Strike off at once all Sinecures Great and Small, all useless Places, and all Pensions whatever, not paid for Professional Services. . . .

III. To take off Ten Millions of Indirect and Ordinary Taxes on Consumption, Labour, Manufactures, &c, by Laying a Tax of 10 per cent. on all Real, that is, Permanent Property, above a Hundred-a-Year. . . .

IV. To give up as a bonus to the landed proprietor five millions of poor-rates . . . by a direct government tax to that amount on sporting dogs, pleasure and coach-horses. (19: 151–56)

17. "National Distresses—Princely Donation of Lord Viscount Dudley and Ward," "The Political Examiner. No. 442" (*Examiner* 8 Sept. 1816: 561–62).

18. Howe annotates the lacuna as: "The poet-laureate?" (7: 380). Surely Gay's "Tom. Tipple," however, is a poor match for the upright Southey, and Hazlitt never shrank from making his references to the Laureate quite explicit (7: 24–27, 168–209, and passim).

19. McFarland finds Hazlitt's poetic allusions "remarkable for their frequency, for their inaccuracy, and for their irrelevance," part of an attempt on Hazlitt's part to compensate for a "lack of [university] education" (66–68). As my analysis here attempts to demonstrate, Hazlitt's allusions were, in this instance at least (and I would venture to maintain in much of his writing), not only relevant but essential to his rhetorical strategy.

20. The *Examiner* cost 10d an issue, and to its circulation of approximately 3,500 copies could be added the extended readership of circulating libraries and shared subscriptions. Coleridge's pamphlet, by contrast, was advertised at 1s 6d; unfortunately the actual sales of *The Statesman's Manual,* when finally published, are not available, though it did not reach a second edition.

21. See Spacks for a provocative study of the important cultural function of "gossip," of which "banter" is one historically specific manifestation.

22. See Jones, *Hazlitt* 256–57 for an alternate account of Hazlitt's stylistic allusion in this passage. Noting his reading in *Henry IV* at this time, Jones describes this "stringing of satirical beads" as "verbally inventive vilification in the style of Falstaff."

23. George quotes a contemporary witness: "The highest triumph of the English dandy is to appear with the most wooden manners . . . and to contrive even his civilities so that they are as near as may be to affronts, . . . to have the courage to offend against every restraint of decorum, . . . [and] to treat his best friends if they cease to have the stamp of fashion, as if he did not know them, 'to cut them' as the technical phrase goes" (164).

24. In the only other remaining response to Hazlitt's preview, Charles Lamb refers to this line in a letter to William Wordsworth with a display of shock appropriate to the moral sensibility of his correspondent: "O horrible license beyond the old Comedy—" (224). With this, Lamb offers a very different and quite suggestive line of enquiry for the cultural and generic precedents of the public invective of the Regency. Certainly Hazlitt might have been flattered to think he was outdoing Aristophanes, if indeed he and Lamb had not already discussed this possibility. For in this same letter, after calling such writings as the present one Hazlitt's "violent strainings," he goes on to declare "I get no conversation in London that is absolutely worth attending to but his" (225). Meanwhile, with reference to Coleridge's proposed sermon, Lamb offers this telling commentary: "[Coleridge has] left for publication as I hear a prodigious mass of composition for a Sermon to the middling ranks of people to persuade them they are not so distressed as is commonly supposed. Methinks he should recite it to a congregation of Bilston Colliers,—the fate of Cinna the Poet would instantly be his" (224).

25. *Morning Chronicle,* qtd. in Cook, introduction xlvi.

Chapter 3

1. "Riots in the Metropolis," *Times* 3 Dec. 1816. For the most detailed historical account, see Thompson 633–36. The Spafields meetings of 15 November and 2 December were infiltrated by Castle, the government spy and agent provocateur, as was the committee to organize the Spitalfields weavers; Castle attended the meeting with plans in place to attack the Bank and the Tower (634). According to James Watson, who was arrested after the riot for looting gun shops, Hunt had attempted to pacify the meeting (635n. 1).

2. The same advertisement appeared again on 25 and 27 December in the *Morning Chronicle,* and in the *Times* on 27 December.

3. Butler 90. See also McVeigh: "Of all Coleridge's prose works, perhaps *The Statesman's Manual* . . . has been treated the most lightly. . . . Today, to those aware of its existence at all, [it] has often seemed faintly absurd, its very title suggesting a quaint self-parody of Coleridge's prosy middle-age" (87).

4. A good example is Hodgson's subtle deconstructive analysis of this passage in a chapter titled "Coleridge's Rhetoric of Allegory and Symbol" (4–10).

5. On the "higher" or "historical criticism" of the Bible at this time, see McGann 5–6, and Prickett passim.

6. On the general issue of literacy, Coleridge does advocate, elsewhere in the sermon, a comprehensive system of national education—if only because "the inconveniences that have arisen from a thing's having become too general, are best removed by making it universal" (6: 39–40).

7. White, introduction xxxi, xxxin. 2; Coburn 6: 3–4n. 1. Coleridge emends the title page of Copy L to read "Addressed to the Higher Class of Society, but more particularly to the Learned," and then he notes in the margin of this emended copy, "So it was ordered to be printed, and so, I believe it was advertised" (6: 3–4n. 1). Yet as we have seen, the advertisement in the *Times* contained no such late revision, though it appeared a full three weeks after Coleridge was aware of the necessary changes. It is significant that in his editor's introduction, White seems to accept Coleridge's belief "that the work had been advertised, as an address not merely to the higher classes, 'but more particularly to the Learned,' " thus implicitly laying blame on those, like Hazlitt, who had read the advertisement but nevertheless went ahead and "made merry

over C's claim" in the text (xxxin. 2). Here again, however, White has neglected to consult the advertisement itself.

8. As White notes, Patrick Colquhoun was well-known as both a metropolitan police magistrate and a collector of statistics, having most recently published *A Treatise on the Wealth, Power, and Resources, of the British Empire, in Every Quarter of the World* (1814) (6: 38n. 2).

9. Coleridge adds a bantering footnote to this term (later quoted by Hazlitt) which depicts the reading public as uniformly witless and uneducated (6: 36–38n).

10. See especially "Appendix C" on "Reason and Religion," which goes on to define "Will," "Conscience," "Understanding," and even "Imagination" (6: 59–63).

11. This is the central "Problem of Conveying Belief," according to Wayne Anderson, and one that threatens to subvert "the entire enterprise of *The Statesman's Manual*" (30). In his view, Coleridge can only solve this difficulty by recourse to a "metadiscursive analysis" (30), involving overt "allusions to the circumstances and problems of composing the text" (29); the self-conscious "effort to specify and condition the kind of reader he requires" (29); and such rhetorical strategies as ellipsis, displacement, and deferral.

12. For Hazlitt's full quotation of this passage (and his commentary on it), see chapter 4.

Chapter 4

1. The *Examiner*'s isolation as a liberal journal was made worse by a coincidence of surnames: the name "Hunt" had become a liability by false association with the "Orator" held responsible for the riots. "We shall repeat nothing further here respecting Mr. HUNT of Bristol, and our having no connexion with him," writes Leigh Hunt defensively in his editorial immediately following the riot. "We are heartily sorry to see the cause of Reform injured by the interference of such men" (*Examiner* 8 Dec. 1816: 769).

2. Jones points out that Hazlitt's work for the *Examiner* at this time amounted almost to editorial collaboration, his writings regularly filling about one-third of the entire paper. On 15 December 1816, for example, his "Literary Notices. No. 19" appeared on the front page as the leading article; he also contributed to this issue a brief "political essay" titled "Buonaparte and Müller" (7: 130), and two theatrical reviews—"Two New Farces" (18: 210–11), and his famous review-essay of "Coriolanus" (4: 214–21) (Jones, "Three Additions" 359–60).

3. Stoddart's virulent prose was considered a liability even to the *Times* itself; perhaps as a result of the *Examiner*'s "Illustrations," he was fired at the end of December (Jones, *Hazlitt* 260, 263).

4. Hazlitt's analysis of "political apostacy" is subtler than the lurid imagery of "prostitution" might suggest. The pressures of conformism and ideological isolation are evident in his essay of 22 December: "It requires some fortitude to oppose one's opinion, however right, to that of all the world besides," he writes. "Nothing but the strongest and clearest conviction can support a man in a losing minority" (7: 138). The prosaic difficulty of remaining a stubborn political dissenter thus becomes the moral norm against which is measured "the degeneracy of modern apostates and reformed Jacobins, who find the applause of their king and country doubly cheering after being so long without it, and who go all lengths in adulation and servility, to make up for their former awkward singularity" (7: 138).

5. The April 1816 edition of the *Quarterly* (15: 29), which had appeared in August, contained two lengthy articles by Southey on "La Vendée" and the "State of the Poor" (Shine 51–52).

6. "Mr. Coleridge and the Edinburgh Reviewers," the *Examiner* 24 Nov. 1816: 743.

7. Coleridge writes, "In the Scriptures, [history and economy] are the living *educts* of the Imagination, that reconciling and mediatory power, which incorporating the reason in Images of the Sense, and organizing (as it were) the flux of the Senses by the permanence and self-circling energies of the Reason, gives birth to a system of symbols, harmonious in themselves,

and consubstantial with the truths, of which they are the conductors" (6: 28–29; qtd. by Hazlitt, 7: 120).

8. In *The Statesman's Manual,* this passage reads: "in the reign of Rehoboam, his *successor.* But I *should* tread on glowing embers" (6: 33; emphases added).

9. It was part of Jeffrey's general editorial practice to edit and overwrite all essays admitted to the *Review;* he would later refer specifically to the "retrenchments and verbal alterations" he had made to this article in particular (Reiman A: 494; Jackson 318). Though by definition undetectable, these silent "retrenchments" were most likely made in those parts of Hazlitt's essay touching directly on political issues, an area already firmly under the control of Brougham and the other Whig ideologues.

10. Hazlitt had had three previous review-essays accepted and published: "Standard Novels and Romances," "Sismondi's Literature of the South," and "Schlegel on the Drama" (16: 5–99).

11. *Morning Chronicle* 24 Feb. 1817. Houghton (456) records the 14th, but the advertisements in both the *Chronicle* and the *Times* on this date state "In a few days will be published. . . ."

12. Indeed, as White notes, Coleridge sent presentation copies of both *The Statesman's Manual* and *A Lay Sermon* to his erstwhile friend Southey at the *Quarterly,* requesting the favor of a review, yet "when Southey's library was sold, the copies of the lay Sermons were still uncut" (introduction xxx).

13. Delegates from Hampden Clubs all over the country met on 22 January with Cobbett, Hunt, and other Radical leaders to produce a unified petition for reform with half-a-million signatures. This achievement, however, was nullified at a blow by the stone or bullet that smashed the Regent's carriage window on 28 January. Possibly instigated by agents provocateurs, this event was the catalyst for the new Parliament's agenda of reaction and repression. (Thompson 619–20, 636–40; White, *Waterloo* 148–59).

14. In addition to the suspension of Habeas Corpus, a "Seditious Meetings Act" made all "reforming Societies and Clubs" illegal, and gave local magistrates the power to prohibit any meeting over fifty (Thompson 639). Most important for Hazlitt, political writers could now be detained under the warrant of a secretary of state (White, *Waterloo* 157).

15. On 11 February ("Published This Day," *Times* 10 Feb. 1817, where it is announced that it "will be published on Tuesday" [11 Feb. 1817]).

16. *Edinburgh* 27 (December 1816): 373–90 and 310–38, by John Allen and Henry Brougham respectively (Houghton 456). Other articles in this edition include reviews by Leigh Hunt of Nott's *Surrey and Wyatt,* and by Brougham of Byron's *Childe Harold Canto the Third.*

17. See chapter 5.

18. In another part of the review, responding to Coleridge's attack on the "READING PUBLIC," Hazlitt reminds Coleridge of how he had seen in the 1790s a "little shabby volume of Thomson's *Seasons* lying in the window of a solitary alehouse at the top of a rock hanging over the British Channel" and had declared "That is true fame!" For Hazlitt this remains a compelling image of free dissemination, cultural enfranchisement through literacy, and the democracy of taste: "If he were to write fifty Lay-Sermons, he could not answer the inference from this one sentence, which is, that there are books that make their way wherever there are readers, and that there ought everywhere to be readers for such books!" (7: 125).

Chapter 5

1. Southey had recommended in his *Quarterly* article that the government take "effectual means for silencing those demagogues who are exciting the people to rebellion" (Oct. 1816; 16.31: 254).

2. Coburn 3.2: 470. All references to Coleridge's essays on *Wat Tyler* will be by volume and page number only.

3. See Hoadley and Manogue, and also Foot ("William Hazlitt's Reply"). Raimond treats

the play itself as one of Southey's "Early Writings," but he only touches briefly on the "affair" it caused in 1817.

4. Though William Winterbotham held the original manuscript in 1817, Sherwood, Neeley, and Jones published from another pirated manuscript, whose owner they refused to disclose (Manogue 111).

5. Hazlitt names this genre, for example, in his first review of Southey in 1814. Having dispatched the "Laureate's poetical politics" in his "Carmen Triumphale," he notes that "Mr. Southey announces a new volume of Inscriptions, which must furnish some curious *parallelisms*" (*Morning Chronicle* 7: 27).

6. Thompson 539; Jones, *Hazlitt* 271–72. Cobbett's defection is one index of the serious implications of the suspension of Habeas Corpus for reformist writers. With Cobbett's departure, William Hone (publisher of Hazlitt's *Political Essays* in 1819) became the unofficial leader of Radical reform in the press (Thompson 640). Despite Thompson's cogent distinction between Hazlitt and Cobbett on the basis of style and hence reading audience (746–78), I would contend that in such passages as this one, Hazlitt makes himself accessible to a much wider audience than just "the polite culture of his time" (747).

7. Hoadley 85n. 16. The wide dissemination of the play continued up to, and well beyond, a standard 1835 edition in the "Lee's Library for Labourers" series, which, as Hoadley points out, "particularly realised Southey's fears that Wat Tyler would be used for propaganda." Thus while a romanticized literary history has suppressed the affair, *Wat Tyler* in fact went on to become a classic in the counter-canon of nineteenth-century working-class literature.

8. See chapter 4, note 12.

9. The *Courier* articles are dated 17 Mar. 1817, 18 Mar. 1817, 27 Mar. 1817, and 2 Apr. 1817.

10. Indeed, as Holmes notes (83), Coleridge's first printed allusion to pantisocracy was in "Address to a Young Jack-Ass" (*Morning Chronicle* 9 Dec. 1794), later satirized by both the *Anti-Jacobin* and Byron in *English Bards,* where Coleridge is "The bard who soars to elegize an ass" (line 263, Byron 116).

11. Coleridge's second *Lay Sermon* had appeared ten days earlier ("Coleridge's Second Lay Sermon," *Times* 21 Mar. 1817). No doubt the appearance of this work in the very midst of the *Wat Tyler* affair explains why Hazlitt did not review it, electing instead to contest Coleridge's higher-profile views on the same issues as they were raised by the struggle over Southey's play. *A Lay Sermon* attracted only two reviews, one of which was written by Coleridge himself (3.2: 461–65), the other by Henry Crabb Robinson (Jackson 278–84).

Chapter 6

1. See Fogel; also Bate, introduction, *Biographia* li.

2. This struggle was intensified by the fact that Hazlitt's first book of literary criticism—*Characters of Shakespeare's Plays*—was published in the same month (July 1817) as the *Biographia.* Moreover, Jeffrey's favorable review of *Characters* appeared directly adjacent to Hazlitt's review of the *Biographia* in the same edition of the *Edinburgh*—as if juxtaposed for polemical effect (28: 472–88).

3. See the introduction.

4. Close readers of the *Edinburgh* would note that this view was corroborated in the adjacent review of *Characters of Shakespeare's Plays,* where Jeffrey quotes the essay on Coriolanus: " 'Shakespeare seems to have had a leaning to the arbitrary side of the question. . . . The imagination is an exaggerating and exclusive faculty. The understanding is a dividing and measuring faculty. The one is an aristocratical, the other a republican faculty. . . . [Poetry] aims at effect, it exists by contrast. It is everything by excess' " (Edinburgh 28: 481).

5. See especially the essay "What is the People?," first published in the *Champion* two months later in October 1817. As Cook notes, this essay was also an intense and allusive "contest"

with Burke ("Hazlitt" 144). Yet far from characterizing Radical discourse as "poison," Hazlitt's aim is to co-opt the energy of Burkean rhetoric for the purposes of a Radical redefinition of "the people" and a vigorous reassertion of their "common and equal rights" (7: 262).

6. However closely it may or may not adhere to the high standard of veracity set in his footnote, Jeffrey's claim that he had no knowledge of Hazlitt's writings for the *Examiner* has the effect of emphasizing the widening divisions between reading audiences of the British public sphere. Jeffrey's adjacent review of *Characters of Shakespeare's Plays,* moreover, though clearly positive, is nevertheless condescending: Hazlitt has written a "very pleasing book" and one of "very considerable originality and genius," but it is a book written "more to show extraordinary love than extraordinary knowledge" of Shakespeare, and "we think, of course, that our own admiration is, on the whole, more discriminating and judicious" (*Edinburgh* 28: 472).

7. Hazlitt refers, of course, to the letter from a "judicious friend" in chapter 13, suggesting the omission of the metaphysical "Chapter on the Imagination" (7.1: 300–4). In generic terms, this remarkable letter bears comparison to Hazlitt's letter from "SEMPER EGO AUDITOR" in its skillful balancing of lyric and satirical elements, and its addition of brilliantly ironic discursive complexity to the project at hand. Yet by August 1817 such a letter may well have seemed a telling capitulation to the authority of review-criticism. Writing on behalf of "*the* PUBLIC," Coleridge's "friend" declares that his "*readers will have both right and reason to complain*" because, among other things, his "*speculations on the esemplastic power would be utterly unintelligible*" (7.1. 302–3). In the context of the criticism established by Hazlitt and others, this last word was more likely to have played into Coleridge's negative public image than to have challenged it with a subtler irony.

8. Delivered beginning January 1818 at the Surrey Institution, and—in another remarkable coincidence—on precisely the same nights as Coleridge's lecture series on drama and poetry at the London Philosophical Society. See Jones, *Hazlitt* 282, for an excellent account, and chapter 7.

9. As noted above, the exact authorship of this passage remains moot.

Chapter 7

1. Subscribers to the Surrey Institution were mostly Dissenters, Quakers, and evangelicals (Baker 253; Coburn 5.1: 487). Among other examples, Hazlitt forgives Swift at the end of his sixth lecture "for being a Tory," because his legacy as a moralist is superior to that of "some others" who have left behind only "the shining example of an apostate from liberty" (5:111).

2. *Examiner* 8 Mar. 1818: 154; qtd. in Jones, *Hazlitt* 283.

3. "Hazlitt and Jeffrey," *Blackwood's* 3 (June 1818): 303.

4. *Morning Chronicle* (1819); qtd. in Cook, introduction xlvi.

5. "Hazlitt Cross-Questioned," *Blackwood's* (Aug. 1818): 549–53. For two excellent accounts of the impact of Lake School gossip, see Jones, *Hazlitt* 154–60, 297–300; also Foot, "Hazlitt's Revenge" (where "Revenge" is ironic: Hazlitt's only "revenge" on such gossip, in Foot's view, is judicious praise of their poetry in public journals).

6. Rev. of *Round Table, Quarterly* 17 (Apr. 1817): 154–59; rev. of *Characters, Quarterly* 18 (Jan. 1818): 458–66; rev. of *Lectures, Quarterly* 19 (June 1818): 424–34. See also rev. of *Political Essays, Quarterly* 22 (July 1819): 158–63.

Epilogue

1. See Cook, "Hazlitt" 137–40.

2. Chandler also identifies this connection, calling the *Political Essays* "a crucial forerunner to the essays later collected in *The Spirit of the Age*" (14). While he also clarifies the contrast between the two works, he alludes to the generic link by noting that "the 1819 volume includes several character sketches anticipatory of *The Spirit of the Age*" (181).

3. Jones, for example, notes that "the apostasies of Coleridge and Wordsworth" are not named in the essay, but they may have obtruded themselves "even more readily with the subscribers to the *Liberal* . . . in 1823" than they would now ("First Flight" 37).

WORKS CITED

Altick, Richard D. *The English Common Reader: A Social History of the Mass Reading Public, 1800–1900.* Chicago: U of Chicago P, 1957.

Andersen, Wayne C. "The Prince of Preparatory Authors: The Problem of Conveying Belief in Coleridge's *The Statesman's Manual.*" *Wordsworth Circle* 15.1 (Winter 1984): 28–31.

Aspinall, Arthur. *Politics and the Press c. 1780–1850.* 1949. Brighton: Harvester, 1973.

———. "The Social Status of Journalists at the Beginning of the Nineteenth Century." *Review of English Studies* os 21.83 (1945): 216–32.

Baker, Herschel. *William Hazlitt.* Cambridge: Harvard UP, 1962.

Barker-Benfield, G. J. *The Culture of Sensibility.* Chicago: U of Chicago P, 1992.

Bate, Walter Jackson. Editors' introduction, Part 1. *Biographia Literaria.* By Samuel Taylor Coleridge. Ed. J. Engell and W. J. Bate. London: Routledge; Princeton: Princeton UP, 1983. Coburn, vol. 7. xli–lxvii.

———. Editor's introductions to "William Hazlitt." *Criticism: The Major Texts.* Enlarged Edition. New York: Harcourt Brace Jovanovich, 1970. 281–92.

Beer, John. "Coleridge, Hazlitt, and 'Christabel.' " *Review of English Studies* ns 37.145 (1986): 40–54.

Belsey, Catherine. "Literature, History, Politics." *Literature and History* 9.1 (Spring 1983): 17–27.

———. "Towards Cultural History—in Theory and Practice." *Textual Practice* 3.2 (Spring 1989): 159–72.

Blunden, Edmund. *Leigh Hunt's "Examiner" Examined.* New York: n.p., 1928.

Butler, Marilyn. *Romantics, Rebels, and Reactionaries: English Literature and its Background, 1760–1830.* New York: Oxford UP, 1981.

Byron, Lord (George Gordon). *Byron's Poetical Works.* New Edition. Ed. John D. Jump. Oxford: Oxford UP, 1970.

Campbell, James Dykes. *Samuel Taylor Coleridge: A Narrative of the Events of His Life.* London: Macmillan, 1896.

Carlson, Julie. *In the Theatre of Romanticism: Coleridge, Nationalism, Women.* Cambridge: Cambridge UP, 1994.

Carnall, Geoffrey. "The Impertinent Barber of Baghdad: Coleridge as Comic Figure in Hazlitt's Essays." *New Approaches to Coleridge: Biographical and Critical Essays.* Ed. Donald Sultana. London: Vision; Totowa, NJ: Barnes & Noble, 1981. 38–47.

Chandler, James. *England in 1819: The Politics of Literary Culture and the Case of Romantic Historicism.* Chicago: U of Chicago P, 1998.

Christensen, Jerome. " 'Like a Guilty Thing Surprised': Deconstruction, Coleridge, and the Apostasy of Criticism." *Critical Inquiry* 12 (Summer 1986): 769–87.

Coburn, Kathleen, gen. ed. *The Collected Works of Samuel Taylor Coleridge.* 16 vols. London: Routledge & Kegan Paul; Princeton: Princeton UP, 1969– .

———. "Who Killed *Christabel?*" *Times Literary Supplement* 20 May 1965: 397.

Coleridge, Samuel Taylor. *Biographia Literaria.* Ed. J. Engell and W. J Bate. 2 vols. London: Routledge & Kegan Paul; Princeton: Princeton UP, 1983. Coburn, vol. 7.

———. *Collected Letters of Samuel Taylor Coleridge.* Ed. E. L. Griggs. Vol 4: 1815–1819. Oxford: Clarendon, 1959.

———. *Essays on His Times in The Morning Post and the Courier.* Ed. David V. Erdman. 2 vols. London: Routledge & Kegan Paul; Princeton: Princeton UP, 1978. Coburn, vol. 3.

———. *Lay Sermons.* Ed. R. J. White. London: Routledge & Kegan Paul; Princeton: Princeton UP, 1972. Coburn, vol. 6.

———. *Poetical Works.* Ed. Ernest Hartley Coleridge. Oxford: Oxford UP, 1912.

Constable, Archibald. Letter to Walter Scott. 8 Aug. 1816. MS 789 fo. 615. National Library of Scotland, Edinburgh.

Cook, Jonathan. "Hazlitt: Criticism and Ideology." *Romanticism and Ideology: Studies in English Writing, 1765–1830.* David Aers, Jonathan Cook and David Punter. London: Routledge & Kegan Paul, 1981. 137–54.

———. Editor's introduction. *William Hazlitt: Selected Writings.* Ed. Jonathan Cook. Oxford: Oxford UP, 1991. ix–xxxviii.

Courtney, Winnifred F. "The Champion." *British Literary Magazines: The Romantic Age, 1789–1836.* Ed. Alvin Sullivan. Westport, CT: Greenwood, 1983. 98–104.

Duff, J. D., ed. *D. IVII JVVENALIS, Satvrae XIV: Fourteen Satires of Juvenal.* Cambridge: Cambridge UP, 1929.

Dulcken, H. W., ed. *Arabian Nights.* Secaucus, NJ: Castle, 1984.

Eagleton, Terry. *The Function of Criticism From the Spectator to Post-Structuralism.* London: Verso, 1984.

Elledge, W. Paul. "The Liberal." *British Literary Magazines: The Romantic Age, 1789–1836.* Ed. Alvin Sullivan. Westport, CT: Greenwood Press, 1983. 220–28.

Erdman, David. "A New Discovery: The First Review of *Christabel* Edited by David V. Erdman." *Texas Studies in English* 37 (1958): 53–60.

Evans, Eric J. *Britain Before the Reform Act: Politics and Society 1815–1832.* London: Longmans, 1989.

The Examiner; A Sunday Paper, on Politics, Domestic Economy and Theatricals. London: John Hunt, 1808–81.

Foot, Michael. "Hazlitt's Revenge on the Lakers." *Wordsworth Circle* 14.1 (Winter 1983): 61–68.

———. "William Hazlitt's Reply to Thomas McFarland or Caligula's Red Cap." *Wordsworth Circle* 19.3 (Summer 1988): 145–50.

Gaull, Marilyn. *English Romanticism: The Human Context.* New York: W. W. Norton, 1988.

Gay, John. *The Beggar's Opera. Eighteenth-Century English Literature.* Ed. Geoffrey Tillotson, et al. New York: Harcourt Brace Jovanovich, 1969. 518–49.

George, M. Dorothy. *Hogarth to Cruikshank: Social Change in Graphic Satire.* New York: Walker, 1967.

190

Works Cited

Gilmartin, Kevin. " 'Victims of Argument, Slaves of Fact': Hunt, Hazlitt, Cobbett and the Literature of Opposition." *Wordsworth Circle* 21:3 (1990): 90–96.

Gravil, Richard and Molly Lefebure, eds. *The Coleridge Connection.* New York: St. Martin's, 1990.

Greenberg, Mark L. "The Yellow Dwarf." *British Literary Magazines: The Romantic Age, 1789– 1836.* Ed. Alvin Sullivan. Westport, CT: Greenwood Press, 1983. 434–40.

Griggs, Earl Leslie. Introduction to Letter 1025. Coleridge, *Letters* 4: 668.

Habermas, Jürgen. *The Structural Transformation of the Public Sphere: An Inquiry into a Category of Bourgeois Society.* 1962. Trans. Thomas Burger. Cambridge: MIT Press, 1989.

Hayden, John O. Introduction. *British Literary Magazines: The Romantic Age, 1789–1836.* Ed. Alvin Sullivan. Westport, CT: Greenwood, 1983. xv–xxv.

Hayter, Alethea. "Coleridge, Maturin's *Bertram,* and Drury Lane." *New Approaches to Coleridge: Biographical and Critical Essays.* Ed. Donald Sultana. London: Vision; Totowa, NJ: Barnes & Noble, 1981. 17–37.

"Hazlitt and Jeffrey." *Blackwood's Edinburgh Magazine* 3 (June 1818): 303–6.

Hazlitt, William. *Characters of Shakespeare's Plays.* Howe, vol. 4: 165–408.

———. *Lectures on the English Poets.* Howe, vol. 5: 1–168.

———. *The Letters of William Hazlitt.* Ed. Herschel M. Sikes, William H. Bonner, and Gerald Lahey. New York: New York UP, 1978.

———. *Political Essays, With Sketches of Public Characters.* Howe, vol. 7.

———. *The Round Table.* Howe, vol. 4: 1–164.

———. *The Spirit of the Age.* Howe, vol. 11: 1–184.

Henderson, Andrea. "Revolution, Response, and 'Christabel.' " *ELH* 57 (1990): 881–900.

Hoadley, Frank T. "The Controversy over Southey's *Wat Tyler.*" *Studies in Philology* 38.1 (June 1941): 81–96.

Hodgson, John A. *Coleridge, Shelley, and Transcendental Inquiry.* Lincoln: U of Nebraska P, 1989.

Holmes, Richard. *Coleridge: Early Visions.* 1989. New York: Viking Penguin, 1990.

Houghton, Walter, ed. *The Wellesky Index of Victorian Periodicals.* Vol. 1. Toronto: U of Toronto P, 1966.

Howe, P. P., ed. *The Complete Works of William Hazlitt.* 21 vols. London: J. M. Dent, 1930–34.

———. *The Life of William Hazlitt.* 1928. London: Hamish Hamilton, 1947.

Jackson, J. R. de J., ed. *Coleridge: The Critical Heritage.* New York: Barnes & Noble, 1970.

———. Editor's introduction. *Coleridge: The Critical Heritage.* Ed. J. R. de J. Jackson. New York: Barnes & Noble, 1970. 1–19.

Janowitz, Anne. "Coleridge's 1816 Volume: Fragment as Rubric." *Studies in Romanticism* 24 (Spring 1985): 21–39.

Johnson, Paul. *The Birth of the Modern: World Society 1815–1830.* London: Widenfield and Nicholson, 1991.

Jones, Stanley. "First Flight: Image and Theme in a Hazlitt Essay." *Prose Studies* 8.1 (May 1985): 35–47.

———. *Hazlitt: A Life From Winterslow to Frith Street.* Oxford: Oxford UP, 1989.

———. "Three Additions to the Canon of Hazlitt's Writings." *Review of English Studies* ns 38.151 (1987): 355–63.

Kelly, Gary. "The Limits of Genre and the Institution of Literature: Romanticism between Fact and Fiction." *Romantic Revolutions: Criticism and Theory.* Ed. K. Johnston et al. Bloomington: Indiana UP, 1990.

Klancher, Jon. *The Making of English Reading Audiences, 1790–1832.* Madison: U of Wisconsin P, 1987.

Lamb, Charles, and Mary Lamb. *The Letters of Charles and Mary Lamb.* Ed. Edwin W. Marrs, Jr. Vol. 3: 1809–1817. Ithaca: Cornell UP, 1978.

Lindop, Grevel, "Lamb, Hazlitt, and De Quincey." Gravil and Lefebure, 111–32.

Magnuson, Paul. *Reading Public Romanticism.* Princeton: Princeton UP, 1998.

Manogue, Ralph A. "Southey and William Winterbotham: New Light on an Old Quarrel." *Charles Lamb Bulletin* ns 38 (April 1982): 105–14.

Marrs, Edwin W., Jr., ed. *The Letters of Charles and Mary Lamb.* Vol. 3: 1809–1817. Ithaca: Cornell UP, 1978.

McFarland, Thomas. *Romantic Cruxes: The English Essayists and the Spirit of the Age.* Oxford: Clarendon, 1987.

McGann, Jerome J. *The Romantic Ideology: A Critical Investigation.* Chicago: U of Chicago P, 1983.

McVeigh, Daniel. "Political Vision in Coleridge's *The Statesman's Manual.*" *Wordsworth Circle* 14.2 (Spring 1983): 87–92.

[Moore, Thomas]. "Coleridge's *Christabel.*" Rev. of *Christabel; Kubla Khan, a Vision; The Pains of Sleep,* by S. T. Coleridge. *Edinburgh Review* 27 (Sept. 1816): 58–67.

Morison, Stanley. *The English Newspaper: Some Account of the Physical Development of Journals Printed in London Between 1622 and the Present Day.* Cambridge: Cambridge UP, 1932.

Morning Chronicle. London: 1769–1855. N. pag.

Peacock, Thomas Love. "An Essay on Fashionable Literature." *Memoirs of Shelley and Other Essays and Reviews.* Ed. Howard Mills. London: Hart-Davis, 1970. 93–113.

Post, John D. *The Last Great Subsistence Crisis in the Western World.* Baltimore: John Hopkins UP, 1977.

Raimond, Jean. "Southey's Early Writings and the Revolution." *Yearbook of English Studies* 19 (1989): 181–96.

Reiman, Donald H., ed. *The Romantics Reviewed: Contemporary Reviews of British Romantic Writers.* 3 parts (A–C). New York: Garland, 1972.

Rooke, Barbara E. Editor's introduction. *The Friend,* by Samuel Taylor Coleridge. Coburn, vol. 4.1. xxxv–cv.

Rudd, Niall, trans. *Juvenal: The Satires.* Oxford: Clarendon, 1991.

Ruddick, Bill. "Recollecting Coleridge: The Internalization of Radical Energies in Hazlitt's Political Prose." *Yearbook of English Studies* 19 (1989): 243–55.

Sage, Victor. Editor's introduction. *The Gothik Novel: A Casebook.* Victor Sage, ed. London: MacMillan, 1990. 1–28.

Schneider, Elisabeth. "Tom Moore and the *Edinburgh* Review of *Christabel.*" *PMLA* 77.2 (March 1962): 71–76.

———. "The Unknown Reviewer of *Christabel.*" *PMLA* 70.3 (June 1955): 417–32.

Schoenfield, Mark. "Voices Together: Lamb, Hazlitt and the *London.*" *Studies in Romanticism* 29 (Summer 1990): 257–72.

Siskin, Clifford. *The Historicity of Romantic Discourse.* New York: Oxford UP, 1988.

Southey, Rev. Charles C., ed. *The Life and Correspondence of Robert Southey.* Vol. 4. 1850. St. Clair Shores, MI: Scholarly Press, 1969.

Southey, Robert. "A Letter to William Smith, Esq., M.P., from Robert Southey, Esq." *The Life and Correspondence of Robert Southey.* Ed. Rev. Charles C. Southey. Vol. 4. 1850. St. Clair Shores, MI: Scholarly Press, 1969. 370–90.

[———]. "Parliamentary Reform." Rev. of *The Monthly Magazine,* Cobbett's *Political Register,* [and other reformist publications]. *Quarterly Review* 16.31 (October 1816): 225–78.

———. *Wat Tyler.* 1817. Introd. Jonathan Wordsworth. Oxford: Woodstock Books, 1989.

Spacks, Patricia Meyer. *Gossip.* Chicago: University of Chicago P, 1986.

Sullivan, Alvin. Editor's preface. *British Literary Magazines: The Romantic Age, 1789–1836.* Westport, CT: Greenwood, 1983. vii–xi.

Swann, Karen. "Literary Gentlemen and Lovely Ladies: The Debate on the Character of *Christabel.*" *ELH* 52.2 (Summer 1985): 397–418.

Thompson, E. P. *The Making of the English Working Class.* London: Victor Gollancz, 1963.

Works Cited

Times of London. London: 1788–1820. N. pag.

Wallins, Roger P. "The Examiner." *British Literary Magazines: The Romantic Age, 1789–1836.* Ed. Alvin Sullivan. Westport, CT: Greenwood, 1983. 150–58.

White, R. J. Editor's introduction. *Lay Sermons,* by Samuel Taylor Coleridge. Coburn, vol. 6. xxix–xlvii.

———. *Waterloo to Peterloo.* 1957. Hammondsworth: Penguin, 1968.

Williams, Raymond. *The Long Revolution.* New York: Columbia UP, 1961.

Woodword, Sir Llewellyn. *The Age of Reform, 1815–1870.* Second ed. Oxford: Clarendon, 1962. Vol. 13 of *The Oxford History of England.* 15 vols. 1936–65.

Yarlott, Geoffrey. *Christabel and the Abyssinian Maid.* London: Methuen, 1967.

I N D E X

agency: cultural, 64, 65; ideological, 16, 59; political, 58, 87, 120, 176. *See also* authority

allegory: and symbol, in *Statesman's Manual,* 69, 90, 93, 183n. 4; and symbol in *Wat Tyler,* 124. *See also* "Coleridge's Christabel, Mr." (Hazlitt, *Examiner*): allegory in

allusion: Hazlitt's use of 44, 62, 182n. 19; as index of projected audience, 59

Anderson, Wayne, 184n. 11

anonymity. *See* review-criticism: and anonymity

Anti-Jacobin Review, The, 122, 140, 181n. 5, 186n. 10

Association for the Relief of the Manufacturing and Labouring Poor, 52–53; Coleridge's proposed donation to, 51, 52, 53

authority: biblical, 72, 75, 76, 91–92, 93; cultural, 12, 44, 58, 73, 76, 98, 128, 140, 146, 148 (*see also* conversation: and cultural authority; genres, discursive: and cultural authority; genius: and cultural authority); moral, 126, 155;

mystification of, 36, 44, 46, 60; and patronage, 39; and performance, 16, 100; of poetry, 144; political, 54, 67, 68, 72, 75, 76, 77, 137; and prophecy, 73; public construction of, 16, 41, 53; spiritual, 82, 83. *See also* review-criticism: ascendent authority of

authorship, in Regency. *See* marketplace, literary; poets

autobiography, 149, 150, 152, 169

Baker, Herschel, 14, 49

Bamford, Samuel, 67

banter: as genre of Regency discourse, 16, 50, 62, 66, 85, 103, 104, 106, 133, 166; and gossip, 64, 182n. 21. *See also* conversation; "table-talk"

bardolatry. *See* genius

Bate, Walter Jackson, 132–33, 179n. 1

Beckford, William, 30

Bible, The: First Kings, 88, 92, 93, 95; and higher criticism, 72, 183n. 5; *Isaiah,* 93; New Testament, 75; Old Testament, 75, 76; prophecy in, 73; as